Assays

Kenneth Rexroth

A New Directions Paperbook

Library of Congress Catalog Card Number: 61-14899
Manufactured in the United States of America
New Directions Books are published by James Laughlin at
Norfolk, Connecticut. New York Address: 333 Sixth Avenue (14)

ACKNOWLEDGMENTS

The author and the publisher acknowledge with thanks permission to reprint the following material, which first appeared in the magazines or books named. Some of the titles have been changed.

"Sung Culture," *Portfolio* and *Art News Annual* No. 3, 1960.

"Who Am I, Where Am I Going? ? ?", *The Urbanite, March* 1961.

"The Poet As Translator" was first presented as a lecture at the University of Texas and included in a symposium volume on translation published by the University of Texas Press.

"The Holy Kabbalah," introduction to *The Holy Kabbalah* by A. E. Waite, University Books Inc., New York.

"American Indian Songs," *Perspectives USA* No. 16, Intercultural Publications Inc.

"Turner and Whistler," *Art News*, November 1960.

"What's Wrong with the Clubs," *Metronome*, May 1961.

Part 3 of "Lawrence Durrell," *The Griffin*, © 1960 by The Readers' Subscription Inc.

"Gnosticism," introduction to *Fragments of a Faith Forgotten* by G. R. S. Mead, University Books Inc., New York.

"The New Poetry," *The New York Times Book Review*, February 12, 1961.

All of the following essays first appeared in *The Nation*, in the issues noted: "Science and Civilization in China," November 10, 1956; "The Letters of Van Gogh," December 13, 1958; "Mark Twain," March 7, 1959; "The Students Take Over," July 2, 1960; "Henry James and H. G. Wells," August 16, 1958; "Simone Weil," January 12, 1957; Part 2 of "Lawrence Durrell," June 4, 1960.

Parts of "Notes on Historians" first appeared in *The Nation*, and parts of "Poets Old and New" first appeared in *The Nation* and *The New York Times Book Review*.

The translations of Sappho's "Orchard" fragment are reprinted in "The Poet As Translator" by permission of the publishers: J. M. Edmonds' translation from the Loeb-Sappho volume, Loeb Classical Library, Harvard University Press, Cambridge, Mass.; Henry Thornton Wharton's translation from *Sappho*, copyright 1920 by Brentano, New York, by permission of Coward-McCann, New York; T. F. Higham's translation from *The Oxford Book of Greek Verse in Translation*, Oxford University Press, New York.

Contents

Assays

Sung Culture

Spring Night

The gold incense burner has gone out.
The water clock has stopped.
A chill breeze sends a shiver through me.
Spring troubles me and threatens my sleep.
Against my balcony, the moon casts the shadows of flowers.*

So wrote the great statesman and reformer Wang An-shih (1021-86). His political opponent, the leading Sung poet and calligrapher, Su Tung-p'o (1036-1101), wrote:

Flower Shadows

It piles up, thick and formidable, on the marble terrace.
The pages, called again and again, try to sweep it away.
Just then the sun comes out and carries it off.
But never mind, the next moon,
The shadow will come back.

My, weren't they cultivated for politicians!, you think. Yes, but not precisely in the way you think. These are both political poems and refer to the influence of eunuchs, foreigners and nongentlemen of the court and to the respective authors' antagonistic parties of reform. It is as though, in the days of Dienbienphu, Mr. Eden had written:

*The translations of poetry are from the author's *One Hundred Poems from the Chinese,* New Directions, 1959.

On the balcony overlooking the mountains,
Muguette, the most accomplished and learned concubine,
In red, white and blue gauze trousers powdered with gold lilies,
Serves, with delicate, weak gestures, the Lord of the West
The precious viands of the land of golden elephants.
Alas, she has placed them so near the edge of the inlaid table
That they may spoil the embroidered waves on his robe of state.

The Sung Dynasty (960-1279) was like that. It was overcivilized, but it adopted its own overcivilization as a mask. A great deal went on behind the filmy scrim of gauze and mist and incense smoke. In some ways the Sung was more tough-minded and realistic and even middle-class than any other period in Chinese history until the last, the Manchu (Ch'ing) Dynasty (1644-1912). It is in the Sung Dynasty that what we consider the specifically Chinese sensibility first came to flower. All those patterns of response to life that had developed through the earlier centuries of Chinese civilization stiffened slightly into an over-all design.

However much we try to escape them, we always tend to view Chinese history through the eyes of the Confucian scholar-gentlemen who first wrote it. They are passionately legitimist. They speak of dynasties in periods of chaos when there were no dynasties. They persist in looking at the very courts before their eyes as embodiments of the Confucian Utopia ruled by the priest-king of the harvest and surrogate for the people, although often the actual court was as polyglot as Charlemagne's and as little "sprung from the local soil." They dismiss whole cultures, for instance the northern proto-Mongol contemporaries of the Sung, as barbarians. And always they hold up as the ideal man the civilized, non-violent scholar-gentleman, with his human-heartedness and his head full of memorized texts for all contingencies. Other classes may have ruled the State and made vital contributions to the culture. They have hardly a literary or historical existence.

Han (206 B.C. to A.D. 220) and T'ang (A.D. 618-906) culture was imperial and syncretistic. Sung culture was national and synthesizing. Only in Sung times did the cultural base become narrow enough, only then was there sufficient lack of distraction from outside, for what we mean by "Confucianism" or, even more loosely, what we mean by "Chinese civilization" to set in the molds that have persisted to this century. Outlanders, what would later be Tibetans, Mongols and Manchus, had been the statesmen who had built the inner Asian empire of China for the T'ang. The T'ang fell in a welter of brigandage and ephemeral "dynasties," and as the Sung emerged and unified China, they drew in upon themselves and eventually left the inner Asian empire to the outlanders. They retreated from the old Chinese borderlands and finally from the homeland, to "South of the River"—once a land of long-haired savages, recently filling up with emigrants from "China." Here the gentlemen-scholars, undisturbed among their own people, could refine and intensify their peculiar culture, much as the Cockney prisoners could build an England more English than England in nineteenth-century Australia.

It is not altogether true that the Sung were beaten out of North China. Their shift to the South was partly economic. Islam had closed the oasis trade routes and had opened the monsoon trade through the Southern seas. It was partly hedonistic, as though older Caucasian New Yorkers should leave the city to Puerto Ricans and Negroes come North seeking opportunity, and themselves all migrate to Southern California, "for the climate" and for a new and different kind of opportunity.

This vast cultural shift had several results you might not expect and might never gather from the legitimist, orthodox histories. The standard of living rose sharply. Peasants on new land, townsmen in new trades and industries, all were better off than in the glorious days of T'ang. A huge middle class of merchants and other literates who were not scholar-gentlemen literati came into being. Soon luxuries were widespread. Prices began a steady rise. Inflation set in and increased sharply till the fall of the dynasty. Against all this the scholar-gentlemen set their faces and built their Confucian Utopia into Chinese society as a durable myth. But they did not do this without first incorporating philosophical Taoism as transmuted by popular folkways from the woods and springs and high places, and both popular and philosophical Buddhism from India, into the very foundations of what purported to be a purely aristocratic and ethnocentric system. So the society that developed in Sung times was at once adventurous and fluid, conservative and anachronistic.

This is a long introduction, but without it, to understand the period is impossible. In Sung times things are never what they seem, and this is not just due to Buddhist skepticism. Sung society and culture are permeated with contraries and contradictions which are never resolved, but, at the worst, are suspended and at the best, beautifully transcended. This is just as meaningful in pottery as in politics. The Sung synthesis, which looks so idle and dreamy on the surface, so precious and frail, is actually extremely dynamic—full of strength and tension.

A very fetching surface it must have been though. Hangchow, the Southern pleasure city turned capital, set amid waters and hills, wreathed with parks and canals and whimsical bridges, the great lake dreaming off into infinity, and the streets, in Baudelaire's phrase, "lit with prostitutes." It was like Baudelaire's Paris, the Paris of the Second Empire when all important business and politics were transacted in salons and brothels, but most of all it was like Tiepolo's Venice—the Venice of Browning's *Toccata of Galuppi's*.

Read the poem again; it's sentimental, but so was Gaspara Stampa and so too was Su Tung-p'o in not a very different way:

As for Venice and her people, merely born to bloom and drop,
Here on earth they bore their fruitage, mirth and folly were the crop:
What of soul was left, I wonder, when the kissing had to stop?

"Dust and ashes!" So you creak it, and I want the heart to scold.
Dear dead women, with such hair, too—what's become of all the gold
Used to hang and brush their bosoms? I feel chilly and grown old.

Sentimentality is a middle-class quality. It is especially one of the aristocratized middle class where it occurs.

Su Tung-p'o was the greatest of the poets of Sung and the greatest poet of sentiment China ever produced. He was one of the greatest calligraphers of all time, and on his style is reared a whole tradition of Japanese fluent calligraphy. He was master of the abstract brush stroke—a painter of bamboo leaves in misty moonlight, so famous that half the bamboo scrawls in Hong Kong art shops are attributed to him to this day. While he was governor of Hangchow he was the lover of Su Hsiao-hsiao, one of the most beautiful prostitutes of Chinese legend, whose tomb was still venerated beside the West Lake of the city until our own time.

A soft breeze from the East scarcely ripples the pale water.
North of the Lake, south of the Lake, the Blue mountains vanish in warm mist.
Pairs of ducks play on the mud flats.
Orioles sing, mating in the new leaves.

By Sung standards this is an intensely erotic poem. It is love-making in a universe which neither is nor is not, in which the only reality is the unconditioned Void, of which it cannot be said that it is either real or unreal, and behind which lies pure undetermined consciousness, thought which does not think:

I drift alone in the middle of the Lake.
There is no rush to moor to, nor bottom to hold an anchor.
Nothing is visible beyond the prow of my little boat.
I take the wine from the picnic basket and slowly get drunk,
while my rod hangs untended over the dim water.

The demon king Ravana asked for teaching and Buddha showed him all the mountains and palaces and jewels and harem maidens of all the universes. Suddenly Ravana's sensibility was overturned and he was utterly alone, and Buddha laughed. Why did he laugh? Because he knew that duality and nonduality are both delusions. Peace is the single point of suchness which is beyond all conditions. And then all the Buddhas and Bodhisattvas and gods and demons and people and beasts and things laughed in all the universes. So opens the Lankavatara Sutra. Again, Buddha, once while he was preaching, picked a flower and smiled, and only the disciple Kasyapa understood why he had smiled. According to tradition, Kasyapa by similar meaningless acts taught Bodhidharma, who brought Ch'an Buddhism (or Zen as it is known in Japan) to China riding on a reed.

Does this mean that the great artists and poets of Sung were all Ch'an Buddhists? They were not. Most of them were not Buddhists at all. They were mostly Confucianists, scholar-gentry who specially prided themselves on the orthodoxy of their caste philosophy. But Confucianism had changed. The welter and flow of ideas of the last two or three hundred years had created a new "universe of discourse," a new consciousness of the popular mind. Indian ideas and notions from the animistic folk background of China had mingled with and profoundly altered the old Confucian orthodoxy.

Sung times produced the two great founders of Neo-

Confucianism, Chu Hsi, China's greatest "philosopher" in our sense, and Lu Hsiang-shan, Chu's leading opponent. They not only made Confucianism a more systematic philosophy, they turned it into a personal discipline of the sensibility. To use Western philosophical jargon, which is misleading but will do, Chu and Lu both developed reality from Not-Being, the unconditioned, through the interaction of form (*li*) and potentiality (*ch'i*). For Chu, these two metaphysical principles always interacted, although the world of form was, eventually, one—pure, empty—the Void of the Buddhists. For Lu, form was always primary, its substantiation an illusion. The only trouble with this glib summary is that both thought of *li* (form, principle) as itself a realm of potentiality in our sense and *ch'i* as really a sort of bare matter, serving as a principle of individuation. For Chu, man's mind was a combination of *li* and *ch'i*. For Lu, man's mind had strayed from the world of *li*, pure form, to which it had originally belonged, and the aim of the wise and good man was to find his lost mind or true nature again by quiet meditation and begin to understand its relation to the whole. At the end would come, without words or ideas, the sudden illumination, the knowledge that the individual was in fact the totality. In the words of the Upanishads—"That art thou."

Far more important to them than the metaphysics they had developed, the Ch'an Buddhists, the Neo-Confucianists, all cultivated a specific kind of sensibility, a special life attitude. This sensibility is the ideal of the Bodhisattva, the being who turns away, on the brink of vanishing into Nirvana, out of quiet, "indifferent" love, and vows that he will not enter into salvation until he can bring all other beings with him. This he does with a smile of "indifference," realizing that all beings, animals, flowers, things, atoms, have the Buddha nature, and yet realizing that there is neither being nor not-being, neither Buddha nor not-Buddha, neither Nirvana nor not-Nirvana, neither illusion nor not-illusion. This ideal reaches its most developed form in Buddhism, true, and finds its most perfect expression in the weary, oversophisticated, smiling faces of the Sung paintings of the Bodhisattvas. But, toned down and made more "practical," it is very close to the ideal of the scholar-gentry. Both Neo-Confucianism and the Bodhisattva ideal involve a real sense of responsibility behind their language of indifference. The difference with orthodox Hinduism is marked. For Arjuna in his chariot in the Bhagavad-Gita, action and inaction become one and the same, but for the Chinese this becomes a scarcely concealed imperative to the moral, socially responsible action that has ever since been identified with Confucianism.

So Su Tung-p'o was not just a dreamer of mists and mountains and foggy bamboo leaves; he was a great administrator with a love and devotion for the people of Hangchow, to whom he became a kind of demigod. And, like a modern, altruistic, overcivilized English civil servant, he was acutely conscious of the pathos of his responsibility and the gulf that it created between him and those given into his charge.

. . . The rich prepare banquets.
Silk and brocade decorate their halls.
The poor have hardly anything to offer.
Instead, they try to hide
The family mortar from the tax assessor.
I am a stranger in this neighborhood,
Where gay processions fill the streets and alleys.
I, too, sing the old folksongs.
But I sing to myself. No one sings with me.

And again, Su's opponent, the great reformer Wang Anshih, who for a while put into effect the Utopian, semisocialistic measures of this idealized Confucianism:

In midsummer, leaning on my thorn stick,
I climb up the rocky trail
Where the leaf shadows make a darkness at noon.
I stop and listen to the quiet voice of the water.

The Sung sensibility was polarized between quiet meditation, a gentle sinking into the indeterminate profundity of an Absolute which was never absolute, and intense, active curiosity about all the manifold of life and things, which led to investigations into the riddles of nature.

This was the time when Chinese science came into its own, the full midsummer of an efflorescence of observation, speculation and technology. Printing, invented shortly before, came of age, and Sung books and style are still considered the best. T'ang stories had been as simple as the Brothers Grimm; true fiction in the vernacular begins with Sung. A whole new kind of poetry, at once freer and more complexly musical, developed—of this Su Tung-p'o is the acknowledged first master. Back to Sung is traced the beginning of modern drama, and the quieter, more subtle plays of the present repertory are still known as "Sung," although most of them are much later. Music, to which Confucius had attributed at least as much importance as ever did Plato or the Pythagoreans, was analyzed and systematized, and again, the quietest, subtlest, most civilized—to our ears—music is still known as Sung. It is likely that some of the solemn choral dances of the Japanese court date back to Sung China, little altered today. Taoism was also revived and provided with a systematic mythology and a philosophy, and it is from Taoist researches and speculations of this time that alchemy and related protoscientific practices grew and, in the case of alchemy, spread over the world. Great illustrated herbals, pharmacopoeias and manuals of medicine, acupuncture, massage, physiotherapy were compiled, as well as encyclopedias, not unlike our own, which developed six hundred years later. Chinese merchants sailed all the southern seas, at least as far as India and the Persian Gulf, and may have reached the African coast.

Painting shows the same polarity. In fact, Sung painting can be described most succinctly by saying that it sought two goals. The portrait painter, the painter of flowers, birds, animals, detailed or, so to speak, close-up studies of landscape, the genre painter of human activities, all strove to concentrate with such intensity on the realization of the subject, the Other, off there opposite their eyes, that the integument was burst asunder and the Buddha nature shown forth. This accounts for the extraordinary surface tension of Sung paintings like the famous *Two Geese* in the British Museum, so reminiscent of our own Arp or Brancusi, and, of course, it accounts for the overpowering sense of individuality in Sung portraiture, surpassed, I suppose, in our own world only by the Romans.

Especially after the conquest of the north by the Chi-Tan from the desert, on the other hand, when Southern Sung landscape almost dissolved in dream, the landscape painters sought to portray the essence of the Ch'an, Neo-Confucian or Taoist metaphysics of ultimate reality. It is significant that this type of painting, committed in principle to an aesthetic of the formless, rises to its highest achievements in a number of extremely individualistic painters. Tung Yüan's *River Landscape* in the Boston Museum establishes a kind of classic norm as early as A.D. 1000. Note that along with his fantasy, mists and illimitable waters, Tung Yüan is an acute observer of geological forms. A perfect example of a U-shaped glacial trough of the Yosemite type is the *Fishing in a Mountain Stream* by Hsu Tao-ning, also from about A.D. 1000, in the Nelson Gallery, Kansas City, Missouri. The strange, almost false-naïve calligraphic paintings of Mi Fei—sugar-loaf mountains, wet windy pines, marshy meadows, all swathed in mist—are painted with discreet, horizontal spots of the brush, in a technique so obvious and so personal as to be utterly inimitable.

Ma Yüan, whose lovely fan painting *Bare Willows and Distant Mountains* is perhaps the most famous Chinese painting in America, also painted a *Fisherman Alone in His Boat*, now in Japan, an archetypal illustration of an archetypal Ch'an poem . . . just a little boat, low in the water, a single figure, a drifting line, and the slight surge of the water stretching away. In a Chinese collection there is a long scroll attributed to Hsia Kuei, *A Myriad Miles of the Yang-Tse,* whole passages of which consist of nothing but the expanse of illimitable water. Other passages, however, are of rocks, whirlpools and rapids, and busy with traffic and folk life.

Many of the paintings of the school of Hsia Kuei are specifically portrayals of the act of "quiet meditation," a sage reclining by a waterfall or a still pool, or looking out from cliffs across endless, formless distance, and sheltered by a gnarled, stunted, highly individualistic pine. This type of painting, at least for my taste, culminates in Fa-ch'ang's *Eight Views of the Tung-T'ing Lake* and in the ink-blot painting of Ying Yu-chien, in his *Eight Views of Hsiao Hsiang.* The most famous section of this latter scroll, *Haze Dispersing from around a Mountain Village,* anticipates the ink blots of the great Japanese, Sesshu, and his followers, and is certainly one of the most remarkable paintings in all history.

There is a small group of paintings, mostly by one or the other of the great artists I have already mentioned, which, it seems to me, combine all the qualities of both main types of Sung painting, the capturing of the absolutely generalized and of the intensely particular—the Buddha Nature and the Unformed Void. Chief among these is the simple and stupendous painting of Fa-ch'ang (Mu Ch'i), five Japanese persimmons in varying stages of ripeness in an irregular row, and slightly to the fore, another, the smallest, persimmon. This is certainly the most nearly perfect expression of the aesthetic principles of the Sung period, whether derived from Ch'an Buddhism or Neo-Confucianism. All similar Western paintings, those Italian bottles of Morandi, for instance, come up to it, topple over into it and vanish. Here is one of the greatest achievements of the mind and skill of man, and inconceivably simple. There is a *Woman in White* with a wicker basket and fly whisk in the Freer Gallery, Washington, D.C., which is more than one of the world's most haunting portraits. The folds of her robe conceal her feet so that she seems to float in bottomless space. The quiet surface tension of the forms is almost unbearable. As you stand before it and watch it (and I use this verb advisedly), its still rapture catches you up and marks your mind indelibly forever after. And last, by another unknown Sung painter, a dog in the Boston Museum, a painting of a being so lonely, so poignant and yet so sure, that it might have been painted by a Bodhisattva himself, as he smiled "indifferently," turned away from promised bliss and lifted his first soul out of Hell.

This special poignancy is itself the Sung sensibility par excellence, and it finds expression in poetry too, notably in Su Tung-p'o's "Gold Hill Monastery," "Terrace in the Snow," and Lu Yu's "I Walk Out in the Country at Night" and the poems by the poetesses Li Ch'ing Chao and Chu Shu Chen (which can be found translated in my own *One Hundred Poems from the Chinese*). In the poetesses the sense of vertiginous ecstasy reaches a point verging on hysteria. Here is another poem by Li Ch'ing Chao:

The lascivious air of Spring
Overflows the narrow garden
Beyond my open windows.
Across the pulsating curtains
Confused flower shadows flicker.
All alone in the summer house,
Wordless, I stroke a rose jade lute.
Far off in the lingering early
Twilight a cliff falls from a mountain.
The faint wind breathes with a light rain,
Delicate as a falling shadow.
O, pepper plant, you do not need
To bow and beg pardon of me.
I know you cannot hold back the day.

No art requires more refined perception than pottery. Here all forms are at least as subtle as the subtlest Brancusis and the slightest error of taste jars like a noisy racket. It is not surprising then that the Sung Dynasty produced the greatest pottery ever made. Pure, ethereal celadons, Tingware plates that look as though they had been made on the moon, stoneware bowls and jugs with brown hare's fur or oil-spot glaze, Chün ware with a purplish mottled glaze like the breast of a bird, these are among the loveliest and the most subtle things in all the world, natural or man-made. It was in Sung times, too, that the control of the ceramic process to produce just the right kind of accident began—crude, irregular pots with blemishes in the glaze—as though they had been made by some half-blind, stumbling old peasant in a bonfire on the windy fields of Heaven. Fortunately, Sung pottery has influenced all the world since and, although not everyone can own a great Sung painting, anyone can have a pot of Japanese or American stoneware that embodies much of the achievement of the Sung potters.

And last, as a token of farewell, I would like to conclude with a tiny jade pitcher-shaped vase in the British Museum. There is nothing to it, it is only three and a half inches high, with a ring handle and a little ornamental band. It looks rather as though it might have held a royal baby's milk. But it is infinitely subtle, so much so that if you look too long at it in its case in the British Museum, it will hypnotize you. Its color is even more subtle than its form, the mottled olive and khaki and gray of the plugs of jade placed in the ears and nostrils of the distinguished dead. This little vase looks as though it might have lain against the heart of the buried Kuan Yin at the end of one or her many incarnations.

Who Am I?
Where Am I Going???

Two documents on my desk. A cross-country phone call from an enthusiastic young woman, and now a letter: "We would like an article about how the old order has changed. The old problems have, more or less, dissipated. Race is less and less becoming a reason for inclusion or rejection. We do not want anything about whether the New Negro is real or a myth. (We say we are here by showing it.) Nor do we wish the article addressed to Negroes." The other document—the morning newspaper story that Dick Wright is dead of a heart attack in Paris.

It has been a long time since I first met Dick at the Left Ball of the Chicago John Reed Club. The old order has changed, not once, but several times, and in many ways. Richard Wright knew it, and he knew that he had not changed with the times, at least as a writer of fiction. He knew he had stayed away too long, from his country first, and finally he realized he had stayed away too long from his race as well. He was a great writer, first because he was a brave man, second, because he told the truth. He never fell for any part of the Social Lie.

He accepted no part of the sticky web of compromises—the tangle of contradictory and contrary compromises—that make up the hoax of "race relations." He didn't just reject the various levels of sophistication of Uncle Tomism. He knew that the Left and Liberal solutions were just elaborate psychodramas for the civilized misfits of both races.

Curiously enough, though, he never saw through the fraud of French racial equality until the last years of his life. It is so easy to sit on the *terrasse* of the Deux Magots with Sedar Senghor and Françoise Sagan, while the waiter bows and scrapes and the women come and go, talking of Ionesco.

It slips your mind that it's still "Boy!" in Brazzaville, except for world-famous writers, and the new kasbahs of Paris are worse than the old slums of Natchez and Mobile.

Even after you learn—it's like back home, where, of course, you despise the Crow-Jimism of the Negrophiles—but, after all, you are treated very well indeed in the Faubourg Saint Germain, and you certainly are not in New Orleans.

The last few times I met Wright we didn't quarrel, but we had some pretty hot arguments—nobody enjoys being told he is living in the past. I think the Bandung Conference brought Dick up to date with a jerk. The book he wrote on it is the best piece of reportage he ever did.

Bandung had a curious effect on him. Talking to all those hundreds of colored people, from all over the southern half of the world, he realized that he was, in a sense, a "White Man" himself. Their job was to throw off the burden of totally foreign exploiters and to revivify old civilizations, or to raise still barbaric ones to new levels of civilization, differing in essence from that of Western Europe.

His struggle, and the struggle of the American Negro, had been for full participation in Western Civilization. His colleagues at Bandung expected that he would hate the white imperialist for the same reasons they did, and they were puzzled and disoriented when they found out that the two emotional areas didn't overlap at all.

Marcus Garvey to the contrary, "museum reproductions" of African sculpture on the over-mantel to the contrary, all of their goals and solutions lay in quite different regions from Wright's.

Richard Wright told the truth about "living Jim Crow," a truth most of the well-bred Negroes of his day were unwilling to admit, not just publicly or to white people, but even to themselves. His first books were greeted with paeans of adulatory masochism by *white* critics. They thoroughly dismayed the hincty "upper classes" whose doings fill the Society columns of the Negro press.

Today the goals of Wright's protest have all been won—in principle—*but in principle only*. Today the struggle is no longer against the lynch rope, the blowtorch, tar and feathers; those victories lie behind us, morally—but morally only. If you are being raped in the kitchen or burned alive in the woods, it is small consolation to know that all the world condemns your persecutors as evil men.

If the problems of the Negro in America are defined in terms of the melodramatic climaxes of Richard Wright's stories, perhaps they have, more or less, but mostly less, dissipated. But have these ever been the major problems facing the average individual? As I write this, all you have to do is switch on the television; there, coming from the streets of New Orleans, are "the old problems." Saying they are gone won't dissipate them.

Where is race becoming less and less a reason for inclusion or rejection? Greenwich Village? The New School for Social Research? The United Nations? Unfortunately, the average Negro, and even the average professional and middle-class Negro, in America is not so situated that he can take advantage of the tolerant atmosphere of those enlightened environments.

How about an upper-middle-class subdivision in Putnam or Marin Counties? New York, San Francisco and Chicago are looked on as the least Jim Crow cities in the country. How many Negroes are there in the Symphony or the Ballet in those cities? How many Negroes take part freely in the scientific and social life of the professional associations? How many Negro television shows are there? How many reporters on daily papers?

Sure, Negroes will be served in most of the hotel dining rooms. How many are you actually likely to see any night, dining at the Drake, the St. Francis or the Waldorf?

Don't address the article to Negroes. Hmmmm. Sure, the New Negro is real. He has been real since before Frederick

Douglass. But don't think that just because you can go visit friends in a loft off Second Avenue and drink wine and talk about Sartre and de Kooning's return to figurative painting, you have won social acceptance.

Sure, you can have an affair with a fashionable wild man and get written up in a novel. Read the novel—if this is miscegenation, give me celibacy. Unless you prefer to live in a world of make-believe, the problems are just beginning.

There is nothing problematic about lynching, it is simply evil. More subtly, the same is true of any degree of racial chauvinism. The problems *begin* as the crippling evils die away. Aristotle, beginning his *Ethics*, says that the first requirement for ethical action is freedom—a slave is not capable of ethics.

This is not altogether true, but it is true enough. Once the crippling bondage of race caste has been broken; once the actual manacles are gone, then the step by step conquest of complete social viability will go on for a long time raising more problems, even if "better" problems, than it solves.

Don't forget. The end of the road is total social indifference as to race, not in the Five Spot or the Blue Note; not in City College; not in a political rally—and least of all, not for intellectuals, entertainers and celebrities. It means that race won't make any difference if you're a plumber and go to the Plumbers' Convention. It won't make a particle of difference with your neighbors in your apartment house or suburb. It won't make any difference to the kids your kids play with, or to the young men and women your sons and daughters choose to marry.

Who in the name of God believes that we are anywhere near that state of affairs? You can't even start. You can't get to be a plumber.

No. The ghettos are still there, although lately the big cities have taken to flattening them and building $100 a room a month apartments in their places. Integrated of course—at $100 a room a month. The ghettos just move over a few blocks and are worse than they were before.

My friends are the most liberal and enlightened set of the city that prides itself on being the most liberal and enlightened in the country. I almost never meet Negroes at their homes. There are no Negroes whatever in the Ballet or the Symphony—none up front, and damn few in the audience. If there are any Negroes playing a socially active role in the scientific and professional life of the city, I haven't heard of them, although there are certainly plenty who are qualified to do so.

California is full of National and State Parks. I have never seen a single Negro camping, mountaineering, hiking, riding, or fishing in the back country. And, in the course of many years, only perhaps a dozen families camping in the auto camps in the centers of the more popular parks.

Legal segregation is going. Jim Crow is dying. But he isn't dead yet. The struggle against discrimination is just beginning. The conflicts and problems of that struggle, both social and personal, will not be as dramatic as the searing climaxes of the novels of Richard Wright and Chester Himes. The important ones will be so quiet it will be easy for a few favorably situated people to pretend they aren't there at all. They will even come to believe it. But they will be there just the same, and it will take more than ignoring them to make them go away.

The Poet As Translator

When discussing the poet as translator, from time immemorial it has been the custom to start out by quoting Dryden. I shan't, but I will try to illustrate Dryden's main thesis—that the translation of poetry into poetry is an act of sympathy—the identification of another person with oneself, the transference of his utterance to one's own utterance. The ideal translator, as we all know well, is not engaged in matching the words of a text with the words of his own language. He is hardly even a proxy, but rather an all-out advocate. His job is one of the most extreme examples of special pleading. So the prime criterion of successful poetic translation is assimilability. Does it get across to the jury?

If we approach the great historic translations this way it is easy to understand why they are great. It is obvious on the most general survey of English literature that the classic translations of the classics accompany the classics of English, occur in the periods of highest productivity and greatest social—what shall we say? cohesion? euphoria? Tudor, Jacobean, Caroline, Augustan or Victorian, many of the translations are themselves among the major English works of their time. Malory's *Morte d'Arthur*, North's Plutarch, Pope's Homer—and, of course, the King James Bible. All the great translations survive into our time because they were so completely of their own time. This means simply that the translator's act of identification was so complete that he

This essay was first presented as a lecture at the University of Texas and included in a symposium volume on translation published by the University of Texas Press.

spoke with the veridical force of his own utterance, conscious of communicating directly to his own audience.

Of course, many such translations are ethnocentric to a degree—sometimes to the degree that they have turned the original into something totally different. This is not true of many of the greatest translations but it is true of some. Is Fitzgerald a translation of Omar? Here the two cultures are so radically different, all that can be said is that Fitzgerald was probably all of medieval Persia that Victorian England was prepared to assimilate. The only real problem is Urquhart. It is hard to imagine anything less like the benign humanism of Rabelais than this crabbed and cracked provincial euphuism. The point of Rabelais is that he was the opposite of eccentric—he was profoundly, utterly normal. Urquhart produced a Scottish classic, and so for Englishmen Rabelais will always be an oddity. This is unfortunate, but then, is Rabelais' normality normal in the British Isles? I think not. Perhaps his Gallic magnanimity could only cross the Channel tricked out in tartan stripes for a harlequinade.

It is the custom to deride Pope's Homer. Nothing could be less like Homer. But the eighteenth century certainly didn't think so—on either side of the Channel. This was the Homer they were prepared to accept. Of course, Pope was a neurasthenic, a dandy in Baudelaire's sense, or Wallace Stevens's, a thoroughly urbanized exquisite who had professionalized his nervous system. Whatever his formal commitments (Pope was a Roman Catholic) his real system of values was only a specialized hierarchy of nervous response. Certainly, nothing less like Homer could be imagined. But each age demands its own image. The other eighteenth-century Homers are not Homer either; they are just mediocre or bad. Is Butler Homer? I suppose he is for those of us who are rationalist, utilitarian, humanitarian. He is a fine Reform Club Homer. I still prefer Butler to Butcher and Lang or William Morris, let alone T. E. Lawrence. However, it is simply not true that the Butcher and Lang version is any more false to the text than Butler. Butcher and Lang is Homer for the readers of *The Idylls of the King*.

I am not proposing to dissolve all questions of authenticity in some sort of vulgar pragmatism. The text is always there as a control. The recent hair-raising performance of Robert Graves, for instance, both violates the text and fails to transmit anything resembling Homer. This is not Homer for the readers of *Punch;* it is the invasion of the text of Homer by the text of *Punch.* Here we have passed the limits of eccentricity. Pope's whole age was eccentric, as was Urquhart's. But theirs was a viable eccentricity; Graves's is not. It is an unpleasant eccentric eccentricity.

The first question must be: is this as much of Homer, or whomever, as can be conveyed on these terms to this audience? Second, of course: is it good in itself? Lord Derby or T. E. Lawrence are simply not good enough English. Graves is simply in bad taste, and the Heroic Age, by definition, was before bad taste was invented. It is possible, of course, that a given audience cannot assimilate enough of the original to justify the effort to achieve a significant resemblance. How much of *Les Liaisons Dangereuses* could be translated into the world of William Law? How much does Proust mean to a Chinese collective farmer and vice versa? Imagine Dante translated by Dorothy Parker or Shakespeare by Tristan Tzara. You don't have to imagine. Dante has recently been translated by someone not too unlike Dorothy Parker. Read it.

As time goes on all translations become dated. Before the language changes the society changes. The Butcher and Lang Homer is repugnant to us because society has changed, but has not changed so much that it has become strange to us. Pope, on the other hand, speaks a language that, considered purely linguistically, seems closer to our own, but his world has receded so far that we read him for his special and extraordinary insights and distortions. At length language changes so much that it becomes liturgical. This is a natural thing and can never be imitated. The nineteenth century made the mistake of thinking it could. Nothing sounds less like liturgical English than William Morris trying to imitate it. This led to terrible waste—I doubt if Morris's wonderful

Saga Library was ever readable by anybody, and there the great sagas are, locked up in that ridiculous language. On the other hand, we never think of the Prophets as speaking like a committee of Jacobean Bishops; we think of the Jacobean Bishops as speaking like the Prophets. At last the language becomes really foreign. Chaucer's wonderful rendering of the *Consolation* of Boethius sounds splendid to us, and certainly seems by far the best ever made in any language. It didn't sound that way to generations closer to Chaucer, not even as far away as Dryden and Pope. They read Chaucer as still in their own language. We do not, but in another that we have no difficulty translating as we go along. Of course, there is here the special factor: Chaucer was an incomparably finer poet than his original.

What I have been trying to convey indirectly is what the poet does in the living relationship of translation, the actual act. Or at least what I think he does and what I presume I do myself. Although it is not itself a translation, consider such a poem as H.D.'s "Heliodora."* It may seem dated to those who are not old enough to have mellowed to H.D.'s enthusiasms, to those who are not young enough to have never heard of her. Its language is very much the argot of Bloomsbury aestheticism with a strong lacing of the Chautauqua Circuit. Still, I think it does convey, all allowances being made, the excitement of translation of great poetry. It certainly does recall very vividly to me my own experience—my first translation from the Greek, a whole evening till after midnight spent in the continuously exalted discussion of one small Sapphic fragment with a friend who was then an undergraduate student of Paul Shorey's.

Here is the H.D.:

Heliodora

He and I sought together,
over the spattered table,

*"Heliodora," *Collected Poems of H.D.*, Liveright, New York, 1929, and *Selected Poems of H.D.*, Grove Press, New York, 1957.

rhymes and flowers,
gifts for a name.

He said, among others,
"I will bring"
(and the phrase was just and good,
but not as good as mine,)
"the narcissus that loves the rain."

We strove for a name,
while the light of the lamps burnt thin
and the outer dawn came in,
a ghost, the last at the feast
or the first,
to sit within
with the two that remained
to quibble in flowers and verse
over a girl's name.

He said, "the rain-loving,"
I said, "the narcissus, drunk,
drunk with the rain."
Yet I had lost
for he said,
"the rose, the lover's gift,
is loved-of-love,"
he said it,
"loved-of-love,"

I waited, even as he spoke,
to see the room filled with a light,
as when in winter,
the embers catch in a wind
when a room is dank;
so it would be filled, I thought,
our room with a light
when he said,
(and he said it first,)
"the rose, the lover's delight,
is loved-of-love,"

but the light was the same.

Then he caught,
seeing the fire in my eyes,
my fire, my fever, perhaps,
for he leaned
with the purple wine
stained on his sleeve,
and said this:
"did you ever think
a girl's mouth,
caught in a kiss,
is a lily that laughs?"

I had not.
I saw it now
as men must see it forever afterwards;
no poet could write again,
"the red lily,
a girl's laugh caught in a kiss";
it was his to pour in the vat
from which all poets dip and quaff,
for poets are brothers in this.

So I saw the fire in his eyes,
it was almost my fire,
(he was younger,)
I saw the face so white,
my heart beat,
it was almost my phrase;
I said, "surprise the muses,
take them by surprise;
it is late,
rather it is dawn-rise,
those ladies sleep, the nine,
our own king's mistresses."

A name to rhyme,
flowers to bring to a name,
what was one girl faint and shy,

with eyes like the myrtle,
(I said: "her underlids
are rather like myrtle,")
to vie with the nine?

Let him take the name,
he had the rhymes,
"the rose, loved-of-love,
the lily, a mouth that laughs,"
he had the gift,
"the scented crocus,
the purple hyacinth,"
what was one girl to the nine?

He said:
"I will make her a wreath";
he said:
"I will write it thus:

I will bring you the lily that laughs,
I will twine
with soft narcissus, the myrtle,
sweet crocus, white violet,
the purple hyacinth, and last,
the rose, loved-of-love,
that these may drip on your hair
the less soft flowers,
may mingle sweet with the sweet
of Heliodora's locks,
myrrh-curled."

(He wrote "myrrh-curled,"
I think, the first.)

I said:
"they sleep, the nine,"
when he shouted swift and passionate;
"*that* for the nine!
above the hills,
the sun is about to wake,

and to-day white violets
shine beside white lilies
adrift on the mountain side;
to-day the narcissus opens
that loves the rain."

I watched him to the door,
catching his robe
as the wine-bowl crashed to the floor,
spilling a few wet lees,
(ah, his "purple hyacinth!")
I saw him out of the door,
I thought:
there will never be a poet
in all the centuries after this,
who will dare write,
after my friend's verse,
"a girl's mouth
is a lily kissed."

What H.D. was doing in this rather precious and somewhat dated little drama was objectifying the story of her own possession by the ghost of Meleager while translating his *stephanos,* his proem to his anthology. Whatever else she has done, she has conveyed the poignancy of that feeling of possession and the glamour of the beautiful Greek words as they come alive in one's very own English. Most of the epithets can be found in the lovely 147th Epigram of the 5th Book, and who will ever forget the first time he ever saw them, bright with their old Greek life on the page? That 147th Epigram has been translated by most of those who have taken the Anthology to English, but only H.D. brings over the glamour and excitement of the language.

Now let us look at a selection from the great number of translations of Sappho's "Orchard," the poem I translated so long ago under identical emotional circumstances, and finally my own.

. . . And by the cool waterside the breeze rustles amid
the apple-branches, and the quivering leaves shed lethargy;

J. M. EDMONDS

And round about the cool water gurgles through apple-boughs,
and slumber streams from quivering leaves.

HENRY THORNTON WHARTON

And by the cool stream the breeze murmurs through apple
branches and slumber pours down from quivering leaves.

COX

Cool waters tumble, singing as they go
Through appled boughs. Softly the leaves are dancing.
Down streams a slumber on the drowsy flow,
My soul entrancing.

T. F. HIGHAM

Through orchard-plots with fragrance crowned
The clear cold fountain murmuring flows;
And forest leaves with rustling sound
Invite to soft repose.

JOHN H. MERIVALE

All around through branches of apple-orchards
Cool streams call, while down from the leaves a-tremble
Slumber distilleth.

J. ADDINGTON SYMONDS

By the cool water the breeze murmurs, rustling
Through apple branches, while from quivering leaves
Streams down deep slumber.

EDWIN M. COX

. . . about the cool water
the wind sounds through sprays

of apple, and from the quivering leaves
slumber pours down. . . .

K. REXROTH

I hold no brief for my own translation, but at the time I did it, it was an entirely original experience with me, or rather, I should say, with us, for, as was the case with H.D.'s poem, there were two of us working on it together—and neither of us was familiar with any other English version. That evening was one of the memorable experiences of my life, just because of the completeness of projection into the experience of that great dead Greek woman. On inspection of these various versions it is obvious that what matters most is sympathy—the ability to project into Sappho's experience and then to transmit it back into one's own idiom with maximum viability.

There is a special factor here, something that comes up in almost all translations of Sappho from Catullus to our own day. There is a special, vertiginous exaltation in Sappho's language, not only in the phrases of a poem like the one to Anactoria, which is about such a state, but even in the very few words surviving in some of the fragments. Both H.D. and those two very exalted ladies who called themselves Michael Field not only felt this but they all wrote poems which are expansions of tiny fragments of Sappho, and which in each case attribute to the inspiring fragment precisely this supernatural luster. Is there any basis for this in fact? It is easy to see what an Englishwoman of Sappho's temperament could do with Fragment 27, *optais amme,* "you burn me . . ." but is there anything actually inflammatory about Fragment 106: *Met' emoi meli mete melissais,* "Neither honey nor bees for me." Does it bear H.D.'s almost hysterical expansion? I think not. Actually it means, "If I can't have roses without thorns I won't have them at all," and is a proverb quoted by Sappho. Here is a poem by Michael Field which is an expansion of Fragments 109 and 110: *Kotharos gar o chrysos io* and *Dios gar pais est' o chrysos/'kenon ou* *sees oude kis/ dardaptois. o de damnatai/ kai phrenon brotean kratiston.**

Yea, gold is son of Zeus; no rust
Its timeless light can stain.
The worm that brings men's flesh to dust
Assaults its strength in vain.
More gold than gold the love I sing,
A hard, inviolable thing.

Men say the passions should grow old
With waning years; my heart
Is incorruptible as gold,
'Tis my immortal part.
Nor is there any god can lay
On love the finger of decay.

This is a rather lovely little poem, perhaps the best in the Michael Field volume of reconstructions of Sappho, *Long Ago*. But it is not Sappho—it is very specifically the *fin de siècle* Lesbian sensibility that flourished alongside the poetry of Wilde and his friends. It is part of the same myth as *Les Chansons de Bilitis* and the poems of Renée Vivien. The amusing thing about it is that the Greek "originals" are not originals at all, but paraphrases in Sappho's metre from indirect references in Pausanias and a scholiast on Pindar. The Sapphic legend was so powerful that anything was enough to set off her late-born sisters. Here sympathy achieves a kind of translation when the source does not even exist. In a few of the translations of the "Apple Orchard" lack of sympathy leads to ludicrous effects—to words (for instance, "gurgles") that would never have occurred to anyone who bothered to project himself imaginatively into Sappho's experience.

Still there is the question of the awesome luster of Sap-

*Transcription from the Greek texts in The Loeb Library *Lyra Graeca* volume, edited by J. M. Edmonds. The Scholiast on Hesiod ascribes 110 to Pindar.

pho's simplest words. Is it there or do we read it into her fragments? Partly it is a function of attention. If you isolate two sentences of a skillful description of passion or of Nature and say, "Pay attention, these are by the greatest lyric poet who ever lived," the mind will find values in them which may have been there, but which would normally have been passed over. Prisoners with nothing else to do, their eyes focused on the stained ceilings of their cells for hours, can find more there to look at than they might in the Sistine Chapel. True, Sappho's apple orchard or her waning moon have all the intensity of Japanese *haiku,* but so do Frances Densmore's schematic translations of Chippewa and Teton Sioux poetry—and, we should never forget, so do hundreds of mediocre English translations of Japanese *haiku* themselves, which transmit none of the special virtues of the originals. I am afraid that I must admit that the supernatural gleam that seems to emanate from the *oio polu leukoteron* of Fragment 62, "far whiter than an egg," is a delusion, on a par with the mystical vision which comes with staring too long at an unshaded electric bulb or from taking one of Aldous Huxley's pharmaceutical nirvana-producers. But, still, in Sappho as in Homer, the simplest sentences do have a wonder, never equalled again in the West and never translated to any other language.

I am going to give you a little anthology of translations, all of them I think successful. They are not all successful for all the same reasons, and one of them is definitely eccentric, but I think they all exemplify a very high degree of imaginative identification with their originals:

The River Merchant's Wife: *A Letter**

While my hair was still cut straight across my forehead
I played about the front gate, pulling flowers.
You came by on bamboo stilts, playing horse,
You walked about my seat, playing with blue plums.

*"The River Merchant's Wife: A Letter," *Personae,* New Directions. Copyright 1926 by Ezra Pound.

And we went on living in the village of Chokan:
Two small people, without dislike or suspicion.

At fourteen I married My Lord you.
I never laughed, being bashful.
Lowering my head, I looked at the wall.

Called to, a thousand times, I never looked back.
At fifteen I stopped scowling,
I desired my dust to be mingled with yours
Forever and forever and forever.
Why should I climb the look out?

At sixteen you departed,
You went into far Ku-to-yen, by the river of swirling eddies,
And you have been gone five months.
The monkeys make sorrowful noise overhead.

You dragged your feet when you went out.
By the gate now, the moss is grown, the different mosses,
Too deep to clear them away!
The leaves fall early this autumn, in wind.
The paired butterflies are already yellow with August
Over the grass in the West garden;
They hurt me. I grow older.
If you are coming down through the narrows of the river
Kiang,
Please let me know beforehand,
And I will come out to meet you
As far as Cho-fu-Sa.

RIHAKU (LI PO)
EZRA POUND

The Shadow of the Orange-Leaves

The young girl who works
all day in her solitary chamber
is moved to tenderness if she
hears of a sudden the sound of
a jade flute.

And she imagines that she
hears the voice of a young boy.

Through the paper of the
windows the shadow of the
orange-leaves enters and sits
on her knees;

And she imagines that somebody has torn her silken dress.

"TIN-TUNG-LING"

STUART MERRILL'S ENGLISH OF JUDITH GAUTIER'S FRENCH

Lugete, O Veneres Cupidinesque

Weep, weep, ye Loves and Cupids all
And ilka Man o' decent feelin':
My lassie's lost her wee, wee bird,
An that's a loss ye'll ken, past healin'.

The lassie lo'ed him like her een:
The darling wee thin lo'ed the ither,
And knew and nestled to her breast,
As ony bairnie to her mither.

Her bosom was his dear, dear haunt —
So dear, he cared no long to leave it;
He'd nae but gang his ain sma' jaunt,
And flutter piping back bereavit.

The wee thing's gane the shadowy road
That's never travelled back by ony:
Out on ye, Shades! ye're greedy aye
To grab at ought that's brave and bonny.

Puir, foolish, fondling, bonnie bird,
Ye little ken what wark ye're leavin':
Ye've gar'd my lassie's een grow red,
Those bonnie een grow red wi' grievin.'

CATULLUS

G. S. DAVIES

Me Nive Candenti Petiit Modo Julia

White as her hand fair Julia threw
A ball of silver snow;
The frozen globe fired as it flew,
My bosom felt it glow.

Strange power of love! whose great command
Can thus a snow-ball arm;
When sent, fair Julia, from thine hand
Ev'n ice itself can warm.

How should we then secure our hearts?
Love's power we all must feel,
Who thus can by strange magic arts
In ice his flames conceal.

'Tis thou alone, fair Julia, know,
Canst quench my fierce desire;
But not with water, ice or snow,
But with an equal fire.

FROM THE PETRONIANA
SOAME JENYNS

*Chorus of Troizenian Women**

At high-tide,
the sea—they say—
left a deep pool
below the rock-shelf:
in that clear place
where the women dip
their water-jars,
my friend steeped her veils
and spread the scarlet stuff
across the hot ridge
of sun-baked rocks:
she first brought word

*"Chorus of Troizenian Women," *Collected Poems of H.D.*, Liveright, New York, 1929. By permission of Norman Holmes Pearson, copyright owner.

of my mistress:
"She lies sick,
faint on her couch
within the palace;
her thin veils
cast a shadow
across her bright locks.
I count three days
since her beautiful lips
touched the fine wheat—
her frail body
disdains nourishment:
she suffers—
some secret hurt
hastens her death."

Surely, O young queen,
you are possessed
by Pan, by Hecate,
by some spirit
of the Corybantic rites,
or by Cybele
from the hill-rocks!
or have you sinned,
that you suffer thus,
against Artemis?
Have you offered
no sacrificial cakes
to the huntress?
For she walks above earth,
along the sea-coast,
and across the salt trail
of the sea-drift.

Or is it that your lord,
born of Erechtheus,
the king most noble in descent,
neglects you in the palace

and your bride-couch
for another in secret?
Or has some sea-man,
landing at our port,
friendly to ships,
brought sad news from Crete?
or some great hurt
binds you to your couch,
broken in spirit.

EURIPIDES
H.D.

*An Elegy**

I

O youngest, best-loved daughter of Hsieh,
Who unluckily married this penniless scholar,
You patched my clothes from your own wicker basket,
And I coaxed off your hair pins of gold, to buy wine with;
For dinner we had to pick wild herbs—
And to use dry locust-leaves for our kindling.
. . . Today they are paying me a hundred thousand—
And all that I can bring to you is a temple sacrifice.

II

We joked, long ago, about one of us dying,
But suddenly, before my eyes, you are gone.
Almost all your clothes have been given away;
Your needlework is sealed, I dare not look at it. . . .
I continue your bounty to our men and our maids—
Sometimes, in a dream, I bring you gifts.
. . . This is a sorrow that all mankind must know—
But not as those know it who have been poor together.

III

I sit here alone, mourning for us both.
How many years do I lack now of my threescore and ten?

*"An Elegy," *The Jade Mountain,* Alfred A. Knopf, New York, 1929.

There have been better men than I to whom heaven denied
  a son,
There was a poet better than I whose dead wife could not
  hear him.
What have I to hope for in the darkness of our tomb?
You and I had little faith in a meeting after death—
Yet my open eyes can see all night
That lifelong trouble of your brow.

YÜAN CHÊN
WITTER BYNNER

Davies' Catullus has been put down, by a Sasenach, as a charming trick. Perhaps it is, but it is a moving poem in its own right and makes a comparison made many times before—the Celtic Catullus and the curiously Roman Burns. Also, Englishmen never really believe that Scots speak their own language. I perfer to think that Davies was so deeply moved and identified himself so closely with Catullus that he naturally turned to his most natural idiom—the Doric.

Soame Jenyns, not the curator of the British Museum, but the eighteenth-century churchman, seems to me to have achieved something very rare—a perfect translation of the most untranslatable type of Latin verse—those light lyrics and erotic elegies and little satires which are grouped in the *Petroniana* and which have otherwise only been captured by Ben Jonson and Herrick, and in their cases have been actually paraphrases. Not only is the English as close as possible to the metric of "Petronius," but the Latin and the English can both be sung to the same melody, "Phillis why shoulde we delaie?" by Waller with music by Henry Lawes. This can be found in Potter's *Reliquary of English Song*, and you can try it yourself if you like. Jenyns catches not only the tone of the original, but he handles language in exactly the same way. The only thing that is missing is the deep hidden undercurrent of ironic disillusion and memory of blood that haunts all these little poems and that led to their being attributed to Petronius in the first place.

Euripides was certainly a neurasthenic, always in quest of a new shudder of hyperaesthesia, and H.D. of all translators is closest to him in this. It is significant that she was herself so hung up on precisely this entranced intensity of response that she was unable to manage the whole plays—*Iphigenia* and *Hippolytus*—that she attempted, but translated only the high spots. They remain, nonetheless, the most Euripidean Euripides in English.

The greatest translators of Chinese—Judith Gautier, Klabund, Pound—knew less than nothing of Chinese when they did their best translations. In fact, Judith Gautier's lover and informant was a Thai, and himself had only the foggiest notions of the meanings of the Chinese text. Stuart Merrill was America's greatest poet between the New Englanders and the post-World War I moderns. He is practically unknown in this country because he lived and wrote almost exclusively in French. His English is definitely Edwardian or McKinleyan, and suffers from all the vices of *The Yellow Book*. Yet who could quarrel with this "translation"? It is a perfect transmission of one of the dominant themes of Chinese poetry and conveys exactly the neurotic lassitude and weakness of the sex-starved girls and deserted concubines who fill Chinese literature.

Pound worked from the notebooks of Fenollosa, who was himself badly informed by a Japanese whose knowledge of Chinese was already out of date, hopelessly Japonified for even the Japan of their day. Nevertheless this is one of the dozen or so major poems to be written by an American in the twentieth century, and still the best single translation from the Chinese.

I have included Witter Bynner's translation of Yüan Chên's elegy for his dead wife because I think it is, again, one of the best American poems of this country, incomparably Bynner's best poem, and, of all these poems, it conveys an overwhelming sense of identification with the situation of the original author. Mistakes, or at least dubious interpretations of a few words have been pointed out since it was made, and Bynner has discarded all the obliquity and literary reference of the original. Still, I think that from every point of view it is the second-ranking single translation from the Chinese out of all we have so far done.

Not only have the best "translators" not known Chinese, there is only one great translator who has, and only one in the second class—Arthur Waley, of course, and Bernhard Karlgren. Waley is a special case. He is a fine poet who has deliberately limited himself, as a kind of rigorous aesthetic discipline—a little like the self-imposed rigors of Paul Valéry—to translation from the Chinese and Japanese. Karlgren must be a special case, too, because he is the only Sinologist in any language who is any good at all as a translator. Possibly this is because he translates not into his own Swedish but into another foreign language—English.

I think this is due to the primitive state of Sinology. Most Sinologists are philologists. They are all too close to the language as such and too fascinated by its special very un-English and yet curiously very English-like problems ever to see the texts as literature. The grammarian takes over in the decadence of the study of a language; but he also takes over—in fact he is essential—in its infancy. Karlgren does as a matter of fact seem to sit very easy to Chinese; you can hear him ordering a meal in Cantonese or bawling out a bureaucrat in the National Language.

A bit of the GI approach to language—Ou est, les cigarettes, les girls, le restaurant, le W.C.?—would be a great help to contemporary Sinology and would go a long way to overcome the philologists' barbarism. After all, you can do nothing whatever with poetry until you comprehend that it too is about "the necessities of life."

One of the most engaging Hellenists of our time, Robert Byron, believed that all ancient Greek should be given the modern pronunciation. There is something to be said for this. Homer certainly did not sound like the waiter in the corner beanery, but it is possible that he sounded even less like the German and American professors, and it is certainly great fun to sit and eat pie à la mode after midnight and swap quotations with a lonely counterman. Somehow Pericles seems more available. This again is the virtue of the Italian and Roman Catholic pronunciation of Latin. The *Tantum Ergo* of Aquinas, known to children in the slums of Youngstown or Belfast, shades imperceptibly into the chirr of Horace's bracelets and back to the old Saturnian stomp. Communion is as important to the poet-translator as communication. I was taught the correct pronunciation of Latin, but I have never been able to take it seriously. On the other hand, who has ever forgotten the first time, on the streets of modern Rome, that he looked down at his feet and saw SPQR on a manhole cover?

Sympathy can carry you very far if you have talent to go with it. Hart Crane never learned to speak French and at the time he wrote his triptych poem "Voyages" he could not read it at all. His only informant was Allen Tate, a doubtful guide at best in this field, and his image of Rimbaud was an absurd inflation of the absurd Rimbaud myth. Yet "Voyages" is by far the best transmission of Rimbaud into English that exists—the purest distillation of the boyish hallucinations of the "Bateau Ivre."

Sympathy, or at least projection, can carry you too far. All sensible men to whom English is native are distressed at the French enthusiasm for M. Poë, the author of "Jamais Plus." Nobody in France seems to be able to learn ever, that Poe's verse is dreadful doggerel and his ratiocinative fiction absurd and his aesthetics the standard lucubrations that go over in Young Ladies' Study Circles and on the Chautauqua Circuit. The reason is, of course, that the French translate their whole culture into Poe before they even start to read him. They think his formalism is their formalism and his scientific speculation the speculation of d'Alembert. They think the giddy early nineteenth-century misses in Baltimore who swooned over the architectonics of "Eureka" are the same overcivilized courtesans who once bestowed their favors on the brocaded inventors of ingenious mathematical machines and, for that, on homespun Le Bon Franklin. In this they are exactly like the brave French Jesuits whose adroit questions taught the Iroquois to expatiate on the mysteries of the Great Spirit, a deity who had migrated unnoticed through the empyrean across the Atlantic from the court of Louis XV.

Finally, what does all this mean to the poet himself? What has it all meant to me? As Eliot, paraphrasing Dryden, has said, inspiration isn't always at its peak. Today we demand practically unrelieved intensity in poetry. The versified agricultural handbooks of the past are not for us—not even the verse novels of the Victorians. No poet ever could meet such a demand every day in the week. Translation, however, can provide us with poetic exercise on the highest level. It is the best way to keep your tools sharp until the great job, the great moment, comes along. More important, it is an exercise of sympathy on the highest level. The writer who can project himself into the exultation of another learns more than the craft of words. He learns the stuff of poetry. It is not just his prosody he keeps alert, it is his heart. The imagination must evoke, not just a vanished detail of experience, but the fullness of another human being.

Last and not least, translation saves you from your contemporaries. You can never really model yourself on Tu Fu or Leopardi or Paulus the Silentiary, but if you try you can learn a great deal about yourself. It is all too easy to model yourself on T. S. Eliot or William Carlos Williams or W. H. Auden or Allen Ginsberg—fatally easy—thousands do it every day. But you will never learn anything about yourself. Translation is flattering, too. I don't at all like feeling like T. S. Eliot or Allen Ginsberg. All through the world's literature there are people I enjoy knowing intimately, whether Abelard or Rafael Alberti, Pierre Reverdy or Tu Fu, Petronius or Aesculapius. You meet such a nice class of people.

The Holy Kabbalah

There is singularly little on Jewish mysticism of any sort to be found in English. Furthermore, most of it is not very rewarding. Much of it is definitely antagonistic. However Routledge published long ago, 1910 in fact, a book, *Aspects of the Hebrew Genius*, edited by Leon Simon, a collection of essays once given as lectures in the North London Jewish Literary Union. There is a chapter on Jewish mysticism by H. Sperling, and in the very first paragraph he says these tremendous words: "They [the vague mystical yearnings of man] can, however, fitly be compared to that invisible chain that binds husband to wife, parents to children, relation to relation, friend to friend, social unit to social unit. Without these lesser mysticisms society would dissolve into its first atoms; without the larger mysticism man would break away from his Maker and be flung into nothingness." On these words hang all the Law and the Prophets. This is the essence of Judaism. It is also the essence of Jewish mysticism, whether the speculations of Hellenistic Neo-Platonists, Medieval Kabbalists, Polish or Levantine Hasidim, or the sophisticated and fashionable philosophy of Martin Buber.

Kabbalism and Hasidism seem, to a Christian taught in his own religion to view Gnostic and theosophic tendencies as the source of all heresy, to be a kind of Jewish heterodoxy. They are not. Jewish orthodoxy is not defined by the correctness of the answers it gives to metaphysical and cosmological questions. The Torah, the Rites of Passage, the Ceremonies

This essay was an introduction to a new edition of *The Holy Kabbalah* by A. E. Waite. University Books, New Hyde Park, New York, 1960.

of the Holidays, the poetic and narrative books of the Bible, philosophy and fantasy, from Maimonides to Isaak Singer—the consensus of faith is never broken. Kabbalism is nothing but a transcendental way of looking at the "purely formal" rites of circumcision, marriage, confirmation. There is no "Kabbalistic Mystery," however profound, that cannot be found clearly and simply exemplified in the ceremonies of Succoth, the Feast of Tabernacles.

Under the influence of millennia of legalistic interpretation of the Law, and guided by the extreme rationalism of Maimonides and other Jewish scholastics, Judaism has come to seem, at least to the outsider, a "religion of the Book" in the most extreme sense, a code, rather than living faith. This is illusory. All the Talmuds in the world cannot make a religion. Religion is what people do—act and contemplation. Whitehead said it was what man does with his aloneness—a very Protestant, in fact, Lutheran statement, and the expression of a theory rather than of actuality. Even the most extreme neo-Lutheran, Kierkegaard, spent much of his time and energy struggling with the community of the Church of Denmark. The casuistry of rabbis, the exhortations of prophets—we must never forget that these take place in the context of a people, held together in a rite. That, after all, is their only significance—to insure the integrity of the people and the continuity of the rite.

Someone back in the nineteenth century said that religion is what humanity uses to fill in the gap between technology and the physical environment. Historically this was certainly true. But it is a kind of inverse and diminishing definition. Ideally, religion is what would be left after man *knew* everything. Kabbalism, like all other Gnosticisms, does concern itself very much with knowing, with cosmology and cosmogony, the nature and process of the Universe. "You shall know and the knowledge shall make you free." Free for what? Today we are inclined to forget how trapped man was by the recalcitrance of his environment, by puzzling vagaries of the universe. Before the universe could be given significance—

"valued" as we say nowadays—it had to be given coherence. Gnosticism has been accused by its opponents, from Plotinus to the present, of equating coherence and significance, structure and value. This may be true where Gnostic movements have been heretical—split off and isolated from the main body of religious development. Kabbalism is not heterodox. It is a symbolic and aesthetic elaboration af the actual cult of Israel, with which it never loses contact. The Jewish Prayerbook as we have it today is essentially a Kabbalistic document.* *"Credere est orare, orare est cognoscere,"* said the great Roman Catholic modernist, Father Tyrrell: "To believe is to pray, to pray is to know."

When man cannot understand nature, and insofar as he cannot understand it at any point, he is confronted with an actual vacuum, and into this he projects himself. What is sought in Alchemy or the Hermetic Books or the Memphite Theology, or irrational fads like flying saucers, is the basic pattern of the human mind in symbolic garb, as it presents itself in the individual believer, and behind that, in the enduring structures of the human organism itself. As the speculative constructions of religion fall away as explanations of " reality" they assume the character of symbolic masks of states of the soul. If they persist in the practices of a cult, we say they have been etherealized. It is precisely their irrationality which keeps dogma and ritual alive. If they can be reduced to "common-sense" explanations or denials they die away. Only the mysteries survive, because they correspond to the processes of man's internal life, outward visible signs of inner spiritual realities.

To go back to the beginning, Kabbalism dates back into the most obscure past of Judaism. What are the distinguishing ideas of Kabbalism? It is first of all a theory of emanations ("degenerative monism" it is called philosophically). The

*This Prayerbook—*Siddur*—is not something relegated to Sabbath service in the Synagogue. Both man and woman use it day and night. What the Bible was to the Protestant in the great days of Dissent, this *grimoire* of Kabbalah is to the orthodox Jew and his wife.

inscrutable Godhead fills and contains the universe. To become active and creative, God emanated ten *sephiroth* or intelligences. A special prominence is given to one of these emanations, who functions as a female principle in the Deity, a demiurge and a term to creation. This is the final emanation, Malkuth the Queen, the physical manifestation of Deity in the universe. She is thought of as a Divine Woman, the Bride of God (like the Shakti of Shiva). Finally, the "innermost secrets" of the Kabbalah are what are "occult" in all occultism, erotic mysticism and a group of practices of the sort we call yoga—autonomic nervous-system gymnastics. For the Kabbalist the ultimate sacrament is the sexual act, carefully organized and sustained as the most perfect mystical trance. Over the marriage bed hovers the Shekinah. Kabbalism also includes, of course, a group of divinatory and magical practices, manipulations of the alphabet and the text of the Pentateuch, magic spells and rites. All of these elements go back to very early days—to the beginnings of Israel in Palestine, and it is these beginnings which shed most light on both scholarly Kabbalism and popular Hasidism, and, in addition, go far to illuminate the real, the abiding spiritual meaning of Judasim in all times and places.

By and large the special details of Kabbalism which distinguish it from the mainstreams of Jewish thought are what is "occult" in occultism everywhere, and most of the world's religions can be reinterpreted in these terms. They give Kabbalism its fascination but they do not give it its substance. As A. E. Waite so well points out, beneath the glittering and mysterious superstructure of the Kabbalah, which purports to be occult Judaism, lies—Judaism.

Kabbalism is probably the only religious movement of the Gnostic type to come full circle in this fashion, to create mysteries and explain them, to hide secrets and discover them, and come at last back to the greater mystery from which it started, but with deeper insights and wider knowledge. Insight and knowledge of what? In the last analysis of the human soul, of man within himself, united with another in marriage, united with his fellows in love. I suppose certain tendencies and individuals in Catholicism have done the same thing. Bonaventura is a sort of enraptured, orthodox Gnostic. There is the Protestant, Jakob Boehme. In modern times there have been all sorts of rationalizing, philosophizing, psychologizing movements which have in fact accomplished similar ends, from the Theosophists and A. E. Waite himself to Martin Buber and Carl Jung. These are different—either eccentric individuals or modern sophisticated cults. Whoever wrote or gathered and edited the tracts of the Zohar, Kabbalism shows all the signs of being a perfectly natural, Near Eastern Gnostic movement, evolved directly from the local soil, the "clerkly lore" of an "anthropological religion."

It might be wise to note some of these sources. Emanationism is found in the so-called "Memphite Theology," a text dating back to the beginnings of Egyptian civilization. Four pairs of gods emanate from Ptah in a hierarchy of power, and the creative process is described in language which still echoes in the Gospel of John. The very word *Isis* means "throne" and many of her attributes survive in the terms applied to the Shekinah, to Malkuth, to the personified Wisdom of Proverbs and finally, in the titles of the Litany of the Blessed Virgin. Pre-Hebraic Palestine is full of Els (Elohim) and Ba'als (Adonai, the Lord) and they all have consorts, at once wives, daughters and mothers—Asherah, Anat, Astarte, Ashteroth. In Egypt they were identified with Isis, with Hathor, and with Sekhet, wife and daughter of Ptah, the ultimate creator. In the fifth century we discover Anat in an Aramaic Elephantine papyrus specifically described as the consort of Yahweh.

Asherah survives in the Scriptures as a term for the phallic pillars, *mazzeboth*, which stood beside the altars and in the holy places until the fall of the Temple. But she also survives in person and the story of Elijah is the tale of a bitter struggle with Jezebel, a regal priestess of Ba'al-Asherah. Temples of Asherah and Yahweh stood side by side in ninth-century Mizpah. In the seventh century Jeremiah found children in the streets of Jerusalem gathering wood and the fathers kindling the fire and the women kneading the dough to make cakes for the Queen of Heaven. The sacred prostitutes and sodomites of the Goddess appear again and again in the Scriptures. The First Isaiah begets a son with a *zonah*—called a "prophetess" in the King James Version, Jephthah is the son of a *zonah*, Hosea's description of his relations with a sacred prostitute are among the most cryptic in the Bible and as late as the mid-seventh century, under Manasseh, the cult was flourishing. With the Assyrian and later Babylonian and then Persian conquests, Ishtar was substituted for Ashteroth, and, as has been pointed out time and again, the Book of Esther (simply another English transliteration of Ishtar) is an elaborate euhemerization of the spring New Year fertility rites and the *heirosgamos*, the sacred marriage—as the folk rites of Purim are paralleled all over the world at the season.

The most likely interpretation of the Song of Songs is that it is a collection of songs for group marriage rites, focused in the *heirosgamos* of priest-king and priestess, which accompanied the opening of the irrigation channels from the main ditches into the dry fields. In fact, a book which casts great light on the Song of Songs is Granet's *Festivals and Songs of Ancient China*, an interpretation of the erotic songs of the ancient Chinese collection, the *Shi Ching*. Do not misunderstand, this parallelism does not "prove" diffusion from some imagined prehistoric religious center. It shows the fundamental identity of man's response to the great rhythms of life. Nothing is more illuminating than to look up "Shekinah" or "Succoth" or "Wisdom" or "Power" or for that matter any of the other epithets of the *Sephiroth* in a good Biblical concordance, and ponder on the mysterious sentences. Do they just seem mysterious because our attention, with minds full of presuppositions, has been directed to them? I think not. These words are keys which unlock some of the oldest material in the Scriptures, and they survive because of their traditional sanctity. The post-Esdras editors, working over the old documents, might disguise them, but they did not dare omit them, any more than they dared wipe out the memory of the sacred groves and the pillar circles and the high places. At last the Samaritan Gnostic, Simon Magus, with his consort, the Mystic Helen, a temple prostitute out of Ephesus of the Great Mother, comes to meet and struggle with the earliest Christians.

Now, we must understand that we have come to view "orthodoxy" after millennia of narrowing definition. To some extent the prophets, some of them, were "orthodox" in this way, or at least they were so represented after the Persian period. But the people knew nothing about these questions. Religion for them was the whole body of cult *acts,* it was what they *did.* We think of such conflicts in terms of Athanasius *vs.* Arrius, Dominicans *vs.* Albigensians, Calvin *vs.* Servetus, Massachusetts *vs.* the Quakers and witches, and the deliberations of Senator McCarthy's Committee. They were nothing of the sort. True, the prophetic movement of Judaism and later the rabbinical schools, represent the slow evolution of such sharpening distinctions and the purging of old practices. But the average inhabitant of Palestine went right on practicing religion as he found it in place—there—in the cult of his ancestors, and even the evolution of Yahvistic monotheism was an enormously drawn-out process. The ancient folkways have never vanished from Judaism, even at its most reformed, and today—the day I am actually writing this: Purim, C.E. 1960—customs whose broken relics we find at the very bottom of mounds of ruins in the Holy Land linger on in the parlors of the thoroughly assimilated and Americanized "High Society" of San Francisco where I live.

Last night I went to a celebration of the hundredth anniversary of one of the city's most fashionable Congregations—an oratorio—a *Purimspiel—Queen Esther,* given to a packed Opera House, with a very Nordic-looking Esther. At the reception afterward the President of the Congregation said, opening his speech, "This is the happiest day of my life," and the rabbi interrupted, "How about your marriage?" This was a joke, a wisecrack as American as anything on television

—and it brought as much laughter from the audience. But it was something more, and it somehow elicited a slightly different kind of stir—an undercurrent that wouldn't have been there with a Gentile audience. That spontaneous joke had touched one of the great nerve centers of Jewry, the Sacrament of Israel, watched over by and nourished under the wings of the Shekinah, that gesture, the physical embodiment of the turn in the creative process, the moment at which all being, having reached its last term, begins its long return to an inscrutable and holy center from which it came. On the buffet, along with champagne and caviar, were *hamanohren.*

A. E. Waite was an odd fish out of an odder barrel. He was not only one of the few persons in modern times, Jew or Gentile, to write a sensible and sound book on Kabbalah. He was a genuine scholar of occultism who himself came out of the welter of occult sects and movements of the end of the last century. He lived in the world of Eliphas Levi, Stanislas de Guaita, "Papus," Sar Peladan, Mme Blavatsky, A. P. Sinnett, Macgregor Mathers, Wynn Westcott, Annie Besant, and "Archbishop" Leadbeater, and more American oddities and rascals than you could shake a stick at. Some of these people are genuine literary curiosities and still make fascinating reading. Others are unbelievably fraudulent and silly. But, to a man, they are mines of misinformation, rash hypotheses and unsupportable conclusions. They are as far from being scholars as could well be imagined. It is a pity that they all, the whole movement, have never become the subjects of scholarship on a large and really serious scale, because they certainly do represent, like the Marxists or the Neo-Catholics, a significant mass movement of the human mind in its long march out of folly. The subjects they were all interested in are among the most interesting subjects for scholarship that exist, but they produced only two scholars. A. E. Waite and G. R. S. Mead. Mead was a Theosophist, and hence suspect in the halls of scholarship, but his is still the only readable translation of the Hermetic literature in English, he edited a Gnostic tractate, the *Pistis Sophia,* and he wrote an estimable book on Gnosticism, *Fragments of a Faith Forgotten.* There is nothing specially odd or cultish about any of these books. In contrast, the acceptably academic translation of the *Hermetica,* by Scott, is the work of a Higher Critic, and is a violent, shameless, distortion of the text.

Waite *was* odd, cultish and eccentric. He wrote the most dreadful prose conceivable, an awful mixture of Walter Pater, Cardinal Newman, Arthur Machen and plain vulgar pretentiousness. It is the last survival of the last spasms of literary Pre-Raphaelitism. Fortunately, though it was common in its day, there is nothing left around to compare it with except Sebastian Evan's *High History of the Holy Grail,* still to be found on shelves of out-of-print Everyman's Library, and William Morris' slightly lunatic translation of the Icelandic Sagas into a kind of Pre-Raphaelite studio code, today utterly unreadable. Waite, however, is not unreadable. You have to read between the balderdash, but it is easy to get used to. Soon you no longer notice it, and he does have, almost always, something very interesting to say. At last the absurd rituals he uses to say the simplest things come to endear him to you, like the wen on Grandma's nose.

In his autobiography Waite gives the impression that his books all came more or less by accident, as assignments from publishers. I rather doubt that, because throughout his life he seems to have followed a definite program. Eventually, and it certainly seems, systematically, he came to cover all the main aspects or traditions or myths of occultism. His works include: *The Secret Tradition in Alchemy, The Brotherhood of the Rosy Cross, The Secret Tradition in Freemasonry, The Hidden Church of the Holy Grail, The Pictorial Key to the Tarot, Raymund Lull, Louis Saint Martin,* and careful editions of the works of Eliphas Levi and the greatest of the English mystical alchemists, Thomas Vaughan, whose works are mysteriously missing from the bibliographies of Dr. Jung's many books on this subject. Besides all this he wrote a lot of dreadful poetry full of Mystic Veils and Clinking Thuribles, and a couple of general statements of his own philosophy—

as well as a rather cobwebby autobiography. Self-evidently this is a program, a carefully planned work of a lifetime. The remarkable thing about it is that, although coming as it does from an era of windy nonsense and smoky pretense, there is nothing seriously wrong with it. They are all books of wide, painstaking scholarship. Waite went to all the sources he could find, in itself a Herculean labor, and he exposed all the errors of quotation and interpretation in the secondary sources that he could uncover. He is almost always right. Not only is he right, but he never loses, however dear to his heart may be the misty mid-regions of Weir in which he wanders, the true scientific scholar's skepticism. In fact, since he was himself the leader of a "Mystic Circle of Seekers for Illumination," who took his somewhat absurd vows very seriously, he uses this very scholars' skepticism as a mask and a refuge. On the question of the very existence of "Spiritual Alchemy," let alone on the sexual yoga, so plainly illustrated in Chinese works on the subject, for which most alchemy is just a kind of double talk, Waite is noncommittal. He leads you to the sources, quotes and analyzes them for you, and leaves you to draw your own conclusions. So likewise with the Grail legend, so with Rosicrucianism, so with occult Freemasonry, so with that *I Ching* of the Western World, the Tarot cards—he strips away the nonsense, exposes the facts, and leaves you to drew your own conclusions. With charlatans he is merciless. Although he is in a sense a product of the school of Eliphas Levi, he never misses a chance to expose the pretensions of that most fascinating of mountebanks. With St. Martin or Lull he is careful, even reverent, although he does an excellent job of taking apart the complicated Lull legend.

The Holy Kabbalah is his greatest work. Although he was a kind of Christian, even a sort of Liberal Catholic, Kabbalah is, out of all the past, the closest thing to his own philosophy. He wrote three books on the subject, each later one incorporating and correcting its predecessors. He seems to have read everything he could find on the subject in every language he knew, and meditated on it deeply and long. It has been said that he did not read Hebrew, but I doubt this. There is much in *The Holy Kabbalah* which he could not have found in Knorr von Rosenroth's *Kabbalah Desnudata,* or in the very unsatisfactory French translation of the Zohar, the only comprehensive expositions of the Kabbalah itself available to him in any other language than Hebrew. No other Gentile writer on Kabbalism can even remotely be compared to him, and no modern Jewish writers are any better. We have to go back to the great *zaddikim* of Hasidism to find such a thorough Kabbalist, and they, alas, present altogether too many problems of their own to be readily assimilated by anyone in the twentieth century. Kabbalism is the great poem of Judaism, a tree of symbolic jewels showing forth the doctrine of the universe as the vesture of Deity, of the community as the embodiment of Deity, and of love as the acting of God in man. Nobody knew this better than A. E. Waite.

American Indian Songs

The United States Bureau of Ethnology Collection

In all the public and academic libraries in America and in most of the principal libraries of the world, off in a corner somewhere or in a seldom entered room, you can find a good many square feet of bookshelves lined with the olive-green publications of the Bureau of American Ethnology, a department of the Smithsonian Institution. There are forty-seven annual reports, from 1881 to 1932, royal octavo volumes lavishly illustrated, averaging around eight hundred pages each. After the forty-seventh report, the ethnological and anthropological material has been published separately. There are about one hundred and fifty bulletins in octavo; these run from thirty-two to one thousand pages, and include the annual anthropological papers—about ten articles to each volume—published each year since the forty-seventh annual report. Besides this there have been a couple of hundred other miscellaneous publications.

This is the largest body of anthropological literature ever published by one institution, private or public. Although it is readily available to every American citizen in his nearby library and at least to every inhabitant of a national capital elsewhere, it is little known and less read—even by anthropologists. This is not due to the quality of its scientific writing. Many of America's major anthropologists are included, often with their greatest works.

Every aspect of American Indian life and much major archaeological-exploration data can be found somewhere in the publications. Many of the monographs in the annual reports are larger than most books. Many of them treat of aspects of Indian life now perished past recall. There are classic treatments of the life and culture of a whole tribe, like Paul Radin's *Winnebago*, which takes up all the thirty-seventh annual report, and short essays on Indian crafts and ceremonies and detailed, comprehensively illustrated reports of archaeological excavations. For instance, over the years an accumulation of papers on the ethnobotany of various tribes has covered the entire useful native flora of North America. Again, the twenty-first annual report contains sixty-three color plates of Hopi Katchinas, the dance masks and costumes which represent the demigods of Pueblo religion. These were all drawn by native artists just at the end of the nineteenth century. They are the first examples of Pueblo Indian painting and are still the best. Inspired by this first assignment, a whole school of Pueblo Indian painting has grown up and is today very popular in America and is shown periodically in the major art galleries of the country. The modern painting is more sophisticated and superficially more decorative, but none of it compares with the freshness and immediacy of these first examples.

Among the bulletins there are a number of handbooks—*American Indians North of Mexico*, edited by Frederick Webb Hodge; succeeded by *Indian Tribes of North America*, edited by J. R. Swanton; *American Indian Languages*, by Franz Boas; *California Indians*, by A. L. Kroeber; and now, completed only recently, the monumental *Handbook of South American Indians*, in six fat volumes, edited by Julian H. Steward. In addition to all this there are a large number of texts and translations of Indian oral literature—myths, legends, lengthy ceremonies and songs.

Most of the songs, both text and music, have been recorded by Frances Densmore, who has been working in this field for forty-five years, and whose collections of Indian music number more than fifteen volumes (three of which have been published elsewhere), each of the fifteen devoted to a different tribe. Besides the printed text and music, she has usually taken phonograph records as well, and these are part of the immense collection of Indian songs, folk songs, folk tales, and other oral literature held by the Smithsonian Institution and the Library of Congress.

To the best of my knowledge, there does not exist any comparable collection of primitive lyric and music made by one person. I am well aware of the criticisms that have been made of Miss Densmore's work by musicologists. It is of course true that primitive music can only be approximated by our Western notation, but at least she has approximated it, and in most cases with surprising accuracy. Any comparison of her notation with the phonograph records which I have ever made has never shown any serious error, once the validity of using our system of notation is granted. One can make a closer approximation by using special notation, but this too of course is still only approximation.

Over and above its musical interest, Miss Densmore's work is also possibly the largest body of primitive lyric poetry in the original language and in translation in existence. As such, it is of tremendous importance to the student of literary origins, to the aesthetician or critic, and especially to the practicing poet. In spite of this her work is almost completely unknown among literary people, and only one American poet of any importance—Yvor Winters—has ever mentioned her in print or shown any sign of her work's influence.

Although any work done with American Indians in the twentieth century can hardly be called early, Miss Densmore was not too late to catch many primitive customs before they became corrupted or forgotten. For instance, a substantial number of the songs in her first book, *Chippewa Music* (1910), are chants in the ritual of the Mide-wiwin Society (the Great Medicine Lodge)—what in our own civilized world would be called a religious and fraternal organization somewhat resembling Freemasonry, possibly originally the organization of the tribe's medicine men. Societies of this sort are now dying out, and in much of the North American Indian world being replaced by the peyote cult. At one time they flourished; many were intertribal, sometimes over a wide area. Less disturbing than the apocalyptic movements like the Ghost Dance religion, they served the same purpose without getting the Indian into so much trouble. That is, they provided cohesion and consolation, and protected and sustained the Indian in his struggle to adjust to the gradually all-enveloping white civilization. Since Miss Densmore always roots each song in its social context, much of the Chippewa study is also one of the best studies of a nonaggressive intratribal cult society.

In 1915, when she visited the Teton Sioux, the Plains Indians, although defeated and broken, still kept much of their culture intact. There were still plenty of men who remembered the days of the buffalo hunt, and many of the great war chiefs were still alive. The memory of the bitter resistance to the white conquest of the Plains was a living thing to every member of the tribe. Furthermore, the Sun Dance religion, an intertribal movement which the Indian Bureau was attempting, unsuccessfully, to suppress, was still flourishing. It is extraordinary that Miss Densmore, a white woman visiting the tribe under the auspices of the government, was able to collect so much material. Not only was she able to gather some thirty-two Sun Dance songs, but she presents them in a context which is still one of the best studies of the Sun Dance religion. She also gives many songs of the dream societies, of the Sacred Bundles, of personal dreams, which, taken together—song and context—probably give more of the significance of these aspects of Plains Indian culture than anything else ever written on the subject.

Not all of her studies are of still flourishing tribes. She has also sought out tribes represented by two or three families of aged people who still treasured a few fragments of melody which they no longer understood.

Musical form can weather amazingly well the social vicissitudes to which it may be exposed and may survive relatively intact in a fundamentally different cultural setting, or from a bygone age, charged with new life and meaning. Music is one of the most persistent culture elements to be found in primitive societies and the most resistant to change. By and large, Western European music shows far more influence stemming from the American Indian (slight in bulk as that actually is) than his music has accepted from us. Not only is music, song—and with it of course, but sometimes to a lesser degree, the words of the lyric, the poetry—unusually persistent and resistant, but of all cultural intangibles it lends itself most to fairly exact record and quantitative analysis and comparison. However fragmentary, nothing else can give us comparable insight into alien and past modes of life. For instance, nothing gives a sense of historical presence like the words and music, surviving from over half a millennium in the Appalachian Mountain communities, of the ballads of their medieval Scottish ancestors.

The important thing about this half century of careful field work is that Miss Densmore has revealed as clearly as anyone ever has the sources of song in the religious and secular experience of primitive society. A great deal of theory has been written on this subject, but outside of work done by or under the inspiration of Erich Maria von Hornbostel in Germany, too little has been done in the field. No one has accumulated so much living data—the actual substance of song itself—from which it is possible to draw theoretical conclusions and also watch many practical conclusions draw themselves. I should add that Miss Densmore's work is incomparably better than the collections of Natalie Curtis Burlin, Theodore Baker, and others which greatly influenced composers like Busoni and MacDowell in the early years of this century.

I think the easiest way to sum up Miss Densmore's conclusions is to say that songs, like other things which we call works of art, occupy in American Indian society a position somewhat like the sacraments and sacramentals of the so-called higher religions. That is, the Indian poet is not only a prophet. Poetry or song does not only play a vatic role in the society, but is itself a numinous thing. The work of art is holy, in Rudolph Otto's sense—an object of supernatural awe, and as such an important instrument in the control of reality on the highest plane. This, of course, is not an uncommon aesthetic theory, but it is something else again to see it concretely demonstrated by an immense mass of evidence gathered in the field.

Of course, there are those who would not choose, on aprioristic or temperamental grounds, to accept such an extreme conclusion from the evidence. Even so, the crucial importance of song, and hence of the work of art, as the very link of significant life itself, of the individual to his society, of the individual to his human and nonhuman environment, is certainly patent.

It is very significant that the texts of almost all these songs are not only extremely simple, but that most of them are pure poems of sensibility resembling nothing so much as classical Japanese poetry or Mallarmé and certain other modern French and American poets, notably some of the Imagists at their best. It is possible, of course, to say that Miss Densmore greatly simplifies the poem by cutting out repetitions and nonsense vocables. But the Japanese poetry which we think of as so extremely compact on the printed page is similarly sung in extended fashion. Certainly the Indian singer does not feel that he is dulling the poignancy of the transcendental awareness of reality which he is communicating by musical elaboration, but rather the reverse. And, if the song is sung, or the record is available, it is immediately apparent that this elaboration is insistence, not diffusion.

The resemblance to Japanese poetry is indeed startling, particularly in the Chippewa songs. This is not due to the influence of Amy Lowell and other free-verse translators on Miss Densmore. On the contrary, she worked with the Chippewa many years before such Japanese translations and their imitations in modern American verse came into existence. As the years have gone by she has moved on to tribes which do not show the same kind of resemblances either in music or in lyric, for instance the Papago, and this is made sufficiently obvious in the translations. Still, certain things remain. She has analyzed exhaustively the musical constants and variants of Indian song. Each new work in an appendix sums up and compares all past collections with the one at hand.

Are there similar constants in the lyric? I think there are. Western European man characteristically regards himself not only as an independent entity in a fundamentally hostile environment but as the relatively permanent factor in a perishing world and the sole source in it of value. Most Western European poetry is, even in its erotic lyric—"Gather ye rosebuds while ye may"—concerned with the tragedy of the waste of value in a world of fact. There is nothing of this in American Indian poetry. The intense aesthetic realization which precedes the poem is a realization of identity with a beneficent environment. Often this is focused in a dream or vision, waking or sleeping, after long lonely fast and vigil in the forest or desert. An aspect of the environment, an animal or a natural object or force, appears to the Indian, waiting in a trance state, and gives him the song, which remains his most precious possession and the pivot of his life forever after. As such, however simple, these songs always express mutual acceptance and approval of the self and the other, focused but also generalized, amounting to identification. In other words, the holy is not the Judaeo-Protestant "utterly other"—a term of Otto's—but the utterly same. They also express the accompanying emotional state—a feeling of extraordinarily intense hyperesthesia, concentration of all faculties in one realization, and the emotional tone of the realization itself—what we call transfiguration and transcendence—the kind of general sacramentalism we identify with St. Francis's Canticles and certain poems of Wordsworth or Francis Jammes.

It is apparent that the creation of song or poetry, "the creative act," as we say today, occupies a place in American Indian culture similar to what may be called, roughly, yogi practices of concentration and nervous-system gymnastics in the cultures of India and the Far East. This is the identifying link. The brief poems of Hitomaro or Basho, or the lengthy reveries of Su Tung Po, as a matter of fact, share the same attitude toward the creative process and produce a product essentially similar.

It is possible to hold that this is a saner and more civilized approach to life than that commonly exercised by Western man. At least, American Indian song operates, at its best, on the highest possible cultural level: it "enhances life values" at least to the degree attempted by our own most ambitious works of art. In a period when life values of all sorts are seriously threatened, it is not profitable to ignore it.

EXAMPLES OF AMERICAN INDIAN SONGS

Translated by Frances Densmore

CHIPPEWA

Mide Songs

In form like a bird,
It appears.

The ground trembles
As I am about to enter.
My heart fails me
As I am about to enter
The spirit lodge.

The sound of flowing waters
Comes toward my home.

Now and then there will arise,
Out of the waters,
My Mide brothers,
The otters.

Beautiful as a star,
Hanging in the sky,
Is our Mide lodge.

What are you saying to me?
I am arrayed like the roses,
And beautiful as they.

The sound is fading away.
It is of five sounds.
Freedom.
The sound is fading away.
It is of five sounds.

Dream Song of Thunders

Sometimes
I go about pitying
Myself,
While I am carried by the wind
Across the sky.

Dream Song

From the half
Of the sky
That which lives there
Is coming, and makes a noise.

Dream Song

The heavens
Go with me.

My Love Has Departed

A loon,
I thought it was.
But it was
My love's.
Splashing oar.

Love Song

Do not weep.
I am not going to die.

Love Song

He must be very sorrowful,
Since he so deceived
And forsook me,
During
My young days.

Love Song

I will go and talk with
My sweetheart
The widow.
I love
My sweetheart
The widow.

Love Song

You desire vainly
That I seek you.
The reason is,
I come
To see your younger sister.

Love Song

Oh!
I am thinking,
Oh!
I am thinking,
I have found
My lover!
Oh!
I think it is so!

Dance Song

Strike you
Our land
With curved horns.

Death Song

The odor of death,
I discern the odor of death
In front of my body.

War Song

The noise of passing feet
On the prairie.
They are playing a game
As they come,
These men.

Song of the Butterfly

In the coming heat
Of the day
I stood there.

Begging Dance Song

Maple sugar
Is the only thing
That satisfies me.

Dream Song

As my eyes
Search the prairie,
I feel the summer in the spring.

Whenever I pause
The noise
Of the village.

TETON SIOUX

Steam Lodge Song of the Sun Dance Ceremony

A voice,
I will send.
Hear me!
The land
All over,
A voice
I am sending!
Hear me!
I will live!

War Song

A wolf
I considered myself.
But I have eaten nothing,
Therefore
From standing
I am tired out.
A wolf
I considered myself
But
The owls
Are hooting,
And,
I fear the night.

Song on Applying War Paint

At the center of the earth
I stand,
Behold me!
At the wind center
I stand,
Behold me!
A root of medicine

Therefore I stand,
At the wind center
I stand.

Song after Battle

The old men say
The earth only
Endures.
You spoke truly,
You are right.

Song after Battle

As the young men went by
I was looking for him.
It surprises me anew
That he has gone.
It is something
To which I can not be reconciled.

Owls hoot at me.
Owls hoot at me.
That is what I hear
In my life.
Wolves howl at me.
Wolves howl at me.
That is what I hear
In my life.

NORTHERN UTE

Dance Song

On a mountain,
The noise of the wind.

MANDAN AND HIDATSA

Love Song

A certain maiden
To the garden goes.
Lonely,
She walks.

PAWNEE

Buffalo Dance Song

He said, Unreal the buffalo is standing.
These are his sayings.
Unreal the buffalo is standing,
Unreal he stands in the open space.
Unreal he is standing.

Spring Song

Spring is opening.
I can smell the different perfumes
Of the white weeds used in the dance.

Dream Song

Beloved, it is good,
He is saying quietly,
The thunder, it is good.

Ghost Dance Song

The yellow star has noticed me.
Furthermore, it gave me
A standing yellow feather,
That yellow star.

MENOMINEE

Dream Song

In the heavens
A noise,
Like the rustling of the trees.

Love Song

I will keep on
Courting
Until morning.

PAPAGO

Downy white feathers
Are moving beneath
The sunset
And along the edge of the world.

The morning star is up.
I cross the mountains
Into the light of the sea.

A white mountain is far at the west.
It stands beautiful.
It has brilliant white arches of light
Bending down towards the earth.

Healing Song

The sun is rising.
At either side a bow is lying.
Beside the bows are lion babies.
The sky is pink.
That is all.

The moon is setting.
At either side are bamboos for arrow making.
Beside the bamboos are wildcat babies.
They walk uncertainly.
That is all.
The sun is slowly departing.
It is slower in its setting.
Black bats will be swooping
When the sun is gone.
That is all.
The spirit children are beneath.
They are moving back and forth.
They roll in play
Among tufts of white eagle down.
That is all.

In the great night my heart will go out.
Toward me the darkness comes rattling.
In the great night my heart will go out.

Song of an Old Woman in the Cold

No talking, no talking.
The snow is falling.
And the wind seems to be blowing backward.

Song for the Puberty Rite of a Girl Named Cowaka

A poor man takes the songs in his hand
And drops them near the place where the sun sets.
See, Cowaka, run to them and take them in your hand,
And place them under the sunset.

YUMAN AND YAQUI

The water bug is drawing
The shadows of the evening
Toward him on the water.

In Cocori is a young girl
Whose name is Hesucita.
She is a pretty girl.
Her eyes look like stars.
Her pretty eyes are like stars moving.

The owl was requested
To do as much as he knew how.
He only hooted and told of the morning star.
And hooted again and told of the dawn.

The bush
Is sitting
Under a tree
And singing.

The deer
Looks at a flower.

Turner and Whistler

In the little booklet *British Painting,* put out by the National Gallery of Art (Washington, D.C.), it says, "It seems curious, when looking at this vision of radiant light with its blues and golds, to realize that the painter was an uncouth boor, who lived under an assumed name in squalor with his common law wife." Well, well. I guess that's one way of looking at it. Considering its source, it is almost an official statement. Like most official statements it is not quite right factually, but it is an accurate reflection of a common emotional attitude.

Turner is vulgar. I think the man got it wrong way around. There was something rather aristocratic about his flaunting of polite society. Plenty of dukes have lived in squalor in big, dirty rat-infested and leaking houses as Turner did. He didn't, most of the time, "live with" his mistress, he kept her in a cottage up the river, just like a duke. It is his paintings that are vulgar. Out of the painting of Venice in the National Gallery that prompted this remark came seventy years of chocolate boxes. Many of his romantic landscapes are even vulgarer. His water colors and graphic work are least so, but certainly their appeal is very obvious. Can good art be this common in its appeal?

Folk art is one thing—we accept its crudity as "natural" and value its simple, effective design. Naïve artists are, when good, really eccentric rather than naïve. Rousseau's slightly daffy vision of the world can be accepted as a different reality. As styles, however absurd, pass back in time, they cross a dividing line beyond which they become less and less offensive because they are no longer reacted against by our own taste.

This isn't just up-to-dateness. Growth of the sensibility in society always rejects the immediate past and later reorganizes it in different terms, finds new values and meanings in the enduring work and forgets the rest. Styles blend together as they recede. Only trained observers can distinguish between the styles of Augustan and Hadrian Rome. Hadrian's artists considered themselves as revolutionary as the Fauves. "Messages" are first vital, then trivial, then acquire a nostalgic evocative power. Today nineteenth-century British anecdotal painting is popular again. One of my favorite paintings is Ford Madox Brown's *The Last of England.* Alma-Tadema, however, for me at least, has not been lent enchantment by time. A tear dims my eye whenever I regard Henry Farny's *Song of the Talking Wire,* but, closer to home, the funny-paper epics of Stanley Spencer and the WPA muralists leave me slightly nauseous.

Whistler is vulgar. He is vulgar in quite the opposite direction to Turner. He did not, to quote that catalogue, "turn his back on polite society." He was a social lion, a drawing-room pet, almost the first of his type in modern Society. Men like Reynolds or the modern clubman Academician are not pets of Society—they are themselves Society. Whistler was not Society, he was not even a gentleman. He was, in fact, close to being an intellectual gigolo.

An artist who is a gentleman has the dignity and craft secretiveness of a skilled mechanic or a good butler. He never lets on. He never peddles spurious initiations into the mysteries of his trade. He keeps his place and expects his customers to keep theirs. The old Scripps-Howard cartoonist Williams once drew a cartoon all voluble artists should take to heart. A battered old house painter in ragged overalls and walrus mustache is mixing paint. The Milquetoast-type client, interested in future do-it-yourself projects, asks, "What's that you're mixing with the paint?" Says the true craftsman, "Muriatic acid, it makes the paint stick better." Whistler taught idle women to chatter in a bad imitation of artists' shop talk. It is the heritage of Whistler's little ventures in high-toned Adult Education, far more than Karl Marx, which has led modern artists to refuse when asked out, and to bristle at the sight of a pulsating diamond choker.

At this date we come at both Turner and Whistler with a mass of prejudices and preformed judgments. Can we clear them away so that we can look at both without bias? Can good pictures be that pretty? Can a popinjay paint honest paintings? I think the answer to the first question is, "Yes." The answer to the second question is, "Yes." The third question, I am afraid, must be answered, "More or less." Turner, in the noblest sense of the words, knew his place, and kept his mouth shut. His paintings are redeemed by something greater than taste. Whistler, who inaugurated a worship of good taste, could never quite keep his ingrained charlatanism from peeping out of even his most devoted work. It is only one step from Whistler to Aubrey Beardsley, only another to Gustave Moreau, only a third to Dali. Whistler is a dangerous artist to like.

It is good to approach Turner through a large display of his water colors. In the first place, there is the purely mechanical fact that his colors have lasted better in that medium than in his oils. Many of his large oils, especially those in America, have faded terribly. The storm at sea in the Chicago Art Institute, for instance, is about as colorful as a steel engraving. Modern taste has to learn to adjust to his Romantic bravura. This is much easier to do in the more intimate, quiet art of water color. Sheer technical mastery in oil is a little beyond the layman (the world is full of people who still think Dali is a "great craftsman"). No one was ever a greater virtuoso of water color than Turner, and this virtuosity is sufficiently apparent to anyone who has never touched a brush, and is, as in the ink painters of the Far East, a delight in itself. Last, and most important, unless you moved an appreciable part of the Tate Gallery across the Atlantic, it would be quite impossible to organize an exhibition which would show Turner's steady development from picturesque landscape to what today we call abstract painting.

Arranged chronologically, water colors like the *Mer de Glace, Snowstorm on Mt. Cenis, St. Goar on the Rhine, Tell's Chapel, Lake Lucerne* show the steady growth of abstract considerations and the dwindling of picturesque detail. In each one it is necessary to mask a smaller and smaller area of representation and anecdote to obtain pure vortexes of light, cloud, wind and rock. Even in a painting like *Mt. Cenis,* the horses and wagons are there to give scale and set the drama. Eventually these effects are achieved by "painterly" means, and, in the last great water colors, even scale ceases to function. Like much recent painting, they depend on their own local space—the direct action of paint on paper.

It is doubtful if Turner knew much of anything about Far Eastern art. About all he could have seen was bric-a-brac and bijouterie. Yet, of all modern artists, he is closest to the great painters of China and Japan. Even the dim river scene *Mainz,* completely within the European tradition and painted rather early on, has the same feeling as the ink scrolls of the misty Yang-tse Kiang. Late paintings like *Tell's Chapel, Lake Lucerne* pass beyond even the ink-blot "discipline-of-occasion" tours de force of Sesshu and his disciples. This is organic painting of a new kind, dynamic, saturated space, all the forces of which are related like the strains and stresses, the vacuoles, vortices and pseudopods which make up the living processes of an amoeba.

In his life Turner was equally un-Western European. He was a totally devoted craftsman and a modest, unpretentious visionary. His mistresses were illiterate and housewifely. Their neighbors thought he was a retired sea captain. He and his father ran his career like a small but very successful business. He tried to hang on to all his best work, and when he died he left everything to his fellow countrymen. Remote heirs broke his will.

Whistler was not just immodest, he was shamelessly vain. His most conscientious portraits, of his mother and of Carlyle, are really Fantin-Latour, slightly flavored with Vermeer. He gave them ridiculously pretentious titles. They are not *Ar-*

rangements in Grey and Black at all, they are just good, workmanlike portraits. *Arrangements of Rose and Silver* is no such thing, it is a studio portrait of a model in a kimono—a particularly exciting form of cheesecake in those days. Neither is it *La Princesse du Pays de la Porcelaine.* It is hard to understand how Whistler could look at so much Japanese art and talk so much about it and have such trouble seeing it. *Arrangement in Black* is simply a portrait of Sarasate with his fiddle, painted in a combination of the styles of Velasquez, van Dyck and Fantin-Latour. Re-do it in slashing brush work and you have Sargent. So it goes. There is nothing wrong with these paintings—except Whistler's lamentable inability to keep still.

Perhaps the best are the *Symphonies in White* and the other color-music jobs which are really exercises in a peculiar, weak, etiolated, precocious sexuality. They are very odd people, the Victorians. More went on than ever met the public eye. These weary children are not as rough as Lolita, but they are every bit as perverse. One step back, the sick nymphomaniacs of Rossetti and the mawkish boys of Burne-Jones, one step ahead, the silly brothel decorations of Aubrey Beardsley. Whistler's girls are far better, because they are convincing. Looking at them we not only know they once really existed, but we can extrapolate the whole world which produced them. This is no small virtue. But they are not *Symphonies.*

Face to face with the *Nocturnes* it is necessary to draw a deep breath. Whistler thought of them as transmitting the inspiration of Hiroshige and Hokusai. They do not. Those artists were gentlemen craftsmen, much like Turner. Both of them had an accurate and knowing eye and uncannily steady hands. Both were even more vulgar than Turner. Whistler's *Nocturnes* are all annoyingly imprecise. Where is the man standing on that barge? This is not calligraphy—it is just careless drawing. For once I think he was right in his choice of titles. These paintings have the same emotional vagueness, patchouli-scented sentiment and etiolated virtuosity as the less admirable piano works of that diseased and neurotic Pole. Once again, like the oddly sexy girls, these are fashionable paintings, embodiments of the most chic vapors of a bygone day.

Does this mean that Whistler is all bad? No. It just means that it requires a kind of censorship of the sensibility to appreciate him. Like highbrow movies, we have to be always on guard not to be taken in. And like highbrow movies, we have to be on guard in a special way—this is our kind of corn, designed specifically to take in just our caste. In Whistler, at least, it is sufficiently dated so that we can recognize it and perform the necessary surgery.

This leaves us with little more than an entertaining afternoon of sophisticated nostalgia, like three hours spent with *Traviata* or *The Merry Widow*. Some artists, of all periods, are inexhaustible in history. Whole art movements will be indebted to them for centuries to come. With Whistler we can only come away saying wryly, "Curious, life was like that once, at least for some people."

What's Wrong with the Clubs

This is a very presumptuous piece; I don't really know enough about the subject to write about it. You'll probably be better off reading Nat Hentoff's book *The Jazz Life,* because he does know what he is talking about. Anyway, I'd like to explore what trade unions call "working conditions" and, in my opinion dependent on working conditions—and race—the living conditions under which many jazz men have to operate.

Music is an art, and its expression should be a joy, but the brutal fact is that the average jazz musician works far too hard, too long hours, under absurdly bad conditions, for too little pay. All musicians of course know this, but the lay public, including the jazz audience, does not. In San Francisco, where I live, a checker in a supermarket or chain grocery makes over four hundred dollars a month for a five-day week, eight-hour day, with fairly liberal time breaks. He, or she (women get the same wage as men), gets overtime, vacations, depending on the company, and often a considerable number of side benefits. The work is certainly nerve-racking, but the hours are normal, and the customers are ordinarily decent human beings.

Compare this with the lot of the average jazz musician. How many make four hundred dollars a month, every month in the year? How many have any prospects of steady employment at all? How many work in clean surroundings? Granted "meeting the public," even banging a cash register in a grocery, is no fun at best, how do the relations between a grocery clerk and the passing stream of housewives compare with the audience relationship enjoyed by a jazz musician in the average night club? What kind of people by and large go to night clubs? Swindlers, rascals and tyrants may, here and there, run grocery stores. How do the worst of them compare with the average night-club owner? How long would the average night-club owner stay in business if he were selling cornflakes to women with children? And how many grocery clerks have to kick back part of their salary to the owner?

You get the point. The final question of course is, why on earth does anybody go on playing jazz for a living? A lot of people don't. Like nursing, where the girls drop out early, most of them, and get married, jazz is pretty much an occupation of the young. The world is full of house painters, psychiatrists, bell captains, ship captains, who tell you, "I used to play trombone when I was in my twenties." As long as you are young and foolish enough to look on the working conditions of the jazz musician as romantic and glamorous, you may have fun. Come thirty, you've got to be pretty good and pretty devoted, or pretty dumb, to stick it out.

The working conditions of jazz have produced in much of the jazz audience, and in all too many musicians themselves, a kind of mystique—a glorying in the disabilities of jazz employment. Due to the fact that a majority of jazz musicians are Negroes, this has merged with a similar mystique—the glorification of the American Negro for the effects of his disabilities. I have always said of the leading Beat novelist that he has exactly the attitude toward the American Negro that any redneck gallus-snapping Southron chauvinist has. He is considerably less informed about the realities of Negro life than even Senator Eastland, who, I suppose, in his own evil way, does "know Nigras." The Beat novelist just likes them that way. Mailer was right when he said that the hipster was a white Negro—but he neglected to point out that the Negro model the hipster imitates is the product of white imaginations. One of the saddest things I ever saw in my life was a couple of Negro Beat bars out near Thirty-fifth Street in Chicago—misguided young Negroes industriously imitating silly white people imitating Negroes who don't exist. We are all familiar with this sort of thing in jazz. Long ago somebody called it "Crow-Jimism." You can find it on both sides of the color line—Negrophilism is not by any manner of means a purely white phenomenon. It used to be a mass sickness in France, and it's still pretty strong over there.

Did you ever hear Juliette Greco sing "*Dieu est Negre*"? It's about as corny a song as can be imagined—all about Tjeemmy, *le saxophone,* dying in the gutter in Place Pigalle, and saying, as he vomits blood, "God is a Negro." I have seen strong-minded French intellectuals weep in their Pernods as she sings it, totally unaware of its hidden chauvinism. Not only that—but Greco herself believes it so intensely that she carries a powerful conviction. She affects me, although I know that it is all tosh.

It is not easy to be a Negro in America. Discrimination has its effects and they are not all good by any manner of means. Anybody who considers the evil effects of discrimination as virtues is pretty silly, and he is unlikely to be a Negro—unless he has been corrupted, usually financially, by silly Negrophiles. True, there exists, to match Crow-Jimism, a kind of Tom Uncle-ism—Black Chauvinism as a commercial racket. Some people have found it very profitable. A few of them, unfortunately, have been jazz musicians.

Once again, this returns us to the question of the jazz audience relationship. It is because the audience is not a normal musical audience, sitting out there beyond the stand primarily to listen to music, that these stereotyped responses have grown up and been turned into rackets. It doesn't do any good to be "cool" and pretend there is nobody out there. They are out there all right, for better or worse. It doesn't do any good to get up with a horn and pretend that you are Elijah Muhammad and the Vassar girls at the front table are the Georgia mob that lynched your grandfather. You aren't and they aren't.

Jazz is music. Music is not black or white. Leonard Feather demonstrated that the musicians who said they could always recognize the race of anybody on a record not only couldn't tell Negro from white, but often couldn't even tell the race of men they had themselves played with for years. The important thing is to secure conditions where the jazz musician plays music for an audience which is there to listen to music.

Now, true, jazz is not chamber music. At least most jazz is not. Some of the best jazz still is dance music. Certainly most of it is social music—music for conviviality—music which needs a certain kind of audience participation to be most effective. There is nothing unusual about this. This is what all music was, everywhere, until the emergence of "serious" music in modern times and in Western European civilization.

How many clubs provide such a setting? The answer is: how many clubs are primarily in the business of selling music? How many club owners could distinguish between Miles Davis, a glockenspiel and a C clef? The fact is that the night club is a lineal descendant of the speakeasy, and is at least as much an underworld operation, in most cases, as ever was its parent. Jazz is permeated with the underworld. By this I do not mean that jazz musicians are underworld characters. Quite the opposite. The boy who works hard, studying piano or trumpet, gaining scholarships, living in a poor flat in a Negro ghetto, perhaps helped by a mother who works as a domestic, is about as far from the underworld, black or white, as could be. As a matter of fact, a large proportion of Negro musicians come from the middle class; two I know well are the sons of doctors who have always carried on an "integrated" practice. Certainly most musicians in their teens start out as what people call "church" rather than as hippies.

But the exploiters of the musicians are underworld characters, with only a few honorable exceptions. Managers, agents, cheap record companies, owners, bartenders, cocktail waitresses—they all bear a singular resemblance to the people who prey on boxers. Of course, pushing drinks with no chemically analyzable alcoholic content, and all the other little swindles of the trade, produce a grifters' mentality in even the best. An appreciable number of night clubs all across the country are run by the Mafia. Now, spreading out of Vegas, has come a new invasion of the entertainment business by a new kind of crook—naïve, cheap, brassy and rich. Behind them, I suppose, lies the sophistication of the Mafia Old Guard, now the business executives of a major American enterprise. They themselves are straight out of Damon Runyon. I grew up on Chicago's South Side and was taught by my gangster friends that life's greatest motto was, "Keep your nose clean and don't volunteer." These boys are like the comic relief in an old George Raft picture.

What the hell kind of environment is this for the practice of an art? No wonder heroin is a problem among jazz musicians. Is it a problem among abstract painters? Members of the Symphony? Architects? Poets? Oh, I know, the Beat poets used to talk about heroin on TV, but the sight of a luer would make any of them faint, and besides, they couldn't afford it. They were just pretending to be like what they thought Negro jazz musicians were like, man. Dope is a problem in jazz because of the nature of the exploitation of the musician. If I had to work till 4 A.M., picking up casuals in gangster-run joints and living in Harlem or in a filthy pad in the New Village east of 2nd Avenue, I wouldn't take heroin, I'd take prussic acid.

Clellon Holmes's *The Horn* is as good a novel as has been written about jazz. Partly it's based on Lester Young's life—but it doesn't hold a candle to the facts. Cast as a novel, the true story of misery and exploitation would not have been believable. Lester Young was no more neurotic nor "insecure" than a good many painters and poets of his generation, Negro or white, but he is dead and they are still alive. What killed him was a working environment with which no artist but the most powerful could be expected to cope. I met Bird when he started out, and, as they say, a nicer young fellow you'd never want to meet.

What is the answer? I don't think the concert hall is the answer. Jazz is essentially, whatever the cool boys thought, an audience-participation art. The only place I have ever seen musical excitement so directly communicated as by Ornette Coleman in the crowded Five Spot was in a sand shuffle in a country dance in Little Egypt. Performing out here in California a few months later at the Monterey Jazz Festival, the whole group showed signs of acute unhappiness—the vital connection with the audience was gone. Some jazz survives the concert or the jazz festival. It seldom seems to matter to Count where the band is playing, the old gismo flows out regardless. But the concert hall could not have produced Count Basie. Moten, Basie, even Mary Lou came out of as close, as all-involving, an audience relationship—the intense and special dance halls and joints of the old Kansas City circuit—as ever was Congo Square.

Almost by definition the good clubs—the "jazz rooms"—in the States are those that book the Modern Jazz Quartet, Coleman, Coltrane, Mingus. This is not because these are modernist musicians, but because, by and large, a club that books them has an audience primarily interested in music. How many such clubs are there? Damn few, and even some of them are not all that good. Some of them are just night clubs that graduated into jazz rooms without the owners ever realizing it.

I would like to see the revival of the old-time cabaret of the 1900's. Plenty of room between the tables. Good food—not just packets of stale sandwiches to get by the law, but real high cuisine. Really fine wines and imported beers and a de-emphasis on hard liquor—or better, "limited license." No bar whatsoever. Waiters, or at least fully clothed, well mannered waitresses . . . that you have to call to get served. In other words—no pushing at all. Put the nut on the door. Floor show, if necessary, to match the quality of the jazz. There's plenty of this stuff now—Dick Gregory, Moms Mably, Les Frères Jacques, Greco, Montero, Severin Dardan and that group that played the Second City recently—imagine a prestidigitator who took rabbits out of people's ears babbling along like Mort Sahl. . . . Imagine a Negro girl singing songs like those of Apollinaire, Queneau, Prévert, MacOrlan, Carco—the stuff that made Greco famous. Why don't American poets write songs like that? Of course blues singers, too. But a bill that automatically reduces the audience to the kind of people the best jazz is for anyway. John Coltrane is not for drunks.

Of course, there already are a few clubs like that—most of them, significantly, not in New York—The Crystal Palace in St. Louis, the *hungry i* in San Francisco (there are several more in San Francisco), the Second City in Chicago. They are fairly expensive, and they don't feature jazz, but they could, or new places like them could. One of the most important things to my mind is to get the take off the drinks and put it on the door. Another, perhaps more important, is some sort of physical arrangement worked out with the authorities that control the sale of liquor so that older teenagers can have a section where they can drink pop or coffee, eat, and listen. The Blackhawk had a good setup here in San Francisco, but one day, without warning, they got knocked over by the town clowns.

The cops were unjust to the Blackhawk, but you can't expect a copper to know any better. They are right in thinking the average night club is no place for a teenager. It's no place for me either. And it is no place for a musician who considers himself a creative artist.

Science and Civilization in China

These volumes are the first two of seven projected in a detailed and exhaustive history of Chinese science and its relation to general Chinese culture and to the evolution of modern science. Joseph Needham is one of the world's leading biochemists and biologists. He has lived for many years in China, knows the language and literature, has a deep sympathy for the people and their ways, an incredible knowledge of the literature of his subject, and of Sinology generally.

Needham's is the sort of project which, nowadays, if it gets done at all, is done by committees of scholars drawn from all the universities of the world. Yet he moves with ease and confidence in regions where the most highly specialized committees would tread with temerity.

Great synthesizing works of scholarship have an aesthetic appeal, different from but often as great as great works of art. Perhaps because history is itself an art (one of the Muses, said the Greeks), few books are more moving than a vast philosophical history. This is true even when, as in Ignatius Donnelly, Spengler or Arnold Toynbee, the guiding ideas, the philosophy and even the facts, are mistaken, false or wrongheaded. Who is likely to forget those excited nights of adolescence spent with *The Golden Bough* or *The Decline of the West*, or, even in maturity, the impact of the first three volumes of Toynbee? Yet hobbyhorses and foolhardiness do not make for the most enduring qualities in the aesthetics of

Science and Civilisation in China. By Joseph Needham. Cambridge University Press, New York. (Four of the projected seven volumes are now available.)

history. Gibbon's *Decline* is probably the greatest achievement of eighteenth-century Europe; it is also one of the ten great prose works of all time, ranking just below Thucydides, *Genji* and *Don Quixote*. It is also singularly correct and exhaustive. Joseph Needham may not be Gibbon, but he is a very remarkable man, and he has written what is already, less than a third completed, a major monument of historical scholarship, surpassing the science histories of Sarton and Thorndike and Sigerist. In some ways, notably in prose style and organizing ability, in sheer interest and lucidity, it is the superior of any history of science and related subjects since Heath's great work on Greek mathematics.

Science and Civilisation in China is not just an exciting book; its effect is stunning, and this not least because excitement is so unexpected in a field given over, alas, to the worst sort of finicking. For more than twenty years American Sinology has been dominated by individuals and traditions from the old Tsarist academy, where Far Eastern studies were essentially part of the curriculum of military policy, with the resultant narrowness, formularization and bigotry. Considerable work of breadth has been done in recent years, but without exception by scholars independent of the school dominant in the United States, often by persons the academicians consider amateurs and upstarts. This has not been true in Great Britain, but then, Arthur Waley, E. R. Hughes, even Needham himself are dilettantes in the eyes of our Sinologists. I think it is important to explain this to the lay public because it has all sorts of practical consequences in this period when it is a matter of life and death that we grow in understanding of the Far East.

It is hard to think of a better way to approach an alien culture than by a study of its science. Religious concepts, by slight tricks of mistranslation, can be perverted. Confucianism can be assimilated to the demented fascism of Ezra Pound, Taoism to Mary Baker Eddy, Buddhism to Theosophy; but the statement that the five elements are Fire, Water, Wood, Metal and Earth, has a salutary indigestibility about it. Our scientific provincialism is appalling. This is true not only of the layman whose notions of scientific infallibility come from advertising pictures of wise men in laboratory coats inspecting test tubes full of canned beans. It is found at the very top. The physicist Heisenberg, father of the dubious "principle of indeterminacy," says in a recent book that the difference between "our" scientific theories and Newton's or Kepler's is that ours are "correct." If true, it is frightening to look ahead to the onrushing centuries of ever-growing scientific unemployment. This is the worst sort of learned smugness, and nothing is better for it than a long quiet voyage among totally foreign scientific landscapes. Chinese science, both speculative and empiric, is radically, fundamentally different, and demands a willed, sympathetic reorientation of perspective on the nature of Nature.

Too often works of scholarship in fields as remote as this are technically inaccessible to the common reader. Needham's book is not. Although the high scholarship, not just in Sinology, but in dozens of related fields, is patent, it is never oppressive, and it explains itself as it goes along. Furthermore, Needham writes English prose, not the professional thieves' cant of the typical academic "paper."

The first volume is introductory. It has chapters on bibliography, special problems of the Chinese language, written and spoken, geography, geology, history and prehistory and the diffusion, migration and interaction of ideas and inventions between China and the West. Not one of these subjects but is full of booby traps for the rash. Volumes of nonsense have been written, especially by American poets, about the Chinese written character. (Chinese culture has been derived from Egypt, the characters from cuneiform; the Mayan and Inca cultures have been derived from China, even the geography and geology of China have attracted those with more notions than sense.) Needham avoids every pitfall. In almost every instance of dispute he is about as near right, about as judicious a guide, as the uninitiated could wish.

True, he seems to be a Marxist—or at least not unsympathetic. This leads him to give considerable space to the influence of waterworks, canals and dams for drainage and irrigation, and of the system of "ever-normal granaries" on Chinese history and social structure. This is a popular interpretation in China just now and it is unquestionably fruitful. On the other hand the controversy over the nature of Chinese society—is it feudal or feudal-bureaucratic?—is due to the limited vocabulary of Engels, Morgan and Hegel.

It is simply not true that for four thousand years before Mao Tse-tung China was "feudal." This is like nothing so much as the old factional dispute among the Trotskyites over the nature of the Russian state. Needham settles for "feudal-bureaucratic" and passes on to point out that really it is unique and specifically Chinese. Again, when Mao controlled only the Northwest it was the custom to lavish praise on the cultural contributions of the Northern Barbarian Dynasties and to attack the Confucian legitimism of, for instance, the Southern Sung. Now that the Communists control all of China, they have mellowed into a measure of Confucian patriotism. Actually the first position is more nearly correct. Needham wavers, but at this crux quotes Lattimore, written some years back. Similarly, there is little doubt that, Confucian theories to the contrary, China has been greatest when it was a federated empire with considerable autonomy of the parts. On this point contemporary theory is shifting and ambiguous. Needham avoids the issue, perhaps wisely. I am familiar with the wilder Marxist perversions of Chinese history and philosophy. I didn't notice them in Needham. In fact, I feel about his Marxism pretty much the way Lincoln felt about Grant's whisky.

I am going to make a rash statement. I think the second volume is about the best guide to Chinese philosophy in English, or for that matter in any language, including the Chinese. Possibly this is because it fits my own predilections, but then, there is not much to compare. Wilhelm is elementary and sometimes wrong, Wieger is a Roman Catholic and often unsympathetic, Waley and Hughes deal only with the classical period, Fung Yu-lan tends to see all Chinese philosophy as a preparation for his own—and so on. Needham approaches each thinker and school primarily, but not exclusively, in terms of reference to the growth of scientific thought—valid understanding of the world. There are chapters on each of the major schools, but he is most sympathetic to Taoism and Sung Neo-Confucianism. I should say that his interpretation of the latter is radical and stimulating, if not necessarily indisputable. There is a chapter on the basic ideas of Chinese science which completely supersedes Forke's famous *World Conception of the Chinese*, long the standard work.

Finally there is a section on human law and natural law in China and the West which is a masterpiece. Needham's point is that ideas of creation out of nothing, of a divine legislator, are unknown or repugnant to Chinese philosophy, as codified law is unknown to Chinese jurisprudence, and that therefore Chinese scientific thought has been far more organic than mechanical, permissive than authoritarian in its interpretation of Nature's ways. The dominant influence in this volume seems to be the organic philosophy of Whitehead, shorn of its Platonic excrescences. This has been an influence almost entirely for the good. It serves as an available bridge to the comprehension of a world in which Nature works by "doing nothing" instead of by passing laws, in which the universe moves as a great web of interrelatedness of which man and his imperatives are only part. That is basically a true picture of the Chinese universe. It is a universe full of strange and wonderful things. It is a universe Western man is going to have to understand if we are all going to survive happily together on a planet where, whether we like it or not, as Confucius said, "All men are brothers."

The Letters of Van Gogh

What makes a good letter writer? Interesting letters. What makes letters interesting? Simplicity, directness, topicality, insight into oneself and others, spontaneity, and in most cases, genuine intimacy. Letters written for publication may be good literature for other reasons, but they are really just a special form of essay. What we want in a collection of letters is unconscious autobiography. If the writer is a great artist or a profound thinker or an important historical figure, so much the better. Van Gogh certainly fits all these desiderata. He is the ideal letter writer, and his *Collected Letters* is almost as important as his collected paintings would be and much more easily domesticated. They are not only intimate, revealing, beautifully written, but they have a special sort of sweet profundity about them that is unmatched by anyone else. What other letters could provide a popular actor with an extremely successful concert repertory? Yet there is nothing theatrical about them. They are as quiet as a conversation by the fireside in a Dutch parsonage. We think of Van Gogh as a fierce, rabid sort of personality. Perhaps this is all legend. The letters are so gentle, modest—I guess the word is endearing. And every letter is haunted by the pathos of Van Gogh's life.

The correspondence of the great artists and idealists in the history of Western Man is mostly about money. The more unworldly they were, the more it is about money. They found

The Complete Letters of Vincent Van Gogh. Edited by V. W. Van Gogh. Translated by Mrs. J. Van Gogh-Bonger and others. Illustrated. New York Graphic Society, 1959.

it scarce. They worried about it all the time. They nagged and cajoled and begged to get it. The personal correspondence of millionaires is never about money. In fact, it is considered excessively bad form ever to mention money among the rich, except in a place of business between the hours of ten and three.

It isn't just capitalism. We don't have the real letters, but the set pieces, the verse letters of Horace and Catullus, are at least implicitly about money. And it isn't even just Western Man—the Chinese poet Tu Fu is every bit as bad. The poets and artists who did not write letters about money are unknown to history—they did not survive. Everybody knows why this is. Unless the artist is in league with magic, miracle, mystery and authority, as Dostoevski put it, he may even get rich—like Rubens—but he never has what nowadays is known as security. And so he frets and schemes and begs. Blake, Baudelaire, Rembrandt, Michelangelo—Van Gogh is no exception. But if not an exception, he at least differs in several interesting ways.

In the first place, he was not a very revolutionary artist. In fact, his early painting was the conventional "proletarian art" of the period. Sculptors like Meunier and painters like Millet were already rich from doing the same sort of thing. Then he changed to a kind of painting that was becoming quite chic, and which has remained, if not chic, at least extremely fashionable among the more conservative, and which has become fabulously expensive—the brightly colored, highly decorative painting produced on the border or transition zone of Neo- and Post-Impressionism. This is the last period in Western art to be genuinely popular and Van Gogh is the most popular of all. Large color prints of *The Sunflowers, The Postman, The Arlésienne, The Chair, The Poolroom, The Bedroom* and the others can be found decorating the overmantel space, not in the homes of intellectuals, or even the educated, but in the homes of Negro janitors, Filipino bus boys, in the parlors of Polish auto workers in Hamtramck and Hungarian steel workers in Gary.

When the first big Van Gogh comprehensive show came to San Francisco before the Second World War, the Southern Pacific ran a "Sunflower Special," with a blow-up of the picture at the tail of the observation car, on each of its routes into town. The Palace of the Legion of Honor was accessible only after an hour's wait. This went on for weeks and broke all records for art exhibitions anywhere in the world. The intellectuals thought it was simply dreadful and did nothing but bitch. It was back in the salad days of the John Reed Clubs when all the really *au courant* young minds were busy debating the theses of Leopold Auerbach on Proletarian Culture.

The ordinary people who buy reproductions of Van Gogh's paintings and hang them on the wall think they are pretty. They make the sitting room more cheery. It killed Van Gogh to paint them. *Did it?* Is this true? Is Van Gogh some sort of Rimbaud or Dylan Thomas, burned alive in the fire of his own vision? Everybody assumes so, and the assumption is implicit in almost all the immense number of books written about him. I think it is false.

Van Gogh may have been a lay saint, but he was a simple kind of saint, like Brother Lawrence or St. Theresa of Lisieux, not a tormented one, like St. Theresa of Avila or St. John of the Cross or the characters of Dostoevski and Bernanos. Nobody can read these eighteen hundred pages of ingenuous communication and believe anything else unless he is totally blinded by presuppositions. If you believe that everybody must carry around an abysm in his heart, as Baudelaire said of Pascal; if you are like the French Catholic intellectuals who write articles for *Esprit*—"De Sade Belongs to Us!"—if you believe that every notorious evil-liver was seeking illumination and every disastrous life was really a clandestine career of piety; in other words, if you hold the presently fashionable apocalyptic view of human destiny; you can find it in Van Gogh if you are bigoted and persistent enough.

Van Gogh had visions, but of miners and potato-peelers at first and then of sunflowers and chairs, never of angels or demons. They excited him, but they did not trouble him the way Ivan Karamazov's visions of similar simple things troubled him. In his young days he was a lay preacher, not a very successful one, to be sure. He never thought of himself as bringing a torch to the countryside and the slums. His favorite episodes of the Gospel were incidents like the supper at Emaus, the widow's mite, the marriage at Cana. He thought of Jesus not as coming to bring a sword to the heart of an intellectual like Paul, but to bring just a little peace and dignity and rest to exhausted and brutalized human beings in slums and hovels. There is something profoundly Dutch about this kind of unpretentious evangelism. It is in Rembrandt, of course, but it goes back to late medieval Pietism, the Beguines and Beghards, Blessed Jan Ruysbroeck, Thomas a Kempis—a movement which involved the whole society of the Lowlands for centuries and which survives today in sects like the Mennonites. Nothing less like Baudelaire exciting himself with a Black Mass in his mistress's boudoir can be imagined.

What was wrong with Van Gogh then? Why did he do all those crazy things that make such successful movies of his life? Something physical. There is a bit by a psychiatrist in the documents appended to these letters. It is amusing because it is in the jabberwocky of an only recently abandoned school of psychiatry and makes you realize what jabberwocky our own psychiatry will be in another fifty years. And it says absolutely nothing. Van Gogh, on the other hand, had a pretty good idea: "I have been a bit beat the way I used to be in the past, when I had that venereal trouble in the Hague and got myself looked after in the hospital." His friends had a good idea, too—the most obvious explanation. He lived a bachelor life. Artists need somebody to see that they eat. He used to paint all day in the fields without eating, come home and try to satisfy his hunger with some burned beans he had left on the stove and instead go out and quiet the demands of his stomach with liquor—*pastis*, probably, the little absinthe of Provence. By night he was drunk. Still excited by the day's painting and with no place else to go, he went to the whorehouses and raised Cain.

Now you can raise all the Cain you want in a whorehouse if you pay for it, but Van Gogh didn't have the money. This made him very unpopular in Arles and seems to have been one of the chief complaints of the neighbors. Such habits are annoying, but there is nothing apocalyptic about them, nothing even existentialist or eschatological. I have known dozens of the most mundane overworked commercial artists who behaved in exactly the same fashion every night. It didn't make them immortal. The snippet Van Gogh took off his ear may have made him familiar to the readers of the movie magazines; it is irrelevant to his immortality. But normal people eat, marry by the time they are his age, don't go around dressed in filthy shirt and pants covered by a ragged overcoat which has been used all winter as a paint rag. Van Gogh was abnormal; as Hokusai said of himself, he was an old man crazy about painting. He was too busy to bother, and then one day it was too late. A lot of simple things like alcohol, pellagra, spirochetes, possibly slight brain damage dating from his birth (he seems to have had mild epileptiform attacks all his life) converged on him and struck him down. Like people who make the cover of *Time*, he died of overwork.

Much has been made of his relations with his family. It is certainly true—to use our own jabberwocky—that the key to a psychosis is to be sought in the family constellation. I see nothing wrong with Van Gogh's and I have read all these eighteen hundred pages, mostly of very affectionate correspondence with, of course, his brother Theo, but also with all his family. Given the late nineteenth century, a Dutchman, a painter, a large family, a father who is a small-town parson, genteel poverty, the results seem to me, not just exemplary, to use Van Gogh's own estimate of his family, but positively ideal. It won't do to identify Van Gogh with the great revolts of his period. Oedipus Complex, Mother Fixation, Sibling Rivalry. If every twentieth-century American family had as few of these bogeys haunting them as the Van Goghs did, we'd all be a lot better off. Van Gogh is not a kind of self-taught Strindberg in paint, and the attempt to make him such is a sort of historical proselytism.

Of course, most of the letters begin "Dear Theo," and there are those who have made much of this, as they have made much of his last days with Gauguin before the breakdown. In the first place, Theo kept all his letters; they are the ones which survive. In the second place, those who find "a struggle with suppressed homosexuality" in the love of men, brothers or not, united in work to which they are passionately devoted, need to stop reading books and go to work. Gauguin is a worse than worthless witness; the Van Gogh family have disdainfully omitted only his letters from the documents of this collection—and rightly so. Gauguin was that most despicable sort of Bohemian, the artist who sponges on other artists because he hasn't the courage to attempt the rich. Even professional panhandlers and pickpockets would rather starve than prey on their own kind. So such a person is always rotten with guilt, always backbiting and boasting, always trying to kick himself free from his benefactors. Van Gogh's kindly, wistful letters about Gauguin at Arles are far saner than Gauguin's own sickening self-justifications, which are, in fact, quite paranoiac and add up to the claim that he "taught Van Gogh to paint and it was too much for his simple brain to take."

We try to fit Van Gogh's objectives into our own, we try to assimilate his art to our own Post-Surrealist, Post-Existentialist aesthetics. It won't fit. He knew very well what he was doing, step by step. He is still a boy and at home, and has been writing Theo about the Barbizon peasant painters, Millet, Breton and the rest, and the Dutch painters of the working class:

> Uncle Cor asked me today if I didn't like "Phryne" by Gerome. I told him I would rather see a homely woman

by Israels or Millet, or an old woman by Edouard Frère: for what's the use of a beautiful body such as Phryne's?

Eventually, he was to discover that his evangelism was on the wrong track. He realized when he saw the brilliance of Impressionist painting that this was what he wanted. He wanted to do certain things with it and use it for certain purposes. At the height of his achievement during the last days at Arles he speaks again and again of carrying on the work of Monticelli and Brias, the painters of the Midi. Now what Monticelli, like Raffaelli and even Redon did, was to use the broken color of Impressionism for decorative rather than representational ends. Van Gogh knew exactly what he was doing. And for what ends? In a curious unconscious way he seems to have had a premonition of modern color reproduction. (As everybody knows, he was devoted to Japanese prints.) Although he and Theo had to think of selling the paintings to "rich Americans" (for a maximum of $125!), he always writes about them as if they were going straight from his easel to the walls of the simple people who sat for his portraits. And he had discovered that what these people wanted was not a somber, gnarled painting of a starving woman peeling rotten potatoes:

> I have just said to Gauguin about this picture [*La Berceuse*] that when he and I were talking about the fishermen of Iceland and of their mournful isolation, exposed to all dangers, alone on the sad sea—I have just said to Gauguin that following those intimate talks of ours came the idea to paint a picture in such a way that sailors, who are at once children and martyrs, seeing it in the cabin of their Icelandic fishing boat, would feel the old sense of being rocked come over them and remember their own lullabies. Now it may be that it is like a chromolithograph from a cheap shop. A woman in green with orange hair standing out against a background of green with pink

flowers. Now these discordant sharps of crude pink, crude orange and crude green are softened by flats of red and green.

Overworked, undernourished, alcoholic—in those days at Arles, Van Gogh had exalted visions, but they were visions of the utter substantiality of the real. "This, Sir," said Sam Johnson to Boswell as he kicked the rock and solved once for all the Epistemological Dilemma, "is the ineluctable modality of the visible!" Chairs, tables, beds, pool tables, people, fields, trees, flowers, caught up in the simplest decorative patterns, naïve, gaudy, but designed to bring a little peace and dignity and rest and even glory to people with the most ordinary tastes—like the marriage at Cana and the supper at Emaus. Dutch, pietistic, evangelical—the lay evangelism of ordinary reality.

An age that prides itself on its self-consciousness and "alienation" may judge Van Gogh to be a minor painter, a decorator, who produced glorified pin-ups for sailors' cabins, but there is no question about the letters. He was indisputably one of the very greatest letter writers who ever lived. You can't get so refined that you cannot recognize his collected letters as one of the major classics of the world's literature, another of the Hundred Best Books the man forgot to put on that list.

Mark Twain

Was Mark Twain a schizophrenic? Van Wyck Brooks established his own critical reputation with a book proving that he was. T. S. Eliot, who has provided two generations of professors with their slim stock of ideas, said he was. It has often been remarked that he was a *laveur,* at least as far as clothes were concerned. Dressing only in white suits laundered every day, he must have been awful guilty of something awful. From the point of view of a small office in a provincial English Department, with rows of Henry James and Soren Kierkegaard on the shelves and hapless coeds slipping exercises in Creative Writing under the door—from this elevated point of view, Mark Twain certainly looks very *queer.*

I think this is all balderdash. Too few critics of his own kind have written about Mark Twain. What he suffers from in the midst of this twentieth and American century is a lack of peers. He needs somebody like Walter Bagehot or even H. L. Mencken or James Gibbons Huneker. He was a man of the world. He was a man of the nineteenth-century American world where Presidents chewed tobacco and billionaires couldn't spell and vast audiences flocked to hear Bob Ingersoll (whom Twain in this book calls "the silver-tongued infidel") and the labor movement was dominated by another silver-tongued cornball named Terence Powderly, who could do nothing but orate, and "Thanatopsis" was considered the most philosophical utterance in the English language, and a small gang of merciless and ignorant brigands put through

The Autobiography of Mark Twain. Arranged and edited by Charles Neider. Harper & Brothers, New York, 1959.

America's Five-Year Plans, and finally "overtook and surpassed" Europe. He was a man of that world that Henry James fled in uncomprehending horror. We have only to look abroad to understand exactly the kind of world it was. It was a world of driving expansion and brutal hard work that brooked no interference or dissent. A world of "primitive accumulation."

It was the official culture which was schizophrenic, not Mark Twain. The whole meaning of Mark Twain is that he "saw life steadily and saw it whole." T. S. Eliot thought his billiard-room jokes childish. They are pretty bad, but are they as bad a joke as Eliot's essay on Crashaw? Mark Twain's low humor was a technique of adjustment to the broadest possible areas of society. It made him a public figure, it gave him the confidence of Presidents of the United States and of the principal corporations of the United States. And it gave him entrance to the American Home, back in the days before Mom had emasculated that institution. All sorts of people, practically everybody, thought he was very, very funny. T. S. Eliot's essay on Crashaw is a snickering little joke on a very small clique of people who were viable themselves only within a scarcely less minute clique—the few High Church members of the now long dead Bloomsbury circle. Furthermore, it owes its character as humor entirely to its incongruous treatment of the standard undergraduate course in Jacobean and Caroline literature—in other words it is *College Humor* in spats and bowler. In his autobiography Mark Twain tells the story of his absurd brother Orion, who used to cool his brain by kneeling in the full bathtub and immersing his head for two minutes at a time. Once the chambermaid opened the unlocked door and ran screaming "Mr. Orion is drownded!" and his wife said "How did you know it was Mr. Orion?" Who is childish, Mr. Eliot or Mark Twain?

Like Jack London, Mark Twain says he went into writing because it was the easiest work he could find, so easy that at the end of his life he could say he hadn't worked a lick in fifty years—it had all been play. This is the remark of a man thoroughly at home in literature. Anything less like

Henry James's ridiculous prefaces would be hard to imagine. Writers like Mallarmé and James and Flaubert, who are always squawking about how artistic they are and how much it hurts, really accept the judgment of bourgeois society that they are loafers. They are ashamed of being writers and endlessly try to justify themselves. The amateur psychoanalysts of Mark Twain are the guilty ones, straddling their double standards. They can't understand this man who was hail fellow well met with cowboys and duchesses, who told the Kaiser that his cook baked potatoes just like a pocket miner he'd known during the Gold Rush. Since they are terrified even at a cocktail party given by another Literary Personage and have no social presence whatsoever and go into rages when their very freshmen can't see the relevance of the *Summa Theologica* to *Deerslayer,* they think Mark Twain must be a fraud and crazy to boot.

Mark Twain was just a very wise nineteenth-century man. He knew his way around socially in the age of the Robber Barons. He knew how to keep his head above water in the Period of Primitive Accumulation. Corny humor, broad anecdotes, after-dinner oratory, primitive vaudeville roles—the Missouri hayseed abroad, a Connecticut Yankee at King Arthur's Court—these may be protective coloration, but they are not selling out. If it weren't Mark Twain but somebody several centuries previous—or Charlie Chaplin—the highbrows would call it the adaptation of folk forms to serious literature. Because those guffawing, tobacco-spitting travel books that made Mark Twain's reputation in the first place and that gave Van Wyck Brooks fainting spells are fundamentally right. Always Mark Twain points out the human meaning of St. Peter's or the pyramids or the Pantheon. What was the social price paid for the Sistine Chapel when it was painted? What is the social price being paid today? It is true that he sweetened the pills, but the word for this is "mastering the terms of the folk culture." Who objects to it in Charlie Chaplin or Li'l Abner, or, for that matter, Count Basie? That he had to do this is shown by Charles Neider's preface to this very book. At the most, Mark Twain was a mild agnostic, usually he seems to have been an amused Deist. Yet, at this late date his own daughter has refused to allow his comments on religion to be published.

What is there to say about this book? It is a more coherent collection of Mark Twain's random reminiscences than the Paine or De Voto volumes, but it omits some of the political and social criticism that De Voto printed and that is certainly important to an understanding of Mark Twain. It is, of course, a book of Mark Twain in his bedroom slippers. Everybody who has read much of Mark Twain is familiar with this aspect of him because he went around that way most of the time. He was never ashamed to be seen in the maximum state of personal dishevelment. Only people who find it impossible to deal with other human beings unless they have on their social masks find this embarrassing. It is very corny, very male, very smoking car and billiard room. But it is all very normal too. Mark Twain remembered his childhood, and loved his wife and daughters and mourned their deaths just as your own relatives back home in Elkhart, Indiana, did those things in 1906. He didn't do any of those things the way the folks do that you meet drinking Pernods in the Deux Magots. Those people in the Deux Magots find him very square—"straight" is the term in the milieu. They think he didn't really mean it, that something was going on behind the scenes. He meant it. This is not Mark Twain's public mask. It is him. He didn't have a public mask. Like all adults, his contradictions and contraries were simply part of him, like his right and left hand.

If Baudelaire was the greatest poet of the capitalist epoch—and he *was* a mild schizophrenic, a sexual freak and a syphilitic—Mark Twain wrote its saga, its prose *Iliad* and *Odyssey*. And he wrote it because he knew how to survive to write it. He survived because he was an eminently normal man. No wonder it is the favorite prose fiction of the Russians. It is the archetypal epic of precisely the historical period they are now in themselves. Unfortunately, so far, nobody has known how to survive to write that epic in Russian.

The Students Take Over

When the newspapers have got nothing else to talk about, they cut loose on the young. The young are always news. If they are up to something, that's news. If they aren't, that's news too. Things we did as kids and thought nothing of, the standard capers of all young animals, now make headlines, shake up police departments and rend the frail hearts of social workers. Partly this is due to the mythologies of modern civilization. Chesterton once pointed out that baby worship is to be expected of a society where the only immortality anybody really believes in is childhood. Partly it is due to the personal reactions of reporters, a class of men by and large prevented, occupationally, from ever growing up. Partly it is hope: "We have failed, they may do better." Partly it is guilt: "We have failed them. Are they planning vengeance?"

In talking about the Revolt of Youth we should never forget that we are dealing with a new concept. For thousands of years nobody cared what youth were doing. They weren't news. They were minding.

They aren't minding now. That isn't news. They haven't been minding since the days of John Held, Jr., *College Humor* and F. Scott Fitzgerald. In those days they were cutting loose. In the Thirties they were joining up, giving one last try to the noble prescriptions of their elders. During the McCarthy Epoch and the Korean War they were turning their backs and walking away. Today they are striking back. That is news. Nobody else is striking back. Hardly a person over thirty in our mass societies believes it is possible to strike back, or would know how to go about it if he did. During the past couple of years, without caring about the consequences, making up their techniques as they went along, organizing spontaneously in the midst of action, young people all over the world have intervened in history.

As the University of California student said at the recent Un-American Activities Committee riot in San Francisco, "Chessman was the last straw. I'm fed up." It's about time somebody got fed up, because, to mix the metaphor, all the chickens are coming home to roost. It has become only too apparent that we can no longer afford the old catch-as-catch-can morality with which civilization has muddled through to 1960. Sloth, rascality, predatory dishonesty, evasion, bluster, no longer work. The machinery has become too delicate, too complicated, too world-encompassing. Maybe it was once true, a hundred and fifty years ago, that the sum total of the immoral actions of selfish men produced a social good. It is no longer true. Maybe once, societally speaking, if wolf ate wolf long enough and hard enough, you produced a race of intelligent dogs. Not now. Pretty soon we are just going to have a world populated by dead wolves.

Toward the end of his life H. G. Wells remarked that "something very queer was creeping over human affairs." He saw a kind of foolish dishonesty, a perverse lust for physical and moral violence, and a total lack of respect for the integrity of the personality invading every walk of life, all the relationships of men, individual and global. He seemed to be not only troubled, but puzzled. In his own *In the Days of the Comet* the earth passes through the tail of a comet and a beneficent gas fills the atmosphere and makes all men good overnight. You feel that he suspected something very similar might have come upon us unawares out of outer space, but that in actuality the gas had turned out to be subtly and pervasively malignant. It is easy to see what he was getting at. Nobody sees it better today than the young student, his head filled with "the heritage of the ages," taught in school all the noblest aspirations of mankind, and brought face to face with the chaos of the world beyond the college gates. He's got to enter it, college will be over in a few months or years. He is entering it already fed up.

Think of the great disasters of our time. They have all been the result of a steadily growing immoralism. You could start indefinitely back—with Bismarck's telegram or the Opium War—but think of what those men alive have experienced: the First World War itself, a vast "counterrevolutionary" offensive; the Versailles Treaty; Fascism and Nazism with their institutionalization of every shoddy and crooked paranoia; the Moscow Trials; the betrayal of Spain; Munich; the Second World War with its noble utterances and its crooked deals; the horrible tale of fifteen years of peace and cold war; the Rosenbergs; the Hungarian Revolution; and, in the last few months, the rascality that has burst around our heads like exploding shrapnel—U-2, phony Summits, an orgy of irresponsibility and lies. This is the world outside the college gates. Millions of people are asked to enter it cheerfully each June, equipped with draft cards, social-security cards, ballots, job-application blanks countersigned by David Sarnoff, J. Edgar Hoover, Allen W. Dulles, the family physician and the pastor of the neighborhood church. Is it surprising that a lot of them should turn away at the door of this banquet hall, turn in their tickets and say, "Sorry, I'm already fed up"?

Marx believed that our civilization was born in the arms of its own executioner, twins who were enemies in the womb. Certainly ours is the only great culture which throughout its life has been accompanied by a creative minority which rejected all its values and claims. Almost all others have had a huge majority who shared in few, if any, of the benefits of civilization. Slaves and proletarians are nothing new, the words themselves are derived from another civilization. But a society which advances by means of an elite in permanent revolt and alienation is something new. In the last fifty years this elite itself has slowly gone under; it, too, has been overwhelmed by the society it both led and subverted. *L'Homme Révolté* has come to the end of his tether. One by one he has compromised and been compromised by all his thousand programs. Nobody believes him any more, so he has become a commercial stereotype, along with the cowboy and the Indian, the private detective, the war hero, and the bison and all other extinct animals. As the agent at MCA said to me three years back, "Revolt is the hottest commodity along The Street." The programs are used up and their promulgators are embarrassed. Youth is fed up with them too. And why not? Hitler fulfilled the entire emergency program of the Communist Manifesto, and in addition made May Day a legal holiday.

For the Bolsheviks, the good society would come automatically if the right power were applied to the right program. But power and program are not the question: what matters is the immediate realization of humane content, here, there, everywhere, in every fact and relationship of society. Today the brutal fact is that society cannot endure without this realization of humane content. The only way to realize it is directly, personally, in the immediate context. Anything else is not just too expensive; it is wrecking the machinery. Modern society is too complex and too delicate to afford social and political Darwinism any more. This means personal moral action. I suppose, if you wish to call it that, it means a spiritual revolution. Prophets and seers have been preaching the necessity for spiritual revolution for at least three thousand years and mankind has yet to come up with a bona fide one. But it is that kind of action and that kind of change that young people are demanding today.

Myself, past fifty, I cannot speak for the young. I am inclined to think they will fail. But that isn't the point. You might as well be a hero if society is going to destroy you anyway. There comes a time when courage and honesty become cheaper than anything else. And who knows, you might win. The nuclear explosion that you could not prevent doesn't care whether you were brave or not. Virtue, they say, in itself is intrinsically enjoyable. You can lose nothing, then, by striking back.

Furthermore, just because the machine is so vast, so complex, it is far more sensitive than ever before. Individual action does tell. Give a tiny poke at one of the insignificant gears down in its bowels and slowly it begins to shudder all over and suddenly belches out hot rivets. It is a question of qualitative change. Thousands of men built the pyramids. One punched card fed into a mechanical brain decides the gravest questions. A few punched cards operate whole factories. Modern society has passed the stage when it was a blind, mechanical monster. It is on the verge of becoming an infinitely responsive instrument.

So the first blows struck back were tiny, insignificant things. Not long after the last war Bayard Rustin got on a bus in Chicago and headed south. When they crossed the Mason-Dixon Line, he stayed where he was. The cops took him off. He "went limp." They beat him into unconsciousness. They took him to jail and finally to a hospital. When he got out, he got on another bus and continued south. So it went, for months—sometimes jail, sometimes the hospital, sometimes they just kicked him into the ditch. Eventually he got to New Orleans. Eventually Jim Crow was abolished on interstate carriers. Individual nonviolent direct action had invaded the South and won. The Southern Negro had been shown the only technique that had any possibility of winning.

Things simmered for a while and then, spontaneously, out of nowhere, the Montgomery bus boycott materialized. Every moment of the birth and growth of this historic action has been elaborately documented. Hour by hour we can study "the masses" acting by themselves. It is my modest, well-considered opinion that Martin Luther King, Jr., is the most remarkable man the South has produced since Thomas Jefferson—since, in other words, it became "the South." Now the most remarkable thing about Martin Luther King is that he is not remarkable at all. He is just an ordinary minister of a middle-class Negro church (or what Negroes call "middle class," which is pretty poor by white standards). There are thousands of men like him all over Negro America. When the voice called, he was ready. He was ready because he was himself part of that voice. Professional, white-baiting Negroes who thrill millionairesses in night clubs in the North would call him a square. He was a brave square. He is the best possible demonstration of the tremendous untapped potential of humanity that the white South has thrown away all these years. He helped to focus that potential and exert it. It won.

No outside organizers formed the Montgomery Improvement Association. They came around later, but they could never quite catch up with it. It is pretty hard to "catch up with," to institutionalize, a movement which is simply the form that a whole community has assumed in action. Although the force of such action is shaped by group loyalty, in the final analysis it must always be individual and direct. You can't delegate either boycott or nonviolence. A committee can't act for you, you have to act yourself.

The Montgomery bus boycott not only won where Negro Zealotism, as well as Uncle Tomism, had always failed, but it demonstrated something that had always sounded like sheer sentimentality. It is better, braver, far more effective and far more pleasurable to act with love than with hate. When you have won, you have gained an unimpeachable victory. The material ends pass or are passed beyond. "Desegregated" buses seem natural in many Southern cities today. The guiltless moral victory remains, always as powerful as the day it was gained. Furthermore, each moral victory converts or neutralizes another block of the opponents' forces.

Before the Montgomery episode was over, Bayard Rustin and Martin Luther King had joined forces. Today they are world statesmen in a "shadow cabinet" that is slowly forming behind the wielders of power, and the advisers and auxiliary leaders in the councils of Negro Africa. At home in America the Montgomery achievement has become the source from which has flowed the moral awakening, first, of Negro, and following them, of white youth.

Everything seemed to be going along nicely. According to the papers and most of their professors, 99 and $^{44}/_{100}$ per cent of the nation's youth were cautiously preparing for the day when they could offer their young split-level brains to GM, IBM, Oak Ridge or the Voice of America. Madison Avenue had discovered its own pet minority of revolt and tamed it into an obedient mascot. According to *Time, Life,* MGM and the editors and publishers of a new, pseudo avant-garde, all the dear little rebels wanted to do was grow beards, dig jazz, take heroin and wreck other people's Cadillacs. While the exurbanite children sat with the baby sitter and thrilled to Wyatt Earp, their parents swooned in the aisles at *The Connection* or set up past bedtime reading switch-blade novelists. The psychological mechanisms were the same in both cases—sure-fire, time-tested and shopworn.

But as a matter of fact, anyone with any sense traveling about the country lecturing on college campuses during the past five years could tell that something very, very different was cooking. Time and again, hundreds of times, I have been asked, by some well-dressed, unassuming, beardless student, "I agree with you completely, but what shall we, my generation, *do*?" To this question I have been able to give only one answer: "I am fifty. You are twenty. It is for you to tell me what to do. The only thing I can say is, don't do the things my generation did. They didn't work." A head of steam was building up, the waters were rising behind the dam; the dam itself, the block to action, was the patent exhaustion of the old forms. What was accumulating was not any kind of programmatic "radicalization," it was a moral demand.

Parenthetically, I might say that a legend of the Red Thirties was growing up too. Let me say (and I was there): As far as practically every campus except CCNY and NYU was concerned, the Red Thirties are pure myth. At the height of the great upsurge in California labor, led in its own imagination by the Communist Party, neither the Young Communist League nor the Young Peoples Socialist League was able to keep a functioning student cadre in continuous operation on the University of California campus. At least every four years they had to start over again. And the leadership, the real bosses, were middle-aged party functionaries sent in from "The Center." One of them, bellowing with early senility, was to show up at the recent Un-American Activities Committee riot in San Francisco and scandalize the students.

The plain fact is that today students are incomparably better educated and more concerned than their elders. As the young do, they still tend to believe things written on paper. For the past five years, bull sessions have been discussing Kropotkin, Daniel De Leon, Trotsky, Gandhi, St. Simon, Plato—an incongruous mixture of the world's cat bellers—looking for the answer. The gap between the generations has been closing up. Teaching them is a new group of young professors, too young to have been compromised by their actual role in the splendid Thirties, themselves realistic-minded products of the GI Bill; and neither ex-dupes nor ex-fellow travelers, but serious scholars of the radical past. It is only just recently that they have come up, only just recently that the creative minority of students has stopped assuming that just because a man stood at a podium he was *ipso facto* a fraud. So the head of steam built up, the waters mounted behind the dike.

And then one day four children walked into a dime store in a small Southern city and pulled out the plug. Four children picked up the massive chain of the Social Lie and snapped it at its weakest link. Everything broke loose.

Children had won at Little Rock, but they had not initiated the action, they had been caught in the middle in a conflict of equally dishonest political forces, and they had won only a token victory. All the world had marveled at those brave young faces, beautiful under the taunts and spittle. If they had not stood fast, the battle would have been lost; it was their bravery alone that won it. But it was a battle officered by their elders, and like all the quarrels among their elders nowadays, it ended in a morally meaningless compromise.

From the first sit-ins the young have kept the command in their own hands. No "regularly constituted outside authority" has been able to catch up with them. The sit-ins swept the South so rapidly that it was impossible to catch up with them physically, but it was even harder for routinized bureaucrats with vested interests in race relations and civil liberties to catch up with them ideologically. The whole spring went by before the professional leaders began to get even a glimmering of what was happening. In the meantime the old leadership was being pushed aside. Young ministers just out of the seminary, maverick young teachers in Jim Crow colleges, choir mistresses and schoolmarms and Sunday-school teachers in all the small cities of the South pitched in and helped—and let the students lead *them*, without bothering to "clear it with Roy." In a couple of months the NAACP found itself with a whole new cadre sprung up from the grass roots.

The only organization which understood what was going on was CORE, the Committee on Racial Equality, organized years ago in an evacuated Japanese flat, "Sakai House" in San Francisco, by Bayard Rustin, Caleb Foote and a few others, as a direct-action, race-relations offshoot of the Fellowship of Reconciliation (the FOR) and the Friends Service Committee. CORE was still a small group of intellectual enthusiasts and there simply weren't enough people to go around. To this day most Negroes know little more of CORE than its name, which they have seen in the Negro press, and the bare fact that its program is direct, nonviolent action. This didn't deter the high-school and college students in the Jim Crow high schools and colleges in Raleigh and Durham. They set up their own direct nonviolent-action organization and in imitation of CORE gave it a name whose initials spelled a word, COST. Soon there were COST "cells" in remote hill-country high schools, complete with codes, hand signals, couriers, all the apparatus of youthful enthusiasm. Needless to say, the very words frightened the older Negro leadership out of its wits.

The police hosed and clubbed the sit-inners, the Uncle Tom presidents of the captive Jim Crow colleges expelled them in droves, white students came South and insisted on being arrested along with the Negroes, sympathy picket lines were thrown in front of almost every chain variety store in almost every college town in the North. Even some stores with no branches in the South and no lunch counters anywhere found themselves picketed until they cleared themselves of any implication of Jim Crow.

The effect on the civilized white minority in the South was extraordinary. All but a few had gone on accepting the old stereotypes. There were good Negroes, to be sure, but they didn't want to mix. The majority were ignorant, violent, bitter, half-civilized, incapable of planned, organized action, happy in Jim Crow. "It would take another two hundred years." In a matter of weeks, in thousands of white brains, the old stereotypes exploded. Here were the Negro children of servants, sharecroppers and garbagemen—"their" servants and sharecroppers and garbagemen, who had always been content with their place—directly engaged in the greatest controlled moral action the South had ever seen. They were quiet, courteous, full of good will to those who abused them; and they sang, softly, all together, under the clubs and fire-hoses, "We will not be moved." Long protest walks of silent Negroes, two abreast, filed through the provincial capitals. A major historical moral issue looked into the eyes of thousands of white spectators in Southern towns which were so locked in "our way of life" that they were unaware they lived in a great world. The end of Jim Crow suddenly seemed both near and inevitable. It is a profoundly disturbing thing to find yourself suddenly thrust upon the stage of history.

I was at the first Louisiana sit-in with a girl from the local paper who had interviewed me that morning. She was typical, full of dying prejudices, misinformation and superstitious fears. But she knew it. She was trying to change. Well, the sit-in did a good job of changing her. It was terrific. A group of well-bred, sweet-faced kids from Southern University filed into the dime store, hand in hand, fellows and girls in couples, and sat down quietly. Their faces were transfused with quiet, innocent dedication. They looked like the choir coming into a fine Negro church. They weren't served. They sat quietly, talking together. Nobody, spectators or participants, raised his voice. In fact, most of the bystanders didn't even stare rudely. When the police came, the youngsters spoke softly and politely, and once again, fellows and girls hand in hand, they filed out, singing a hymn, and got in the paddy wagon.

The newspaper girl was shaken to her shoes. Possibly it was the first time in her life she had ever faced what it meant to be a human being. She came to the faculty party for me at Louisiana State that night. Her flesh was still shaking and she couldn't stop talking. She had come up against one of the big things of life and she was going to be always a little different afterward.

The response on the campuses of the white colleges of the South was immediate. There had always been interracial committees and clubs around, but they had been limited to a handful of eccentrics. These increased tremendously and involved large numbers of quite normal students. Manifestations of sympathy with the sit-ins and joint activities with nearby Negro schools even came to involve student-government and student-union bodies. Editorials in college papers, with almost no exceptions, gave enthusiastic support. Believe me, it is quite an experience to eat dinner with a fraternity at a fashionable Southern school and see a can to collect money for CORE at the end of the table.

More important than sympathy actions for and with the Negroes, the sit-ins stimulated a similar burst, a runaway brush fire, of activity for all sorts of other aims. They not only stimulated the activity, they provided the form and in a sense the ideology. Nonviolent direct action popped up everywhere—so fast that even the press wire services could no longer keep track of it, although they certainly played it up as the hottest domestic news of the day. The actions dealt with a few things: compulsory ROTC, peace, race relations, civil liberties, capital punishment—all, in the final analysis, moral issues. In no case were they concerned with politics in the ordinary sense of the word.

Here the ROTC marched out to troop the colors and found a line of students sitting down across the parade ground. In another school a protest march paraded around and through and between the ranks of the marching ROTC, apparently to everybody's amusement. In other schools the faculty and even the administration and, in one place, the governor joined in protest rallies against ROTC. There were so many peace and disarmament meetings and marches it is impossible to form a clear picture—they seem to have taken place everywhere and, for the first time, to have brought out large numbers. Off campus, as it were, the lonely pacifists who had been sitting out the civil-defense propaganda stunt in New York called their annual "sit out" and were dumbfounded at the turnout. For the first time, too, the courts and even the police weakened. Few were arrested, and fewer sentenced.

The Chessman execution provoked demonstrations, meetings, telegrams, on campuses all over the country. In Northern California the "mass base" of all forms of protest was among the students and the younger teachers. They provided the cadre, circulated petitions, sent wires, interviewed the Governor, and kept up a continuous vigil at the gates of San Quentin. All this activity was unquestionably spontaneous. At no time did the American Civil Liberties Union or the regular anti-capital-punishment organizations initiate, or even take part in, any mass action, whatever else they may have done. Chessman, of course, had a tremendous appeal to youth; he was young, he was an intellectual, even an artist of sorts; before his arrest he had been the kind of person they could recognize, if not approve of, among themselves. He was not very different from the hero of *On the Road*, who happened to be locked up in San Quentin along with him. As his life drew to a close, he showed a beautiful magnanimity in all he did or said. On all the campuses of the country—of the world, for that matter—he seemed an almost typical example of the alienated and outraged youthful "delinquent" of the post-World War II era—the product of a delinquent society. To the young who refused to be demoralized by society, it appeared that that society was killing him only to sweep its own guilt under the rug. I think almost everyone (Chessman's supporters included) over thirty-five seriously underestimates the psychological effect of the Chessman case on the young.

At all points the brutal reactionary tendencies in American life were being challenged, not on a political basis, Left versus

Right, but because of their patent dishonesty and moral violence. The most spectacular challenge was the riot at the hearing of the Un-American Activities Committee in San Francisco. There is no question but that this was a completely spontaneous demonstration. The idea that Communist agitators provoked it is ludicrous. True, all that were left of the local Bolsheviks turned out, some thirty of them—Stalinists and the two groups of Trotskyites. Even the "youth leader" who, twenty-eight years before, at the age of thirty, had been assigned to lead the YCL, showed up and roared and stomped incoherently, and provided comic relief. Certainly no one took him seriously. There was one aspect about the whole thing that was not spontaneous. That was the work of the committee. They planned it that way. Over the protests and warnings of the city administration they deliberately framed up a riot. When the riot came, it was the cops who lost their nerve and rioted, if rioting means uncontrolled mob violence. The kids sat on the floor with their hands in their pockets and sang, "We shall not be moved."

Spectacular as it was, there are actions more important than the San Francisco riot. Here and there about the country, lonely, single individuals have popped up out of nowhere and struck their blows. It is almost impossible to get information about draft resisters, nonregistrants, conscientious objectors, but here and there one pops up in the local press or, more likely, in the student press.

Even more important are the individual actions of high-school students whom only a hopeless paranoiac could believe anybody had organized. A sixteen-year-old boy in Queens, and then three in the Bronx, refused to sign loyalty oaths to get their diplomas. As kudos are distributed in a New York suburban high school, a boy gets up and rejects an award from the American Legion. Everybody is horrified at his bad manners. A couple of days later two of his prizes are offered to the two runners-up, who reject them in turn. This is spontaneous direct action if ever there was. And the important thing about it is that in all these cases, these high-school kids have made it clear that they do not object to either loyalty oaths or the American Legion because they are "reactionary," but because they are morally contemptible.

The Negro faculties and presidents of the Jim Crow colleges, who not only opposed the sit-ins but expelled dozens of the sit-inners, now found themselves faced with deserted campuses. They were overtaken by a tremendous groundswell of approval of their youngsters' actions from Negro parents, and were dumbfounded by the sympathy shown by a broad stratum of the white South. One by one they swung around, until Uncle Toms who had expelled students taking part in sit-ins during their Easter vacations in other states, went on public record as saying, "If your son or daughter telephones you and says he or she has been arrested in a sit-in, get down on your knees and thank God."

Not only did the New Revolt of Youth become the hottest domestic copy in years, but it reached the ears of all the retired and semiretired and comfortably fixed pie-card artists of every lost and every long-since-won cause of the labor and radical movements. Everybody shouted, "Myself when young!" and pitched in with application blanks. The AFL-CIO sent out a well-known leader of the Esperanto movement who reported that the kids were muddled and confused and little interested in the trade-union movement which they, mistakenly in his opinion, thought of as morally compromised. YPSL chapters of the Thomasite Socialists rose from the graves of twenty years. Youth experts with theories about what their grandchildren were talking about went on cross-country tours. *Dissent* had a subscription drive. The Trotskyites came up with programs. Everybody got in the act—except, curiously, the Communists. As a matter of fact, back in a dusty office in New York, they were grimly deadlocked in their last factional fight. Although the movement was a spontaneous outburst of direct nonviolent action, it didn't quite please the libertarians and pacifists. They went about straightening everybody out, and *Liberation* came out with an article defining the correct Line and pointing out the errors of the ideologically immature.

As the kids go back to school this fall, this is going to be the greatest danger they will face—all these eager helpers from the other side of the age barrier, all these cooks, each with a time-tested recipe for the broth. All over the world this kind of ferment is stewing on college campuses. In Korea and Japan and Turkey the students have marched and brought down governments, and they have humbled the President of the greatest power in history. So far the movement is still formless, a world-wide upheaval of disgust. Even in Japan the Zengakuren, which does have a sort of ideology—the Left communism against which Lenin wrote his famous pamphlet—has only been able to act as a cheerleader. It has failed to impose its leadership, its organization or its principles on the still chaotic upsurge. In France the official Neo-Gandhian Movement, in alliance with certain sections of the Catholic Left, does seem to have given some sort of shape and leadership. I am inclined to think that this is due to the almost total ignorance of French youth of this generation—they had to go to the official sources for information and guidance, they just didn't have enough, themselves, to get started.

Is this in fact a "political" upsurge? It isn't now—it is a great moral rejection, a kind of mass vomit. Everybody in the world knows that we are on the verge of extinction and nobody does anything about it. The kids are fed up. The great problems of the world today are immediate world-wide peace, immediate race equality and immediate massive assistance to the former colonial peoples. All of them could be started toward solution by a few decisive acts of moral courage among the boys at the top of the heap. Instead, the leaders of the two ruling nations abuse each other like little boys caught out behind the barn. Their apologists stage elaborate military and ideological defenses of Marxian socialism and laissez-faire capitalism, neither of which has ever existed on the earth or ever will exist. While the Zengakuren howls in the streets, Khrushchev delivers a speech on the anniversary of Lenin's "Leftism, an Infantile Disorder" and uses it to attack—Mao! Meanwhile a boy gets up in a New York suburban school and contemptuously hands back his "patriotic" prize. He is fed up.

Henry James and H. G. Wells

Everybody knows the famous remark by Wells: "It [any novel by James] is like a church lit but without a congregation to distract you, with every light and line focused on the high altar. And on the altar, very reverently placed, intensely there, is a dead kitten, an egg-shell, a bit of string. . . ." It has been quoted by every high-toned critic in three languages. If it doesn't appear at least once in four numbers in any of our literary quarterlies, I am sure they would penitently refund your subscription. It is supposed to show what an awful boor Wells was, what a dreadful *Socialist*. It does nothing of the sort. In the context of Wells's satire *Boon*, it is pretty good literary criticism.

My mother used to say, "A snob is a person who imitates the manners of the class above him." Characteristic of the snob is social ignorance and insecurity. Perhaps the editors of this collection, by publishing all the James-Wells correspondence and all their critical mentions of each other, intend to show how high-class James was and how low-class Wells. I am afraid they demonstrate quite the opposite. Wells was pretty much a man of the world, at home in the world at all social levels, with a keen eye for the follies and pretenses of foolish and pretentious people of all classes. He wrote about his own work with misleading modesty and with a craftsman's natural instinct to keep his trade secrets from the public. He wrote about other writers with insight and humor. Eventually, in his correspondence with James, he was forced, by James's

Henry James and H. G. Wells. Edited and introduced by Leon Edel and Gordon N. Ray. University of Illinois Press, Urbana, 1958.

hauteur and lengthy elementary lectures on the craft of fiction, from humor to badinage, and finally, to just plain pulling the pompous old man's leg. He has the insouciance and arrogance of what used to be called a natural-born gentleman. James is always pretentious, literary and high-toned. It never occurs to him that this is the way literary people talk to the customers and that it is bad manners to hand such stuff out to one's colleagues. In other words, he believes implicitly in the mask of literary society, as well as what the newspapers call Society with a capital letter, and he acts accordingly, in private, with a presumed peer. In other words, he is a snob.

A lot of tosh has been written about Wells as a "social" novelist, always trying to reform the world via preachy fiction. You would think he was a sort of Upton Sinclair at his worst or a bad "proletarian" novelist. It must be quite a shock for an innocent person, with an honestly empirical approach, to sit down and read his fiction from *The Time Machine* to *The Research Magnificent*, admittedly his best period. His novels are not social novels at all. True, they reflect the society of their time; Ann Veronica, for instance, is a feminist. But *Tono-Bungay* is no more "about" the evils of patent medicines than *Crime and Punishment* is "about" Russian detective methods. All the major Wells novels have exactly the same subject as those of a writer no one would dream of connecting with him—D. H. Lawrence; they are about matrimony, about the mysteries and difficulties and agonies and tragedies and—rarely—the joys of the search for a true "life of dialogue." Wells's characters seek constantly and painfully to realize each other as total persons, and they usually pitifully fail. It is only too true that the Social Lie is precisely the conspiracy of organized society to prevent precisely this, and so there is always implicit a running criticism and sometimes a specific criticism of the frauds by which men live. Wells says depreciatingly that his people are seldom realized. This is false modesty. They are not constructed as artistic artifacts. They struggle to realize each other, and so, in their success or failure, realize themselves poignantly for the reader.

There is a sort of Reform Club myth about the sort of man and writer H. G. Wells was. Read him and see. He wasn't like that at all. I will let you in on a secret. This myth was constructed to teach him his place, to put him down. He was guilty of two unforgivable British sins. He was not just a Socialist, but a shameless *republican.* He several times printed very insulting comments, not about Royalty in the abstract, but about specific members of The Family in person. Almost as bad, he openly cohabited with members of the opposite sex without benefit of clerk or clergy. Furthermore, they were women one might, at any moment, meet socially. It is quite correct to keep a housemaid in Herts or retire one's favorite tart to Twickenham. It is almost *de rigueur,* like the tightly rolled umbrella and the bowler, in precisely the circles that snubbed Wells and made up the myth of the propaganda novelist and upstart son of a servant girl. It must have been excruciatingly embarrassing to his very British colleagues when he took seriously the preachments of two centuries of advanced thought and lived openly out of wedlock in a flat in Hampstead with, of all things, another writer, who was also a lady. And after that scandal he went right on doing the same thing until he was an aged man, over and over again. In other words, he behaved much like some arrogant aristocrat whose pedigree went back before the War of the Roses and who had nothing but contempt for the frauds with which the *hoi polloi* hide their naked shames. Parenthetically, this is exactly the same reason why Ford Madox Ford was practically driven out of England—and one of the leading persecutors of Ford was Henry James. James, always the perfect gentleman, concentrated his venom on Ford's mistress; he was physically afraid of Ford himself.

All the nonsense which Wells viewed with the amused contempt which comes from assured social and artistic position and integrity, James took utterly seriously. In fact, it is this nonsense which he made the major subject of his novels, and which, to "the well-brought-up-person" who knows his way around, gives them their pathos. The people in his novels behave the way the Upper Classes tell the Lower Classes they behave. But nobody has ever behaved this way, which is why there are no real people in James's novels. There can be no realization of each other, no life of dialogue, no realization of the individual character, if characters are nothing but cutouts from the Society Page of a third-rate newspaper. It is for this reason that James, in these letters and articles, describes the craft of fiction somewhat as Ben Jonson, in his theory of "humors," described his plays. Fortunately, he did not write them that way. People are not moral types, they are people, and novels, at least the best ones, are about people. But for James, the Boston Brahmin, the American Millionaire and the British Aristocracy were not just types, they were archetypes. Because, alas, poor James was a provincial snob.

The best thing in the book is a hilarious tale in the introduction about how William James, on a visit to his brother, tried to peek over the garden wall and catch a glimpse of the next-door neighbor, G. K. Chesterton. Poor Henry was prostrated with terror at his very aristocratic brother's nonchalance. He behaved exactly like an overrefined hypersensitive Edwardian housemaid. Wells and William James belong to the literary world of Huckleberry Finn or Don Quixote; Henry James, it must be admited, was only a Ouida in a frock coat.

Lawrence Durrell

1 (1957)

One of the best, and certainly one of the most civilized writers in English today is Lawrence Durrell. He has written a couple of superlative travel books, literary essays, miscellaneous belles-lettres, four volumes of poetry and novels which are quite unlike any other fictions of our day—at least until they produce imitators.

I enjoy Durrell's poetry more than that of anybody else anywhere near his age now writing in the British Isles. In fact, only McDiarmid, Muir and Read appeal to me as much. It is a poetry of tone, the communication of the precise quality of a very precious kind of revery—animalism and skeptic faith recollected in tranquillity. Wallace Stevens wrote with the same emotional subject matter, but his poetry is cooked and strident in comparison with Durrell's easy relaxation. Again, he is gifted with a gentle, unselfconscious eroticism very rare in our nasty and Puritan world—never nastier than among our most advanced *émancipés*.

The poet who has influenced Durrell most is probably the Greek poet Cavafis, the only homosexual writer in history who was not ridden with guilt. Durrell's loves and adventures have been more normal and less random, so that he is saved from Cavafis' heart-rending nostalgia for vanished and vanishing fulfillment. He seems to have come naturally, by easy,

The books of Durrell discussed in these three reviews, written from 1957 to 1960, are published by Dutton, except for *Selected Poems*, an Evergreen paperback.

heterosexual means, to the kind of tolerance of the painful heart that must have cost Cavafis a lifetime of very disagreeable trouble. No one writing verse today can better evoke a scene, a place, a room, a situation, the body of a woman, alive at just that fleeting moment that it lived, with all the meaning of its present and all the pathos of its vanishing. Again, no one can better bow over unspeaking, resonant strings. Durrell's overtones and references would be destroyed by notes. It is just a haunting flavor of Gibbon's Theodora that counts in Durrell's poem to a modern intellectual tart of the same name—lurking in the background with her rumors of bear pits and brothels, like some evanescent herb dimly sensed in a production of morels stuffed with *brochet.* What glitters in the foreground is the gold fleck in the living girl's eye—recorded forever.

Stevens may have liked to think he approached art as the late Aga Khan might have approached a race horse, a *pâté truffé,* a girl or a Chateau Ausone of the year of the comet. Actually, his approach was more that of a New England insurance executive. Durrell is so convincing as a good European he comes close to being a good Levantine. And it is all done simply, with never a mirror—the best kind of legerdemain, without a stick of apparatus. It's not for nothing that he wrote two poems years ago which are still the best ever written in Basic English. The ancestor is Horace. Someday, when the world has calmed down, maybe we will again realize that Horace was the perfect artist he was considered by less troubled times. Right now, Lawrence Durrell is the only person I know who has the indomitable guts to walk in his footsteps.

Just before the war Durrell wrote a novel, *The Black Book.* Nobody who ever read it ever quite got over it. It is the story, told from the inside, of a bunch of thoroughly wretched characters—intellectuals seeking exquisite debauchery. It gets just the right tone. It is so perfect, so dead-pan, you have to think it over before you realize that Durrell himself didn't really mean it. Now lots of people have portrayed the evils of musical beds. I believe quite a few novels nowadays deal with this and related subjects. By and large, scratch a pornographer and a furious Puritan emerges from the tousled bedcovers. Above the bidets of *The Black Book's* disgraceful boudoirs is written in a fine Spenserian hand: "Durrell was here"—there is only the gentle echo of Epicurean malice.

Justine is at least the equal of *The Black Book,* from the comic irony of its title to the tour de force of a tour de force that is its style. It is an imitation of what the French call a *récit* of a weak, pretentious schoolmaster and amateur of the sensibility, who is very busy writing fine writing about his ridiculously self-conscious amours. But the take-off on fine writing is itself fine writing—very fine writing indeed, and the two qualities, the real and its satirical mirror image, are so blended and confused that the exact nature of the "aesthetic satisfaction" is impossible to analyze. Proust managed this sometimes, as in the absurd scene where his hero uses pages to describe the maneuvers by which he managed to spy on Charlus in the lumber room. Durrell is so much more economical; Proust, delighted to discover a spark of humor rising in his humorless mind, usually worked his jokes to death.

Once again Durrell has turned to Cavafis—in fact, *Justine* is almost a novelification (like a versification but backwards) of Cavafis' poetry. It is not just an evocation, but a bodily conjuration of Alexandria—soft, sweet, corrupt and crazy, like some impossibly cloying tropical fruit. Shanghai . . . Alexandria . . . Tangiers . . . only our time has produced these sanatoria with the luxury rooms full of uprooted rotting infants and the corridors full of eyeless beggars exhibiting their stinking sores. Not only is Durrell's Alexandria so real that it envelopes you like a cloud of its own miasmas, but the people—even though we see them through comic distorting mirrors—are more real than real. The realest of all is the proverbial tart with a heart of gold. Both Durrell and I have been taken to task by the same British critics for imagining that this type of girl actually exists. He certainly makes her very convincing. I doubt if he just thought her up. Like all hearts of gold, she dies as pathetically as any Dickens girl. I doubt if the other people have hearts at all—there doesn't seem to be anything inside them but dry *râles* and spoiling orchids. But they are frighteningly like the people you know.

2 (1960)

Sitting down to write this review of Durrell's *Clea,* I have little relish for the job. For a good many years now I have been a devoted, persistent fan of Lawrence Durrell. When *Justine* came out I wrote a very laudatory review for *The Nation.* It seemed the promise of a thoroughly adult job. The characters were a distasteful crew, but certainly they were grownups; the plot was as complex as any of Conrad's, and since the succeeding three novels were announced as treating the same cast through the eyes of three different characters, the whole project promised to be a fabulous network of motives, false motives and imaginary motives. The style was saturated with a whimsical, self-mocking irony, "fine writing" making fun of itself. Altogether, I felt on sure ground when I prophesied a big work by a mature man, one worthy to be set alongside Ford Madox Ford's Tietjens series, the promise of a novel which would be fit reading for a male over thirty-five. Certainly, there aren't very many such. Now, at least this one male over thirty-five is a disappointed man.

What happened? In the first place, I think a purely mechanical mistake. Durell sold *Justine* before the rest of the work was completed, and for the next three years had to produce a book a year against an inexorable deadline. Maybe Dickens or Dostoevski could do this; they hated it and groused about it, but they produced masterpieces that way. It is obvious that Durrell could not. Times have changed. Writers are far more self-indulgent and temperamental nowadays—they are artists, and rigorous business arrangements upset them. Durrell felt frustrated and hemmed in. Each year he put off writing and then wrote carelessly, perhaps even defiantly. What had been complex and subtle and ironic turned into something flimsy, schematic and flashy.

Plotting, which at the start was careful and wise, became

sensational. It not only became sensational, it became frivolous and irresponsible. Perhaps it makes a good hot item for the paperbacks to suggest that the Egyptian Copts and the Jews are in a plot with the Nazis to betray the Arabs and British in Egypt and Palestine—but this is the kind of yarn we associate with Talbot Mundy, not with a serious writer. It is all too easy to envisage a young Egyptian officer in charge of a border post reading that book between hours of duty. This kind of childish meddling with the lives of the innocent should be left to "Steve Canyon" and "Terry and the Pirates." The word for it is cheap—as well as dangerous. One step more and the word is malicious.

The writing has decayed in the same way. Pain and disaster emerged at first from the necessary relationships of the characters; in the later books it is applied from the outside. Clea's disaster with the fish-gun is not tragedy, it is sensationalism, on a par with the highly sophisticated sadism of the pseudo-highbrow French and Italian movies. Furthermore, its gratuitousness shows; they do this so much better in Japan where sentimental agonies have a long tradition of great skill. Gone too is the subtle mockery of fancy writing. The narrator of *Clea* has decided that now he can really "write," at last he is an artist. You won't get far in the book before the horrible suspicion sneaks over you that Durrell agrees with him. I'll take De Quincey.

What is wrong with this writer? He has terrific talent, he is no longer a young man, he has learned all the lessons there are to learn. Is it an incorrigible Bohemianism? Perhaps. I went back and reread *The Black Book*. All the Alexandria tetralogy is there, writ small. It is one of the first and best books of its kind—that long spate of tales of the life and loves of the Underground Man that have become the characteristic literary fad of the last twenty years. It is a tale of a wretched warren of loathsome characters, and like Dostoevski's manifesto, *Letters from the Underworld*, like *Les Liaisons Dangereuses*, like the life and letters of Baudelaire, its moral point is that all such people can do is debauch, in rotten frivolity, the ignorant and trusting innocent. This, in a sense, is the point of the first of the kind, the immensely fashionable parent of the whole genre, that other *Justine* by Sade. The trouble with *The Black Book* is that you can never be sure of Durrell's intention. Did he know what he was doing? How close is he, really, to his characters, the closeness of the artist who understands all, or the embroilment of the participant who understands nothing?

In his preface to the new edition of *The Black Book* Durrell speaks of it as an attack on Puritanism and identifies it with the genre of *Lady Chatterley's Lover*. But *Chatterley* is not an attack on Puritanism at all. It reeks of Puritanism and crippled, self-conscious sex—and of the personal spites and ill tempers of Lawrence as well. Only an adolescent, recently escaped from the Epworth League, could think of it as a pagan manifesto of sexual freedom. So too, *The Black Book* is a tour de force of ingrown Puritanism, and so too, I am afraid, is the Alexandrine tetralogy.

While the four parts of the novel were coming out, Durrell published *Bitter Lemons, Esprit de Corps, Stiff Upper Lip*. These are all concerned with his own life as a diplomatic representative of Great Britain. They all have the same fault, a blissfully unconscious, but none the less absolute ethnocentrism. In *Bitter Lemons* the Cypriots are happy childlike innocents, misled by "demagogues" and the "envenomed insinuations of the Athens Radio." It never occurs to Durrell that they might just want to be free of the British. Only the most unworthy motives are ever ascribed to either the Turkish or Greek leaders, who are always portrayed as "outside agitators," interested only in advancing themselves at the expense of naïve and friendly schoolchildren. The English, on the other hand, are seen as silly, bumbling, out of date, but oh so sane and wholesome and always concerned only with the good of the charges that God has entrusted to them. We've heard all this before; in fact, we can hear it almost any day when a Southern Congressman is sounding off, and what day is one not? *Stiff Upper Lip* and *Esprit de Corps* are unforgivable.

They are written in the most dreadful imitation of P. G. Wodehouse, a favorite author of Durrell, by his own admission. (He reads him in *Bitter Lemons* during negotiations with the Cypriots over their freedom.) It is a bad imitation and so vulgar it makes your flesh crawl. These two books of purported humor explain much about what happened to the splendid plan announced in *Justine*. Possibly, carefully read, they explain everything. British diplomats are noble and silly, Indians, Negroes, Egyptians are sly and rascally children, uniformly portrayed in terms of a Soho pickpocket—the only "native," you feel, reading these disgraceful books, Durrell has ever known personally. This, of course, is not true; he has lived most of his life in the Levant. What is wrong with him? What is wrong with Englishmen?

Meanwhile he has published something else. Grove Press has brought out his *Selected Poems* and there are rumors a *Complete Collected Poems* will be along eventually. These are great poems, lovely, temperate, with every subtle cadence so carefully controlled, so excruciatingly civilized. They reek of the Levant at its best, with all of its best reeks. There is little self-consciousness in them, and little Puritanism, but lots of the weary sensuality and fleshy joy of Greek and Turkish and Egyptian life and love and food and drink. These poems, not *Justine*, really transfuse into the pale British bloodstream the wistful lewdness and wisdom of that great bad Greek, the poet Cavafis, who was one of the most consummate evil livers in all literature. Durrell's poems avoid Cavafis' more lurid sin, but they perfectly transmit his smile and his impeccable taste. I think the poems answer the question, "What's wrong with this initially so ambitious work?" Closeness, or embroilment? Durrell is an old and loyal friend of Henry Miller. So loyal in fact that he recently edited an anthology presenting poor Henry as a Thinker; it would seem that Durrell really believes Miller thinks. This is a fine friendship, well tested through almost thirty years, and it is not fortuitous. Like Henry Miller, Durrell is suspiciously like some character in his own fictions.

3 (1960)

In 1938 Lawrence Durrell sent the typescript of *The Black Book* to Henry Miller, asking his opinion of it, and telling him to pitch it into the Seine when he had read it. Miller took it to his own publishers, the Obelisk Press, who immediately published it. It has been a "banned classic" ever since. It is hard to understand, reading it today, why it should ever have been banned in the first place. T. S. Eliot, Cyril Connolly, everybody who was anybody in those days, greeted it with shouts of joy. Eliot called it "the first piece of work by a new English writer to give me any hope for the future of prose fiction." Although it has a few common colloquial terms for human anatomy and physiology scattered through it and its subject is a sort of hall-bedroom sexual rat race, it is about as salacious as a VD clinic.

It is the story of the denizens of a cheap rooming house in South London, that illimitable expanse of faceless squalor that covers many hundreds of times the acreage of the city that the Upper Classes and the international world of tourism and business know as "London." The two most human people in the cast are foreign students, the rest are lumpenintelligentsia. They are the underemployed or unemployable, devoid of all skills, too poorly educated to be of any good to others, with too much education for their own good.

It is the story of typical representatives of a class who are habitually terrorized by sex, and who therefore use it habitually as an instrument of terror. Sex does not frighten them because it is sex, but because it is humane. If wine, or music, or good food were as important as humane sex is to humane living, these too would occupy the center of attention. Good food, of course, as an instrument of *humanitas* does not terrify any Englishman of any class. Unless he crosses the Channel he never has an opportunity to encounter it. But sex is inescapable. In one form or another, as they say, it persists in raising its head. The characters of *The Black Book* can't cope with it. It obsesses them and frightens them. Their response is a kind of disheveled misery.

It is a study of the etiology of one, and the commonest, kind of Bohemianism. We forget that there are at least two kinds. Mimi's friends in Puccini's opera are the first kind, young artists on their way up. They have the arrogance of young genius. They are poor and immoral. At the end of the story they are mostly very successful, and Mimi is dead. But while it all lasted, they had a good time—love, wine, food, music. This kind of Bohemian is an under- or unemployed intellectual who gives up most of the necessities of the poor so he can enjoy some of the luxuries of the rich. But there is another kind, by far more common, the upstart product of a lower-middle-class Puritan background who discovers himself unable to compete with the world of civilized men which he is trying to enter. This demoralizes him. He rebels. He reads erotic books. He tries pederasty, at least in his imagination. He neglects to shave and often to wash. Above all else he is frightened. This is the character who forms the pattern for most of the people in *The Black Book.* Dostoevski called him the Underground Man. He is a debauched Puritan, an unwisely paroled shopkeeper.

It is the story of a group of people suffering from incurable spiritual malnutrition, and by "spiritual" I mean "physical"—fleshly. These are nervous systems which can never do anything but starve. The joys of life are as unassimilable as crushed rock. Above all else, these are people who cannot assimilate one another. Humaneness is the fine art of enjoying other people. Each of these people is utterly alone, not one knows there is anybody else out there.

All this sounds as if *The Black Book* was not very enjoyable reading. Certainly Dostoevski's *Notes from the Underground* is one of literature's more disagreeable experiences. On the contrary, *The Black Book* is often even funny. It is in the tradition of "bitter comedy," like Jonson's *Volpone* or Machiavelli's *Mandragola*—but then, I suppose, so is Dostoevski's book, in a sense. It is more than just the comic form. I can't imagine anyone less like Mark Twain than Durrell, but in almost everything he writes he shares one salient and splendid characteristic with Mark Twain—he so obviously has such a good time writing. Some of the passages in *The Black Book* are a young author's "fine writing," later to be parodied by Durrell himself in *Justine,* but, unlike so much of this sort of thing, they are never self-consciously written. They flow out of youthful scorn and pity and out of just plain enthusiasm with the newly mastered ability to write. This creates a kind of audience participation, a stylistic excitement not unlike the excitement of jazz.

The dominant mood of *The Alexandria Quartet* is a comic overcivilization. Its world is peopled exclusively by provincial avatars of Oscar Wilde, Whistler, Mercedes d' Acosta, Princess Polignac, Ida Rubenstein, Diaghilev, Nazimova—in other words, a seedy Edwardian glamour, long since vanished from Europe, and gone off to the backlands of the Levant to die. The book smells of something I for one have never smelled, that fascinating substance so popular in the novels my Aunt Minnie read, patchouli. *The Alexandria Quartet* is saved from comedy by its sad irony. If it weren't for its irony it would be a kind of chic, reader-flattering Ouida.

The dominant mood of *The Black Book* is plain rambunctiousness. To press the comparison to jazz, if *The Alexandria Quartet* is like the *Modern Jazz Quartet* playing "Sleepy Lagoon" (I rather hope they never have!), then *The Black Book* is like the King Oliver Band, or, to be very precise—because it deals with exactly the same subject—Jelly Roll Morton playing and singing "I Thought I Heard Buddy Bolton Say."

As George Elliott has pointed out, *The Alexandria Quartet* is romantic to the core. It would be like d'Annunzio if d'Annunzio had had good taste. Everybody is frightfully high class. Even the servants and tramps have an *Arabian Nights* grotesquerie. In *The Black Book,* everybody is low class, the lowest class of all, the homeless upstarts of the lower middle class. The tragic wastrels of Alexandria are sometimes foolish, sometimes silly. The characters of *The Black Book,* in their dirty socks and rayon combinations, are ridiculous. What redeems them is Durrell's own youth—because he has, in abundance, one of the rare, sterling virtues of youth, an all-devouring, all-forgiving angry pity. As Robert MacAlmon says in Hemingway's novel—"Oh, give 'em anger, and give 'em pity."

Durrell seems to be fascinated with the thin sentence of sense in the vast, dull mass of Sade, the notion that the most life-destroying of all poisons is guilt. Guilt flagellates the major characters of *The Alexandria Quartet* with a whip of scorpions. At least they have, most of them, something to feel guilty about. Guilt has emasculated the characters of *The Black Book* at birth. They pay the penalty but are incapable of comprehending, much less enjoying, the crime. This is certainly as pathetic a predicament as could be imagined. There is other pathos, too, of the plain old-fashioned kind. The central story of the book, the vacuous debauching of the vulgar dying waif, Gracie, by her witless debaucher, Gregory, is a kind of malicious parody of the tragedy of Mimi and her lover, the *La Bohème* of hobohemia. It may be sickeningly sentimental in a perverse way, but it is one of the most unforgettable tales in modern fiction.

What makes *The Alexandria Quartet,* of course, as everybody knows, is its structure. It is a tour de force of multiple-aspect narrative. Durrell has said, in several interviews, in England and in France, in *Encounter,* in *France Observateur,* and in *L'Express,* that he had never read Ford Madox Ford's *The Good Soldier* or his Tietjens series. I don't doubt his word, but find the fact astonishing. It would seem that Ford occurred spontaneously to all three interviewers. Certainly he occurred to me. I know of no modern novelist more like Durrell. Very likely he had read Conrad, and possibly the complex, cobwebby novels which Conrad and Ford (then Hueffer) wrote together. Maybe he just naturally thinks that way.

The Alexandria Quartet is a big job, with lots of room to maneuver. *The Black Book* is a volume of about three hundred pages with a small and rather ambiguously defined cast of characters. Yet *The Black Book,* too, is a carefully braided indirect, direct, and third-person narrative. Much of it is cast in the form of a diary by the lamentable Gregory. Circling over and under and around this narrative is another, equally immodest, diary-like in form and substance, purportedly the direct utterance of Durrell himself (he uses his own name). Consequently, the image of the characters is always unstable, they merge and go out of focus and return in altered form. The writing wanders off and explodes in amateur surrealist fireworks, and when it returns, the pattern of the characters has changed again. Gregory himself never appears in the flesh. Durrell is part of the time writing in the same dismal London rooming house, part of the time he is recollecting in replete and guiltless tranquillity in rainy, wintry Corfu (or is it Crete?).

What is important in all this counterpoint is that Durrell, as first-person narrator, gets slowly sucked into the moral world of his shoddy diarist, whom, incidentally, he has never seen, and then, as imperceptibly and gratuitously, escapes. The book ends like *Ulysses*, with an invocation to the existential flesh of the wife in bed beside him, in Greece, on a rainy morning.

The characters in Durrell's first novel are somewhat like idiot brothers and sisters of those in his new one. Their doom is less well upholstered and attended. They are bound for Hell in a third-class carriage. Justine and her friends are headed there in a private car on the Orient Express, but the road is the same doom, the end is the same Hell, just a grubbier slum of that vast city.

Actually, though they are vaguely enough drawn, the people in *The Black Book* are a little more real, at least they are more convincing. Most of us have relatives like them somewhere. My own parents, as a matter of fact, were well-to-do provincial intellectuals, and, I suspect, modeled their lives on characters like Justine and Nessim. Maybe such people really once existed, flirting dangerously among the fine bindings, at a reception of Mrs. Potter Palmer's, away from the crowd, in the dimly lit library, but for me at least, their reality is impaired by "books my mother read." On the other hand, these people reading deep books in their unmade beds in South London are all about us—they have made a number of disagreeable revolutions in our time.

I wonder if Durrell is, even today, aware of who stands out in the book as most real, most convincing? I, for one, think the Peruvian, full of South American animality, demoralized, but still there, and Miss Smith, the African girl who is studying Middle English, but who, someday, when she has mastered the mysteries of Europe, is going back to Africa and her own race. Neither of these people is involved, nor do they need to be involved, in the interpersonal hunger strikes of the others. Soon they will pick up and go, back to a wiser world. Meantime, Lobo can never quite "make it," Miss Smith, calmly and courteously, doesn't even try. They point the moral. It is an old one. I suppose it is an anti-Puritan one, as the book narrowly escapes being an anti-Puritan tract. It is certainly a religious one. Sin is the failure of the organ of reciprocity.

The failure of reciprocity, incongruity, low life, these are the ingredients of classic comedy. So *The Black Book* is a classic comedy. This might only mean that it is a careful concoction following the recipes of Aristotelian and Renaissance cookbooks. It is so much more because it is a lyric comedy, and the lyricism is the voice of Durrell's anger and pity and enthusiasm.

Just incidentally, it is also, along with Miller's *Tropics* and a few other books, one of the first of what has become the characteristic genre of mid-century fiction—the highbrow true-confession story, the mixture of semi-autobiography, diaristic style, interior monologue, random expostulation and prose dithyramb—the artifice of convincing immodesty. The later Céline, Miller, Kerouac, even *Lolita.* Over in France, on lower levels, there are a half dozen published every month. *The Black Book* is still one of the very best.

Gnosticism

There are two "culture clashes" (as anthropologists call them) of great importance in the history of religion. The first was the Persian conquest of Syria, Palestine and Egypt. The second was Alexander's conquest of Persia. They were not just sterile military conquests but wide and deep fusions of culture. Each was like the mixing of two chemical elements with the resulting effervescence, heat, and emergence of new chemical compounds. Out of the first came Judaism as we know it in the Scriptures. Out of the second came Christianity as we know it in the Christian Scriptures and in the writings of the early Fathers of the Church.

Tremendous energies are often released by the mingling of the right disparate elements—chemical explosions, nuclear fission—the strongest "radio star" in the sky is actually a pair of colliding nebulae. So, likewise, the spiritual and intellectual energies released by those ancient culture clashes are still affecting us today. Not only Judaism and Christianity, but Stoicism, Neo-Platonism, Mahayana Buddhism, the later mystery religions, Mithraism, the worship of Isis, Manichaeism, all emerge from this cultural mixing. Even the old orthodox religions in Greece, Egypt, Syria, Persia and India were profoundly changed.

Religion was uprooted, quite literally. It was lifted from the soil of the strictly local rite and cult and was internationalized and generalized. Once you were born in a place and

This essay was an introduction to a new edition of *Fragments of a Faith Forgotten: The Gnostics* by G. R. S. Mead. University Books, New Hyde Park, N.Y., 1960.

worshiped the god of the nearby hilltop and the goddess of the spring under it. They may have been called Zeus or Artemis, but as living deities they are bound to a place, their national character remained an unreal creation of the poets. Even in the Orient, the Great Gods—Amun or Marduk, Isis or Ishtar—owed their generalized worship to the fact that they were gods of the Palace Cult or the capital city. In daily life they were fragmented into hundreds of minor Amuns and Marduks and Ishtars and Isises, gods of the village or the field or the neighborhood. It was these local deities the people worshiped, except for the great national or royal ceremonies.

The uprooting of religion came when men were able to come and go freely through vast empires that stretched from one end of the ancient world to the other. Their deities acquired a theology, a gospel, a general myth and a theoretical justification. Such religions produced a propaganda and missionaries. Eventually there were shrines to Persian and Palestinian and Egyptian saviors on the borders of Scotland; religious sculptors and painters who had learned from Praxiteles and Apelles worked in the Gobi Desert and among the recently civilized Japanese.

Out of this immense seedbed or forcing-shed sprouted all the modern orthodoxies. Out of the same soil came heterodoxy. In fact, until this time the notion of heterodoxy could not exist. The famous Aten worship of Ikhnaten was not a heterodoxy—it was simply a different royal cult. The old folk religions had sanctified the seasons of the year and the rites of passage. The new world religions built on this foundation and gave the myths and practices of the cult an ethical content. At first they gave the individual only significance; later they came to offer him salvation; but this salvation was contingent on the co-operation of the worshiper's will and the assent of his faith. By the time of the first Greek nature philosophers, the world of science and the folk transcendental world had become incompatible. To Socrates, Anaxagoras was impious and crazy in trying to explain the mechanisms of the universe. Heterodoxy came into existence.

It is obvious, is it not, that the propaganda of a foreign or constructed religious cult must be that it will work where the old native faith does not. As against the ancestral faith which is taken on trust but which becomes insufficient to cope with the new facts, the proselytizers of the new religion must guarantee results. Also, the native religion is public by definition. Its rites and myths are an open expression of the entire society and any person who cares to learn the sacred scriptures can understand them. In contrast, the alien religion is occult. It is a secret doctrine because the very knowledge of the doctrine of itself insures salvation, and so it cannot be left accessible to the untested and uninitiated. The secret doctrine includes the actual scientific knowledge of the time, which is directly assimilated to the myth. Perhaps a better way of saying this is that the myth absorbs all the details of the knowledge of the world. So you have a religion which throughout approximates to magic. Its knowledge and its rites are coercive. The faithful can force the universe to the desired conclusion. Prayers are thought of as being as efficacious as chemical formulas. They are spells.

Of course, magical elements of this sort lie at the very sources of all the religions of the ancient world and reach their greatest development in Babylon and Egypt. Maturing civilization gives the magical formulas of the Book of the Dead a personal and ethical interpretation. But the individual crises of the soul which accompany the dislocations, deracinations, and insecurities of men living in world empires reinstate the securities of the primitive spell, the formula, the coercive rite, the knowledge of presumed absolute fact that insures salvation.

Our first record of a mystery religion of the later type is a fourth-century demotic papyrus, found in an ancient polyglot settlement in the Nile Delta, which must have been something like modern Alexandria. It is written in cursive Egyptian, but the language is Aramaic, the *lingua franca* of the Persian and Hellenistic Near East. It is a mystery play, a sacred marriage of the goddess Anat and Baal, after Anat has saved her consort from Mut, the god of death. There is also a trinity of couples and behind them all an overgod, Baal Shamain, the Lord of Heaven. These nine deities do not all come from one place, but from Canaan, Babylon, Assyria and the old Sumerian lands. They have been deliberately put together by some unknown "founder," a connoisseur of Near Eastern religion not unlike our twentieth-century religious window-shoppers. Furthermore, not only does the text handle the Egyptian characters in a most cavalier way, but *it is in code*. No Egyptian or Aramaic scribe could decipher it without the key. In addition, it is not in ordinary current Aramaic of its day, but in an artificial, pseudo-archaic language, like our bad classical translations in "Biblical prose." Before this, only the secrets of devination and astrology were written in cryptogram—because they were thought to have the efficacy of scientific procedures. Here we have a foreign cult in an alien land with a secret ritual, its myth is a recently constructed syncretistic fantasy, its rite is guaranteed to work, its deities parallel the scientific picture of the cosmos. We have, as I said, the first of the mystery religions of the later type known to us, and we have the first intimations of Gnosticism. In the next eight hundred years the pattern would change very little, it would only develop.

Gnosticism as such is only a few years older than Christianity but its origins, or at least the origins of its material, are lost in time. Some of this material it shares with Christianity, but Gnosticism is much more conservative, it uses far more of the past. Christianity takes from the past only a central religious drama, Gnosticism retains a whole cosmology and cosmogony.

Let us take one by one the cardinal points of the Gnostic creed and trace them back to their earliest appearance.

Emanationism is contemporary with the beginning of high civilization in Egypt. The "Memphite Theology" is a tractate from the Old Kingdom. In it, Ptah, the deity whom the Egyptians of Memphis considered the eldest of the gods, has emanate from him four couples of gods, male and female, in descending order of being. Ptah *thought, spoke,* and his word created them. Each god or goddess had no other being than the "heart and tongue of Ptah" and by them all things were made and without them was not anything made that was made. (Ptah himself, incidentally, is represented not with the ordinary body of a man, but as a swaddled mummy with a huge protruding phallus, the combination of life and death.) Earlier still than the Memphite Theology is the Ennead of Heliopolis, where the same four pairs are derived from the creator Atun. This, however, is an ordinary creation myth and does not share with the Memphis tract its remarkable philosophy. The unique idea of emantionism is that the Great God acts only through his emanations.

The war of Good and Evil and the debauching of creation are Babylonian and later Persian ideas. It never seems to have occurred to the Egyptians or the early Semites that there was anything seriously wrong with the world; but Mesopotamian and later Persian religions are haunted by the power of evil. This is an important distinction. The Egyptians were well aware of evil, but they granted it no metaphysical, let alone ontological importance. Isis and Osiris saved men from death. The saviors, the Saoshyanto, of Persian religion save from sin, against which, unaided, man, and all creation with him, could not prevail. We have an abundance of texts which indicate that the Egyptians, like the Quakers, found it relatively easy to be good. Farther east, the Babylonians, then the Persians, and after them the post-exilic Hebrews and then the majority of Christians, seem to have found it difficult indeed.

The Gnostics went still further. Although in Persian religion evil often functions as an autonomous principle, there is no suggestion that creation, matter, or man, is bad as such. This idea, of *the intrinsic evil of the world,* is the peculiar and distinguishing notion of most of the Gnostic cults.

From Persia comes the concept of the universe as a moral battleground, existence in itself as *the struggle of light against darkness.* We are familiar with this language in the New

Testament and among the Jewish sectaries of the Dead Sea Scrolls. With it, into Gnosticism, came a whole physics and metaphysics of light which was to survive in various forms in Western thought for centuries.

Anyone who has ever seen a reproduction of one of the pictures from the Egyptian Book of the Dead is familiar with what is known as the Perils of the Soul, the belief that after death the soul passes before the inquisitors of the Underworld and to be saved must know the proper prayer or spell for each god as well as their secret names. By Persian times in Egypt the Ennead of Osiris had come to take the place of the original principal judges of the dead, although the unfortunate soul had to undergo a minor inquisition from dozens of petty deities or demons. Gnosticism equated these inquisitors of the soul with the cosmic powers, the rulers of the spheres of heaven. The Egyptian progress of the soul through the Underworld was changed to *the ascent of the soul, led by the descended and now ascending savior*, to the empyrean and the bliss of union with the unknown God from whom all creation and creators had emanated. But the magical process by which this ascent is achieved remains the same as in the Egyptian Underworld. The Gnostic soul is saved because it knows the secrets of the heavenly spheres and can give the correct answers.

The Enneads of Heliopolis or Memphis were not equated with the planets and the sun and moon until very late in Egypt. In Babylon, however, similar hierarchies were so identified at an early date. Once Babylonian astrology reached its full development, just before and during the Persian period, this (so to speak) *solar-system religion* spread over the whole near East, eventually to influence not only the Greeks and Romans but also the Celts and Teutons.

The descent of the redeemer goddess, Ishtar or Anahit or Isis, long predates the organization of the pantheon into the solar system, but once the two notions are conjoined it is obvious that the cosmos becomes the theater of a tremendous drama. This cosmogony is not to be disdained. A millennium and a half later it was still meaningful to William Blake.

Other elements—serpent worship, erotic mysticism and ritual, the mystic marriage, the slain redeemer god—all these ideas, as it has so often been pointed out, are nearly universal and in most cases precede the coming of the historic populations into the Near East. They are Neolithic or even earlier. So, too, is *the strong matriarchal or at least antipatriarchal emphasis* of most Gnostic sects.

The gods of Homer and the Greek dramatists and, to a lesser degree, those of the Royal cults of Egypt or Babylon, go their way regardless of man. Gnosticism shares with Christianity, Judaism and Zoroastrianism the concept of creation and redemption as a great drama, focused on man, a drama in which the individual worshiper plays a primary role. Literal dramas of redemption, actual plays, are common throughout the ancient Near East. The Memphite Theology is in fact a play; so is the principle Ras Shamra codex, so is the Aramaic papyrus I mentioned before, so too is one form of the Gilgamesh Epic and of the Descent of Ishtar. Relics of this dramatic form survive in the Song of Songs, Job and Esther. These ancient dramatic performances conditioned the myths they portrayed, and conversely the new dramatic myths provided the framework for the myth as literature and eventually for the Passion of Christ as well as for the drama as a work of art. It is not for nothing that cranks have found in the tragedies of Shakespeare, but especially in *The Tempest,* the disguised rituals of an occult mystery religion. Dramatic episodes survive in the documents of Gnosticism, especially the famous dance and antiphonal chant in the Acts of John. The ancient ritual dramas before the great empires were social —they were concerned with objective reality, fruitfulness of the fields and the turning of the year. Acting in a great royal play in Memphis or Thebes, the Pharaoh is the god incarnate, but he functions only as the focus of Egyptian society, the nation ceremoniously embraces its bride, the land of Egypt. Gnosticism subjectivized the cosmic drama. Simon Magus is the god incarnate, going from place to place in the Levant like an ordinary man, and his bride, the mystic Helen, is literally a girl redeemed from a brothel. The Gnostic saviors are independent operators, come to save individual sinners without any of the sanctions of organized society.

I have dwelt at length on the origins of the mythological and ritual material of Gnosticism for the simple reason that Gnosticism is the main funnel through which these rites and doctrines reach modern times. The mysterious deity of the Templars or the erotic revels of the witches or the ceremonies of the Masons or Rosicrucians, all are aspects of a special heterodoxy that began with Gnosticism. For better or worse, the Gnostics were the founders of what we call occultism.

Occultism is always a minority religion. Were it to become the religion of an empire, and for long enough, it would become folk, social, public, no longer occult.

Some critics have seen Gnosticism as a sort of international secret religion which was scattered all through the Near East in the years just before the Christian Era. They have stressed its Greek, Persian, Babylonian and Egyptian elements and its debt to vulgarized Neo-Platonism and Stoicism, and have tried to dissociate its formation from Judaism and Christianity. I think this is open to question. There is no doubt but that syncretistic cults of all kinds were flourishing in the Near East of those days, but actually we deduce this from Gnosticism, not the other way around. We have very little to substantiate it. There are a few documents, like the Aramaic papyrus from the Delta, but they are synthetic mystery religions, vulgarized Neo-Platonism, magic, Hermeticism, everything but Gnosticism. As a definite entity Gnosticism appears with Simon Magus, Menander and Saturninum, and it appears in an entirely Jewish and Christian context. It is, in fact, generated by the action of Jewish heterodoxy upon the inchoate, formative years of Christianity. Gnosticism has transmitted many ancient ideas to later heretics and occultists, but it received them as transmuted and fused by Jewish eccentric speculation. Most of the elements of all the Gnostic systems

For instance, I myself have spoken of Kabbalism as Jewish and Pseudepigrapha.

For instance, I myself have spoken of Kabbalism as Jewish

Gnosticism. This is more or less true, but in the fantasies of the *Book of Baruch* (not the Book of Baruch of the Apocrypha) we have already a fully developed Jewish gnosis contemporary with the very beginnings of the Gnostic cults. The First Principle, the Ayn Soph of the Zohar, is, of all things, called Priapus in Baruch. He generates Elohim and his consort Eden, and they in turn generate twenty-four angelic forces, male and female couples, who together create the world and Adam and Eve. Elohim, believing himself the Lord, ascends to the summit of creation and is united with Priapus. Eden, left behind, becomes jealous and brings sin and death into the world. Then Elohim through his angel Baruch inspires Moses, Heracles and Jesus to lead men up to Priapus by the path Elohim has discovered; men go up not alone but in union with their spouses. The source of evil in the world is temporary, the result of Elohim's desertion of his bride and the resulting divorce and adultery. Heracles and Moses fail, but Jesus succeeds in teaching the gospel of redemption and himself ascending to God. Where are we? Is Gnosticism Christian Kabbalism? Except for the name of Jesus we are in a completely Jewish world. These are the mysteries of the Zohar and of the Hasidim. The sexual act is the foundation of all existence and its frustration or betrayal or misuse is the source of all evil. The relationship of two specific human individuals is not only reflected in the organization of the cosmos but each, macrocosm and microcosm, affects the other. This is Kabbalism, but is it Gnosticism? Certainly it lacks many of the distinguishing characteristics of Gnosticism: light metaphysics, the perils of the soul, an evil deity, the irredeemable nature of matter; most important, it does not presume to impart a mysterious, secret knowledge with which the member of the cult can coerce reality. Nevertheless, it is out of such a background of Jewish apocalyptic, eschatological and cosmological fantasy, out of the melting pot of religions that was Palestine at the beginning of the Christian era, that Gnosticism arose.

About Gnosticism as such, as it is revealed in the documents which survive to us, it is not necessary to correct George R. S. Mead. Since he gathered his anthology and commented upon it, sixty years of research and new discoveries have gone by, but his picture is still, in its essentials, correct. In recent years we have learned a great deal about one sect of heretical Judaism from the Dead Sea Scrolls, and in the Scrolls we can trace various germinal ideas that the Gnostics were to develop. It was not until 1955 that the *Berlin Papyrus,* Mead's *Akhmin Codex,* was published in its entirety in a critical edition, but Mead's summary of it is still sound. In 1945 a whole library of Gnostic books was discovered at Nag-Hammadi in Upper Egypt, thirteen volumes, forty-eight treatises, more than seven hundred pages. Unfortunately, economic and political vicissitudes have kept most of these from publication. So far only the Gnostic books which are contained also in the *Akhmin Codex* of Berlin, the *Gospel of Truth* and the *Gospel of Thomas,* have appeared. We know the others only through summaries by Jean Doresse. Our knowledge of Gnosticism has been deepened and enriched, but has not been changed in any fundamental way since Mead wrote. And nobody since has better understood what we know.

Fragments of a Faith Forgotten is a masterpiece of lucid, or as lucid as might be, exposition of an unbelievably complicated and difficult and ambiguous subject. Once in a while Mead's sympathies for the Gnostics make him a little sentimental, but he never permits his sympathies to destroy his objectivity. After sixty years he is still the most reliable guide to the corpus of Gnosticism that we have.

It might be desirable to add to what we learn from Mead a few words about the effects of Gnosticism on the evolution of orthodox Christianity. The Synoptic Gospels make of the Incarnation the climax of a *historical* drama. Paul, and to a lesser degree John, and the author of the Epistle to the Romans, constantly using Gnostic terms, reinterpreted in their own way, make of the Incarnation the climax of a *cosmic* drama. Gnostic angelology influenced Dionysius the Pseudo-Areopagite, and through him the whole Catholic and popular mythology of the organization of heaven. Traces of Gnostic cosmology are everywhere in Dante. The peculiar light physics and metaphysics which the Gnostics got from Persia influenced all Scholastic philosophy, and reached its culmination in St. Bonaventura. It reappears again in Jakob Boehme, along with a Gnostic theory of emanations (and who is to say that it does not survive, imperceptible to us, under the surface of the primary assumptions of modern physics?).

As Gnosticism died away in popularity its place was taken by Manichaeism. Out of Manichaeism came Paulicianism, Bogomilism, and out of them both a whole covey of Russian heresies and the famous Cathari of the Albigensian Crusade. In ways that are impossible to trace, much of the mythology of Gnosticism survived, underground, to emerge in the revival of occultism in the seventeenth century.

Finally, what did Gnosticism do for the practicing Gnostic of the first Christian centuries? As long as the Church was without power it was forced to suffer dissent. Some men seem to be naturally heterodox. It is a great phychological consolation to certain kinds of personalities to believe that the official Deity of the Old Testament and the Church is really the Devil. This is not as frivolous as it might sound; it is good for civilization to have Trotskyites around. We have found in our own day that an all-pervading orthodoxy dries up the sources of creativity. Since the official Church was patriarchal and authoritarian, Gnosticism gave expression to those matriarchal and libertarian tendencies which are there, suppressed or not, in all societies.

Furthermore, what the Gnostics projected onto the screen of their profound ignorance as a picture of the universe was in reality a picture of their own minds. Its mythology is a symbolic portrayal, almost a deliberate one, of the forces which operate in the structuring and evolution of the human personality. It is, more than almost any other religious system, because it is of all others, the most invented, the most "made up," an institutionalized panorama of what Jung has called the Collective Unconscious. The whole Gnostic heresy is a sort of socially therapeutic dream. (This notion, as Jung has pointed out, does not involve any mysterious undersoul shared by all men—it is a collective picture because all men respond to life in much the same way, because they all have the same physiological endowment.)

We can operate upon our minds by the manipulation of symbols if not on the cosmos; Gnosticism was fundamentally a magical theory of life, man, the universe, God, morality. The spirit-matter, good-evil, God-creature, omnipotence-freedom dilemmas posed by Christianity, Gnosticism attempted to solve with a magical doctrine of correspondences in which man and the cosmos reflected each other. As such, it was a step in the history of science as well as in the history of religion. It was a wrong step, but one which still influences thought, not just the Theosophists, but those who think that Heisenberg's Principle of Indeterminancy is an ontological discovery rather than a mathematical formula. Alchemy was Gnostic through and through, an attempt to achieve both wealth and salvation by parallel manipulation of the microcosm and the macrocosm. But the philosophy of Alfred North Whitehead is based on the same principle—an enormously sophisticated Smaragdine Tablet. We can learn nothing about the solar system from Gnosticism and little about good and evil in the world, but we can learn considerable about ourselves.

Elsewhere I have already said that G. R. S. Mead shares with A. E. Waite the distinction of being the only true scholars who came out of the great welter of occult sects and movements of the end of the last century. In our understanding of Gnosticism we owe to him not only this anthology but also his edition of the Gnostic tractate, the *Pistis Sophia.* We owe him, too, the only readable translation of the Hermetic literature in English, *Thrice-Greatest Hermes.* Of our total debt to him one must postpone the reckoning. Enough for the present that, after sixty years, he remains our most trustworthy guide to Gnosticism.

The Influence of French Poetry on American

People, especially French and American people, tend to forget that the heart of the United States was once French. Not only was all of Canada and all of the Mississippi drainage from the Alleghenies to the Rockies under the French flag, as everybody knows, but French and French-Indian mountain men had penetrated to the West Coast before any of the officially recognized explorers and discoverers, for whom they were in fact often the guides. Deep in the Northern Rockies is the town of Coeur d'Alene, Idaho. In Nevada, Wyoming, Oregon, many of the leading merchants in the small towns are descended from the French, and they often still name their children Pierre, Jeanne and Yvonne—conspicuous among the recent rash of movie-star first names, dictated by the mysteries of Hollywood "numerology" which cause the Roman Catholic clergy such distress at baptism. Not only are towns all over the Middle West named such things as Prairie du Chien and Vincennes, not only are their leading families named Sublette and Le Sueur and Deslauriers, but—something very few people realize—French life survived intact in hundreds of small isolated communities until well into the twentieth century.

When I was a boy, during the First World War, I took a canoe trip down the Kankakee River from near Chicago to the Mississippi. We passed through many villages where hardly an inhabitant spoke a word of English and where the only communication was the wandering tree-lined river and a single muddy, rutted road out to the highway. There is a

This essay was written in 1958 as an introduction to an anthology of American poets in French translation published in Paris by *Europe*.

book about it, *Tales of a Vanishing River,* and there was a popular humorous dialect poet, Drummond, who used to recite his poems in high-school assemblies and on the Chautauqua Circuit (a kind of pious variety tent show for farmers, now vanished) back in those days. "I am zee capitain of zee *Marguerite* vat zail zee Kankakee." This was not off in the wilds somewhere—it was a long day's walk from the neighborhood of Studs Lonigan.

Midwestern Naturalism of the first quarter of the century was essentially a French-inspired movement. Its sources were in Zola and Turgenev, and in a lesser, but then more popular writer, Maupassant. In Theodore Dreiser, Zona Gale, Willa Cather, Hamlin Garland, down to Vardis Fisher and H. L. Davis in our own day, the very conception of the "family epic" is Balzacian, modified by Zola, and the locale is in each case—even Idaho and Eastern Oregon—a land first trod by French moccasins. Zola and Balzac taught the novelists of the early twentieth century method, Flaubert and the Goncourts taught them style. Not only is *Main Street* a flimsy and unironic imitation of *Madame Bovary,* but Sinclair Lewis never realized how very like Carol Kennicott's Gopher Prairie were the small French towns which broke the hearts of thousands of self-dramatizing Duses of the Second Empire.

I myself was born in South Bend, Indiana, on the site of an old portage of the *voyageurs,* and in sight of a monument to the Chevalier de La Salle, whose flowing locks in pigeon-limed bronze were my first intimation that people had not always looked like twentieth-century Americans.

Henry James, of course, owed everything to Flaubert—the conception of the novel as an extraordinarily complex organization of what a later generation was to call "abstract art." This is a false conception—there is nothing "abstract" about a novel—and the French influence in Henry James and his like is literary and artificial. Actually, he writes like an etherealized Trollope or Jane Austin. Nothing in criticism, unless it is some of the dreadful blunders of Sainte-Beuve, or the silly enthusiasms of Poe, is quite so comic as Henry James' book on

French novelists, with its utter inability to understand what those novels were about. They might as well have been in Swahili or Etruscan for all Henry James understood them, for the simple reason that his life and background were totally different. The Midwest Naturalists responded to French nineteenth-century literature because it was about a life they could recognize as very much like their own, and its values and aims were theirs.

Baudelaire to Rimbaud, Balzac to Ibsen, there is one factor operating in Western European literature too seldom recognized, and for the suffering authors it was sometimes the most important. This is de-provincialization—the struggle for metropolitan community with the new, emancipated and uniform standards of a new level of capitalist culture. It is seriously open to question if the system of values represented by the lycanthrope Borel is superior to that of Charles Bovary. It is just more citified. By the end of the First World War, Ben Hecht in Chicago, who had just gone through the Munich Commune, thought of himself as completely a member of the same City State as Ernst Toller, Louis Aragon, Blaise Cendrars or George Grosz. In 1923 Sam Putnam, Lawrence Lipton and myself, led a Dadaist movement in Chicago known as "The Escalator" which was quite as lunatic as anything ever managed by Max Ernst or Francis Picabia or Tristan Tzara. Notice the names—German, Catalonian, Rumanian—the Western European City State community has not only arrived, it has grown sick of itself.

Where did Norah go when she escaped from the Doll's House? She went to town and got a job. Henry James' characters go to art galleries to resolve their mysterious tragedies. His women are already completely emancipated—as emancipated as the authoress or the heroine of the *Princesse de Clèves*. But this is artificial; like Malraux' art, it is writing which has fed on writing. In the long run archaism in the arts is of interest only to the very refined—it is a brave and very precious sort of soul that finds Abadie and Violet le Duc more exciting than Phidias, and Sacré Coeur more fun than Amiens. When the chi-chi has died away, cannibalism is an uncommon curiosity, in art as in anthropology.

It should be made clear, in a sort of parenthesis, that the New England tradition so ably reinstated by Van Wyck Brooks is neither characteristic of the rest of America nor really essentially British in inspiration. It is a reflection of the dominance of the German universities in the first half of the nineteenth century. Emerson, Longfellow and their friends were typically Teutonic in so many ways, and even Thoreau is not Rousseau in the woods near Boston but Rousseau as filtered through the German Romantic notion of natural self-sufficiency—a very different idea from Rousseau's essentially communal concept. As a matter of fact, the only Englishman all the New Englanders liked, and who liked all of them, was that most Teutonic Scot, Carlyle.

This brings us to Whitman. It is true that Whitman filled his poems with pidgin French. It is also true that his poem on the defeat of the Commune is the best poem, in any language, that still unhealed schism in the French soul inspired. It is true that he looked to what he thought of as the French spirit as the leader in a revolution of morals—especially sexual morals. But I am afraid he thought of France entirely in terms of Fourier, Proudhon, St. Simon, Blanqui—the mother of free communes and free love. America in those days was dotted with Fourierist Phalanxes, Etienne Cabot's *Icaries,* and similar French communalist experiments. The American Warren ran a Time Store in Cincinnati which not only anticipated Proudhon by several years, but which actually made "mutualism" work.

France, of course, in Whitman's day was not the France he imagined. That France existed largely in books read by cranks. It was in America that it came to life in Group Marriage, Comradely Love, Vegetarianism and Funny Money. Whitman, I am afraid, for all the doctors of comparative literature try to do with him, is an autochthone, a real original, and if his roots are anywhere except in the pre-Civil War North with its swarming cranks, reformers and humanists, they are in Isaiah.

Which brings us back to poetry and the twentieth century. How many Americans would be prepared to admit that the greatest American poet of the turn of the century did not write in English at all, but in French? How many have ever heard of him? Hardly any. I am referring of course to Stuart Merrill. Yet who is there to compete with him? Trumbull Stickney? George Santayana? I do not care for Edwin Robinson or Robert Frost myself, so I would say that Stuart Merrill remained the best American poet until the end of the First World War, with the sole exception of Carl Sandburg. Of course, if you prefer, you can have Vielé-Griffin.

One of the most hilarious examples of intercultural error known to me is G. E. Clarcier's statement: "Merrill . . . fondant aux Etats-Unis le mouvement socialiste." The American Socialist movement is at least as old as Babeuf—and the Social Democracy of his day never heard of Merrill. Alas, he was what the Bolsheviks call "a petty bourgeois dilettante," although a very admirable one, but he loved to entertain French admirers around café tables with fairy tales of his career as a revolutionist in the States.

Before we go on, two minor points should be cleared up. Frost and Robinson are presented in the contemporary academy in America as intensely American writers. They are nothing of the sort. Robinson is a rather vulgar imitator of the early nineteenth-century British narrative poet Crabbe, when he does not imitate those incredibly soft and sentimental productions, the narrative poems of Tennyson. Robert Frost discovered himself as a British Georgian poet. In his young days he lived near and was greatly influenced by the man who has slowly emerged as the best of the Georgian poets—Edward Thomas—and he belongs squarely in that tradition.

Now we come full circle. Who was the idol of the Georgian poets? Francis Jammes. Now that the dust of the explosions of the epoch from Apollinaire to Georges Schéhadé is dying away, it does not sound so incredible to recall that the great international influences in poetry in the early years of this century were Jammes and Verhaeren. They wrote about different things in different ways, but they were two faces of the same coin, two poles of the same literary universe—the world of H. G. Wells and Theodore Dreiser, of Gerhart Hauptmann and Romain Rolland, the world which was given international viability in the criticism of Georg Brandes, and which found poetic expression in the English language in figures again as diverse as John Masefield in Britain and Carl Sandburg in America. The Marxists are perfectly right, incidentally, in pointing out that this literature, realistic if not naturalistic, and always with at least an undercurrent of social criticism, is the last artistic expression of capitalist culture to believe in its own health. All artistic expression after these times starts by *calling itself* decadent. Recently, when the Nobel Prize went to modern Russia for the first time it went to a poet who, whatever his varying favor with the Bolsheviks might be, was for one thing the leading living disciple of Francis Jammes.

Literary epochs play leapfrog with one another. French poetry after Apollinaire ignored the recent past and went back to Rimbaud and Mallarmé—finding in them of course not Symbolism, but a revolutionary syntax of the mind. The most powerful current immediately before the First World War was programmatically anti-Symbolist. If this was true in France it was even more true in the English-speaking world where Rimbaud, Verlaine and Mallarmé meant the sentimentalities of Oscar Wilde and Ernest Dowson, and the pallid *Art Nouveau* descendants of the Symbolists, the disciples of Maeterlinck, seeking the blue flowers of their souls under purple and green lights on a stage masked in heavy scrim, like pea soup.

Derème, Toulet, Carco and the poets of *Le Divan* could be thought to have had a considerable influence in America. There certainly existed a large number of poets, more or less their contemporaries, who wrote much like them. The average literate poet of the early years of this century owned and read the *Mercure* anthology. But I doubt if this was a real influence. Rather it was what biologists call "convergence." Modern taste has never revived these writers, and today the average young American poet has never heard of them. There is nothing to compare to the revival of Toulet and Carco in France—let alone to the remarkable contemporary reputation of O. V. Lubicz-Milosz. Arthur Davison Ficke, even the still living and quite good Witter Bynner, are largely forgotten, and only Edna St. Vincent Millay survives, read by passionate high-school girls.

Did Edna Millay read Renée Vivien or Lucie Delarue-Mardrus? Although she was married to a French intellectual, I would be willing to wager a considerable sum that she never heard of them. Instead, she attempted what is probably the worst translation of Baudelaire—a personality utterly beyond her—in any language. Again, as part of the revolt against provincialism and for a world-wide liberated urban culture, I imagine she thought of herself as standing for French values against New England Puritanism. But, alas, even worse than Whitman, I fear she thought of French culture pretty much the same way as a G.I. out for the night in Gay Paree. It is very simple—Tristan Derème is read today in France and Arthur Davison Ficke is not read in America for the reason that Derème is an incomparably better writer.

The best poet of the *Divan* style in America is the critic Edmund Wilson, who has a genius for conveying the very taste and smell of old, unhappy, far-off seductions—a regular heterosexual Cavafis. His rigorously unsentimental contemporaries refuse to take him seriously as a poet.

Similarly, a large body of bad Parnassian or Verlainean verse might be extracted from bygone American magazines, but like minor and provincial French verse of the same kind it is better left forgotten. On the other hand, there is in America, as in France, a vast amount of good, but forgotten, provincial verse. For two generations the American hinterland has produced innumerable poets of the kind and quality of Pomairols.

While discussing this period it occurs to me to ask: Where was the Prince of Poetry in those days? The God of the Closerie des Lilas, did he have no influence in America? I think Paul Fort is too intensely French to travel. In certain formal and syntactical ways, yes, but in any real sense, no. Amy Lowell wrote a book titled *Six French Poets* (Regnier, Samain, Spire, Fort, Jammes and Verhaeren). In it she pays tribute to Fort. She borrowed several devices from him, notably what she called "polyphonic prose." Unfortunately, although she was an extremely powerful personality—a little like Gertrude Stein—she was not one of America's best writers and her influence never extended much further than the reach of her personality. "Polyphonic prose" was never taken up by anyone else.

Amy Lowell does, however, bring us to the first major climacteric in twentieth-century American poetry, the Imagist movement. This was a bona fide movement of the Parisian type, with members, leaders, its own tradition, its own magazine and annual. For this reason any number of doctoral theses have been written demonstrating its connection with French poetry. I think this is so much waste paper. The connection is almost nonexistent.

Did Imagist theories of free verse owe anything to the tireless propaganda of Vielé-Griffin? I think not. There is a simple, obvious reason why not. *Vers libre* is "*libre*" of the French alexandrine and the syllabic structure of French poetry. American free verse is free of the accentual pentameter and the quatrain. In fact, as free verse in America became more sophisticated, it often adopted syllabic structures, as in Marianne Moore, whose verse is not free at all, but counted. Of course, poetry in the English language has always been free in Vielé-Griffin's sense. The rules of classical French poetry have no counterpart in even the strictest English prosody.

Imagism is part of the world-wide movement of the time —anti-Symbolism. If we had nothing but the Imagist Manifestoes to go by, we might think it was very like the poetry of Reverdy—that it was "literary Cubism." It was not. It was much more conventional syntactically and it was actually, however anti-Symbolist its program, influenced at second and third hand by certain Symbolists, notably Gourmont and

Laforgue, who were favorites of two of the leaders, Richard Aldington and Ezra Pound. The notion of any intelligent influence can be dissipated instantly by a perusal of Ezra Pound's essay on leading French poets of those days, in which he names as the great hope of French poetry—Max Elskamp! This at the height of the careers of Apollinaire and his colleagues! Pound himself was a sort of late-born Symbolist, actually an *Art Nouveau* poet—the last of the Pre-Raphaelites. A bitter struggle broke out between Pound and Amy Lowell for leadership of the Imagists, and partly it revolved around who knew best what was the latest thing from Paris, France. Amy Lowell was a little out of date—Spire and Fort were gettiug *usé* in 1920—but at least she knew French poetry. But Pound was on the scene, he drank with Georges Fourrest and flirted with models who had slept with Willy, and he seized the loudspeaker of authority and clung to it. And today many an American Ph.D. thinks Pound is the "founder of Imagism and the first American to introduce modern French poetry to the United States." Georges Fourrest and Max Elskamp!

One American Imagist who was thoroughly conversant with the French poetry of his time was John Gould Fletcher. In fact his major work, a series of reveries called *Blue Symphony, Red Symphony, Green Symphony,* etc., can best be characterized as a deliberate attempt to turn Imagism into a kind of Neo-Symbolism. It is not easy to pinpoint any one French poet as the inspiration for these poems. None of the later Symbolists fit exactly. There are ideas derived from Merrill, Vielé-Griffin, St-Pol Roux, as well as the early work of Salmon and Apollinaire. But basically the resemblance is closest to the Belgians, and it is my opinion that the school of Maeterlinck is not Symbolist at all, but a literary parallel to *Art Nouveau* in the plastic arts. The theories behind John Gould Fletcher's practice, however, came straight from Remy de Gourmont . . . as might be guessed from the very idea of symphonies in color. The *Blue Symphony* in particular was very influential in its day and prepared the way for the long philosophical reveries which are so characteristic of modern American poetry—Eliot's *Waste Land,* Pound's *Cantos,* Williams' *Paterson,* Zukofsky's *Poem Beginning "A,"* Lowenfels' *Some Deaths,* Tyler's *Granite Butterfly* and much of the work of Conrad Aiken. Five long poems of my own are all deeply indebted to John Gould Fletcher. Had he written in French, Fletcher would have been a recognized landmark in literary history. As it was, he went out of fashion in his middle age, was little read, changed his style, much for the worse, and finally, as have thirty other important American poets in the twentieth century—committed suicide.

The British Imagist F. S. Flint, who later gave up writing altogether, did know contemporary French verse very well indeed. His translations of Cendrars, Aragon, Eluard, Soupault, Jacob and the rest, from their classical period, remain the best translations of modern French verse in English, and they were done over thirty-five years ago. They seemed to have no influence on the Imagists, however. They encouraged them in their practice of free verse, but the problems of French poetry in the early Twenties were either over the heads or outside the interests of English and American writers.

The leading Imagist, and the only one still read today, was H. D. (Hilda Doolittle, then the wife of Richard Aldington). She was more influenced by Meleager and the Choruses of Euripides than all of French literature rolled together. Her personality greatly resembles Renée Vivien; some of her poetry has the same scene and subject as *Les Chansons de Bilitis.* But there the resemblance ends. She is a far harder, brighter, cleaner poet than Louys or Vivien—a much better one, if you will.

Imagism was a revolt against rhetoric and symbolism in poetry, a return to direct statement, simple clear images, unpretentious themes, fidelity to objectively verifiable experience, strict avoidance of sentimentality. I suppose this is the actual *programme* of all good poetry anywhere. The Enemy of the Imagists was Tennyson and Victorianism generally. I doubt if anybody writing in France in 1912-25 was consciously engaged in a struggle against Lamartine or Hugo.

There was an important but usually ignored influence. All the Imagists were familiar with Judith Gautier's *Livre du Jade*—that precious minor classic of French letters. From it they got their first intimation of Chinese poetry—a poetry which fulfilled and surpassed the Imagist Manifesto beyond the abilities or dreams of even the best of the Imagists. Amy Lowell's (with Florence Ayscough) *Fir Flower Tablets,* Witter Bynner's *The Jade Mountain* (The 300 Poems of T'ang), Ezra Pound's *Cathay* are translations from the Chinese, and are in each case incomparably their respective author's best work. Judith Gautier not only was almost certainly the first inspiration for this interest, but she provided the Americans with her special interpretations of Chinese poetry—a mood of exquisitely refined weariness and excruciating sensibility which is not, as a matter of fact, characteristic of Chinese poetry until the eighteenth century. None of these authors, including Judith Gautier, read Chinese—yet they made the best translations in any language.

Even those Imagists who could not read *Le Livre du Jade* in French read beautifully translated selections in Stuart Merrill's *Pastels in Prose.* This was a translation of French prose poems from a wide variety of writers, mostly Symbolist, and was an attempt to acclimate the prose poem in America. It is the only work by which Merrill is known to most Americans. It failed in its purpose. Not only have few prose poems of any importance ever been written in English, but from Baudelaire to Léon Paul Fargue there are no good translations from the French. It seems to be a medium singularly unfitted to the spirit of American poetry. In fact, the only important prose poems in America are to be found in William Carlos Williams' *Kora in Hell,* a sort of prose *Vita Nuova* which shows a familiarity with Max Jacob and Fargue.

There is one other curious influence, one of those vagaries of history due to the "personal element" that eludes the strict mechanists. Pound knew Georges Fourrest and tried vainly to write witty epigrams like his—"Here lies George

Fourrest under the sod./ He never feared the cops, syphillis or God." Pound never managed anything as good as that. But F. S. Flint knew a considerable poet then teaching in London —Jean de Bosschère. He introduced him to the other Imagists and their own concepts of free verse probably had some influence on Bosschère rather than the other way around. He certainly had a definite influence on Flint himself, to a lesser degree on Aldington, and probably on Pound's "Villanelle of the Psychological Hour"—the only poem Pound ever wrote in anything like the idiom of modern French verse. Then Bosschère published in London and Chicago in a *face en face* edition, French and English, his *Closed Door.* This contained the famous "Ulysses Builds His Bed," the first competent example of dissociation and recombination of elements in the "cubist" manner that most poets who read no French had ever encountered. Its effect was tremendous. Out of it came the germinal idea for Joyce's great epic. Out of it came the technique of *The Waste Land.* Anthropologists are familiar with phenomena like this in what they call "acculturation" or in "diffusion" of culture elements. Something not of primary importance in one culture will be transmitted to another almost by chance, and find a niche unoccupied in the other culture pattern and proliferate all over the place. It is like the spread of the English sparrow and the starling all over America, or rabbits in Australia. Pascal Covici, then a Chicago book dealer and later one of America's largest publishers, was especially fond of Bosschère and published practically everything he wrote, while Cendrars is, to the best of my knowledge, except for his *Anthologie Negre,* represented only by a poor translation of *L'Or,* made long ago. Such are the exigencies of the diffusion of culture and of comparative literature.

Meantime, literary cubism was coming into existence in English. Gertrude Stein's *Tender Buttons* and the abstract dissociative poems of Walter Conrad Arensburg antedate the fully developed style of Reverdy by ten years or more. Both were wealthy Americans who had lived for long periods in France and who were very much alive to what was going on in the most advanced circles. Arensburg gave up writing, became the leading exponent of the Baconian heresy—the idea that Bacon wrote Shakespeare—to prove which he spent thousands. He was a close friend of Marcel Duchamp, and, aided by Duchamp, he built one of the two or three largest collections of modern painting in the world—now in the Philadelphia Museum. (It contains almost the entire *oeuvre* of Duchamp himself.)*

Until just before the Second World War, when she became a great world celebrity like the Aga Khan or Brigitte Bardot or Princess Margaret, Gertrude Stein published her books at her own expense and was read only by a tiny coterie, mostly of Americans living abroad. She is one of the most intensely American writers that ever lived. Her words, her ideas, her materials, all are the purest Americanese, and even her extraordinary syntax is simply a development of tendencies latent in typically American speech. Yet she is also an American writer whose work stands fully in the mainstream of French poetry from Apollinaire to Surrealism.

Arensburg and Stein both lived abroad, they both wrote for small coteries of sophisticates, they both contributed to the magazine *Others* edited by Alfred Kreymborg, and it is with this magazine and the group that grew up around it that modernism in American poetry really begins. William Carlos Williams, Wallace Stevens, Marianne Moore, Mina Loy, T. S. Eliot, Conrad Aiken, Marsden Hartley, Wallace Gould, Alfred Kreymborg himself, Maxwell Bodenheim, and the socialist poets Lola Ridge and James Oppenheim, the anarchist Arturo Giovannitti, dozens of others—Kreymborg produced them all suddenly on the literary stage in America, like a conjurer pulling rabbits from a hat. The effect

*Incidentally, Arensburg made, some forty years ago, the best translation of "*L'Après-Midi d'un Faune*" in English. In the notes he pointed out that the afternoon which is the putative subject of the poem takes place after the poem is over . . . "*Tard succombent au fier silence de midi:*" I know of no other American writer who ever attached any importance to this line.

on the press and the conventional poetry circles was terrific. It surpassed by far the noise made by the Beat Generation or the alcoholics of the Hemingway-Fitzgerald Lost Generation. American literature was never the same again, and of course today many of these names are modern classics, poets loaded with honors and taught in the grammar schools and endlessly and exhaustively explicated in hundreds upon hundreds of Ph.D. theses. Their influences are, without exception, largely French.

French they may have been. Up to date, except with a few exceptions, they were not. It takes as long almost for new poetic idioms to cross a language barrier as it does for the use of the blowpipe to travel from one tribe to another in the Amazon. The time lag was considerable. Pound had just discovered Laforgue and was translating his prose extravaganzas and singing his praises to all comers. Laforgue is the principal influence on most of these people. All the early work of T. S. Eliot is extremely Laforguean. He now attributes that special spleen and irony to Corbière, but it is extremely doubtful if he had ever heard of Corbière prior to 1920. The real leader of the group to which Eliot and Pound belonged in London was the novelist, polemicist, and very great painter, Wyndham Lewis, and Lewis's narrative style is Laforgue reduced to a formula: "Describe human beings as though they were machines, landscapes as though they were chemical formulas, inanimate objects as though they were alive." This is pretty much the formula of the Laforguean poetry of the English poetess Edith Sitwell too, and she had a considerable influence on American poets. Marianne Moore is a poet very like Edith Sitwell, but without her depth. She not only took over the Laforguean aesthetic, but she wrote in syllabic verse which structurally often resembles specific poems of Laforgue's. Aiken's poetry was much like Laforgue's in its choice of inadequate, spleen-ridden and troubled narrators—the first person of the poem almost always sounds like Eliot's *Prufrock* or a slightly healthier Laforgue himself. But Aiken's long, mellifluous, easy line with its obvious sonorities and sentimental rhythms sounds much more like Valéry Larbaud. Dozens of Aiken's poems are pure Barnabooth.

It is very important to understand that modernist American poetry—and English, as well—of the generation just before and after the First World War, the generation of Supervielle and Cendrars, of Reverdy and Breton—was hopelessly stuck on Laforgue. This peculiar blockage is extremely difficult to understand and merits a long essay—or an American Ph.D. thesis—in itself. Puzzling about this, I comfort myself with the memory that shortly after the Second World War, Roger Caillois informed me that the best American novelist was Horace McCoy.

Actually the Socialist-Populist writers were more aware of contemporary French literature. They read the French socialist and anarchist press and wrote in a sort of international Whitmanesque revolutionary idiom like many of their now forgotten compeers in the French journals of the "movement." I suppose their favorite foreign poets were Verhaeren and the German, Richard Dehmel. But they were aware of what was going on, as the aesthetes of this period were not. They had a living contact with intellectuals in Paris, Amsterdam, Berlin, Munich, Geneva. The Laforgueans had derived their knowledge of the latest thing from courses in French literature at Harvard and I doubt if either Pound or Eliot has ever heard of Herman Gorter to this day. When Gorter and his friends seized power in postwar Rotterdam, weeping men and women recited hastily made translations of his poems from soapboxes to ragged crowds in the slums of New York and Chicago. Mayakofski's poems were translated into American before they were into French. Sandburg wrote one of the first poems to Brancusi in any language, and it is still one of the best.

The large Yiddish-language press, then by far the most civilized journals in America, published translations of poetry from all over the world, and the American Yiddish poet Yehoash was translating Japanese *haiku* and introducing ideas derived from Apollinaire into Yiddish verse before anybody ever dreamed of doing such things in English. A section of New York, utterly unknown to the "real Americans," was an international capital with an international language into which literature from all over Europe was translated, dozens of magazines and newspapers of higher quality than anything in English, and the best theater in the Western hemisphere. It must not be forgotten that almost all Jewish poets of those days still read Yiddish, although they wrote in English, and were thus exposed to international influences unknown to their Gentile colleagues. "Cosmopolitanism" somebody in Russia called it a few years back.

If the proletariat had an international culture, so did the rich. Walter Conrad Arensburg moved from specific imitations of Mallarmé, "*Reflets dans l'Eau*": "The swan existing/ Is like a song/ With an accompaniment/ imaginary . . ." through imitations of Toulet: "Sleepy head/ Lay aside your sandals/ That have fled/ Down a night of candles/ By the bed . . ." to the pure cubism of "A drink into home use indicates early Italian, otherwise the elements of how keep outside. Use what listens on Sundays and catchy elms will oxidize pillows. Blunders are belted in cousins . . ." to "abstract" poems with titles like "Axiom" and "Ohm," which can be compared only with Picabia, but which, quite unlike Picabia or Tzara, were written in dead earnest.

Mina Loy somewhat resembled the early Soupault, although when she wrote her best verse it is unlikely that she had ever heard of him. Later she married the boxer Arthur Craven, a famous figure of the great days of Dada. Gertrude Stein, of course, was plugging away, writing poetry and prose which might well have puzzled Barzun (the father, not the son), but she did not contribute much to literary magazines until ten years later.

Marsden Hartley was one of America's greatest painters. Working in Germany and Paris before the First World War, he was one of the first abstract expressionists and in those days he wrote some rather odd poetry, obviously French in inspiration. When he returned to the States he abandoned all this and painted for the rest of his life in a powerful, rocky, Fauve-like style the landscapes and seascapes and people of his native Maine. His poetry underwent a similar change. It is simple, direct, painfully honest, unabashedly personal. Little appreciated in the long period of academic English-inspired metaphysical verse of the self-styled Reactionary Generation, he is coming back into favor, at least among young poets.

Now we come to the last two poets of this group, whom I have held back because they are by far the best. (A comparative study like this must pass by, at least to an extent, questions of value and concentrate on historical connections. Arensburg, Oppenheim, Bodenheim, several others, are not very good writers. I forgot poor old Bodenheim, by the way. He was a sort of hobo Laforgue, a poor and rather absurd poet who spent his life cadging drinks in the Bohemian quarters of New York and Chicago and living off the fringes of "the movement"—first the anarcho-syndicalist IWW, later the Communists. Like all such pathetic people, he had a rather frightening dissolute integrity of his own. He was, I suppose, the most Laforguean of all, but Laforgue came to him through the worst of all channels, the English Decadents, Wilde, Dowson, Symons—and Ben Hecht!)

To resume the thread—Wallace Stevens and William Carlos Williams are poets of world importance, completely devoid of the provincial, derivative character that marks most of these people. They have, *vis à vis* French poetry, none of that flavor of the backwoodsman seeing Paris for the first time that we associate with even such important figures as Rubén Darío.

Wallace Stevens might be said to have fulfilled and completed Laforgue, more than anyone in French poetry, or any other language for that matter. (Rimbaud does not fulfill Laforgue—no two life attitudes could be less alike.) Stevens shares Laforgue's irony and his sensual wisdom, but he has something Laforgue lacks as a poet and lacked as a man—a very simple thing: good health. The bitterness of Laforgue's irony becomes a tonic rather than a corrosive bitterness in Stevens and produces a skepticism and animal faith, a completely *laique* affirmation beyond the capacity of a dying and unhappily exiled man. The pure Voltairean malice in the Laforgue tradition is revealed in all its innocence and grandeur.

Today it is William Carlos Williams who emerges as the greatest of this group—the classic American modernists—and as America's greatest living poet. He was partly educated in France. He has lived there for extended periods. He knows personally most of the heroic generation of post-World War I poets and has translated a novel of Soupault's. He was a friend of Valéry Larbaud and the American editor of *Commerce.* Intensely personal, local, antiliterary, absolutely devoted to the achievement of a truly American vision, he is none the less the one American poet who ranks with the best of his French contemporaries, who speaks to them as an equal in a language they can understand. I would say too that the ordinary French reader today could get more out of him than from any other American poet except Whitman. It is the true autochthones who circulate most freely in all lands. Williams could be said to belong in the Cubist tradition—Imagism, Objectivism, the dissociation and rearrangement of the elements of concrete reality, rather than rhetoric or free association. But where Reverdy, Apollinaire, Salmon, Cendrars, Cocteau and Jacob are all urban, even megalopolitan, poets of that Paris which is the international market of objects of *vertu*, vice, and art, Williams has confined himself in single strictness to the life before his eyes—the life or a physician in a small town twenty miles from New York. In so doing, his localism has become international and timeless. His long quest for a completely defenseless simplicity of personal speech produces an idiom identical with that which is the end product of centuries of polish, refinement, tradition and revolution.

The next generation, the young men and women who began to write during and just after the First World War, had more connections with France and were more alive to what was actually going on there. The reason was obvious—they were there. Many of them went abroad as soldiers and stayed on, traveling about Europe and living as cheaply as possible off the inflated currencies with their hard dollars. This is the famous Lost Generation. They weren't very lost. They had a ball in Europe. They all started publishing their books and selling their paintings in their early twenties. Most of them came back to the States to enormously successful careers or very highly paid jobs. Ernest Hemingway, on safari hunting rhinoceros, has never looked very "lost" to me.

Although the First World War broke the isolation of America and pulled it into the general orbit of Western civilization, the experiences of Europe in the war actually had little meaning for these young Americans. Malcolm Cowley, one of their leaders, and a poet who became a successful editor and publisher, wrote a book about those years, *Exile's Return.* It is a good book, and a fine study of the mind of his generation of Americans abroad, but it shows less than no understanding of what had happened to the European spirit. A good deal of it is taken up with the high days of Dada. To Cowley, and to most of his well-off friends, Dada was just a continuation of the American-college-boy pranks they had known at Princeton and Harvard. They might be able to write about it, but they could never understand in their hearts that the war and the counterrevolutions that followed it had destroyed the foundations of the Humanist tradition, that the very word *civilization* had come to stink of blood. Perhaps it was a Nazi who first said, "When I hear the word *culture*, I reach for my revolver." But it was Max Ernst who exhibited a billet of wood with an ax chained to it and the card, "If you don't like this piece of sculpture, you dirty bourgeois, make one for yourself." And who was it who wanted to show, in the same Rhineland Dada exhibition, a loaded pistol mounted in a frame and pointed at the spectator, with a little string on the trigger and the caption: *Please pull.* The state of mind behind this state of affairs was totally incomprehensible to the average American poet drinking Pernods which cost him two and a half cents American money on the *terrasse* of the Dome and congratulating himself on what a rebel he was—against American Prohibition. No happy man has so much *einfuhling* that he can truly comprehend a broken heart.

Still—they did their best. They bought drinks for the leading personages of the period if they could persuade them to visit their tables. They financed literary reviews. They helped stage demonstrations and plays in which people continuously shot off pistols and cranked klaxons. (Ah, the klaxons! The true Mona Lisas of the Twenties! Where would we have been without them?) The exiles were always good for a loan which seemed very sizable on the receiving end, translated into francs, but which was cheap at half the price. They bought a taste of the disorderly old age of a culture. In other words, they were like schoolboys who discovered they could make love to a decrepit and dissolute but unbelievably depraved duchess for less than the price of ten minutes in a short-order whorehouse back home.

Duchesses in dissolution, alas, are over the heads of schoolboys, and so, like Malcolm Cowley, the exiles returned—to good jobs. What had they accomplished, the young men of the Twenties, the expatriates? A good deal, some of it unwittingly. They broke for a moment the continuity of American culture. They introduced to America the alienated and outraged European avant-garde, and although few of them understood what they were doing, there were others, in America and expatriated, who did. They started a tradition of publishing the most vital American writing, as well as a lot of translation from modern French writing, in Paris—a tradition which persists, more or less on dying momentum, to this day. They ran a number of reviews, expensively gotten up by European standards, which may have had little public support but which were studied avidly by every alert writer and painter back home. Similar magazines, necessarily cheaper and less worldly, proliferated all over America.

The Little Review, edited by Margaret Anderson and Jane Heap, started in Chicago and moved to Paris, where it finally died in Gurdgieff's dude ranch in Fontainebleau. *Broom* was founded and edited by Alfred Kreymborg and Harold Loeb in Rome, Paris and Berlin, and eventually was taken over by Malcolm Cowley and Matthew Josephson and moved to America—where it promptly died. *Contact* was edited by William Carlos Williams and Robert MacAlmon and included a book-publishing venture. The *Transatlantic Review* was edited by the dynamic and endlessly fertile British novelist Ford Madox Ford, but published mostly American and French writers. There were many others. At the end there were still plenty, and they and their editors were more closely integrated with European life and more comprehending. Eugene Jolas' *transition* and Sam Putnam's *New Review* were even read by Frenchmen!

Most of these magazines also published good reproductions, and so laid the foundations, not only of modern American abstract art—but of the fabulously successful American art market. Institutions like the Museum of Modern Art, the Arensburg Collection, and the Barnes Collection in Philadelphia, the beautifully organized collection of modern French painting in the Chicago Art Institute, as well as the millionaire art dealers of New York—this would all have been a much poorer thing had it not been for these apostles of acculturation who often had to hide from their printers till money showed up at American Express from Grandma in Sheboygan, Michigan.

Then came the Stavisky riots, the manifesto for the United Front (signed by dozens of American writers and artists in France), the Spanish War, Munich—the thunderous footsteps of the Golem marching toward the door—and everybody left for America . . . except Henry Miller, who didn't have the fare and didn't believe in politics anyway.

Let us give what the American *commerçants* call a brief rundown on the leading poets of that period.

Malcolm Cowley started out as a populist poet, but from

Harvard, not the Middle West. For five years in Europe his work was full of echoes of Apollinaire, Rimbaud, Cendrars, Soupault—(Soupault and Duchamp seem to have been very congenial minds to the Americans)—even Tristan Tzara and Roger Vitrac. Then he went back to the States, wrote the best poem on the death of Sacco and Vanzetti, gave up poetry and became an editor of a political weekly, *The New Republic.*

Hart Crane worshiped Rimbaud, or at least the Rimbaudian legend. He never learned to speak more than a few words of French, but his "Voyages" are the best recreation of Rimbaud that exists in English and his whole life was a sort of acting out of "Bateau Ivre." Formally, however, as a prosodist, he was quite conventional and influenced mostly by early Elizabethan blank verse—probably because he also thought of himself as an avatar of Marlowe. He spent quite a bit of time in France in the last years of his life, but he had more trouble with the police than he did contact with his French colleagues.

Harry Crosby and his wife Caresse ran a very ambitious publishing house, the Black Sun Press. They wrote together a book of beautiful erotic poems, *Sleeping Together,* which bears comparison with the Golls' *Dix Milles Aubes.* Then they returned to America and Crosby shot himself at a drunken party. His work somewhat resembled Artaud's, if Artaud had been mad for the sun instead of the way he was.

Archibald MacLeish lived in Paris in those days and his best poem is "Portrait of a Man," in memoriam to Harry Crosby. It is a very deliberate imitation of Apollinaire's "Zone." Larbaud, St.-John Perse, Apollinaire, Cendrars—especially their use of tourism as a symbolic system—MacLeish was deeply influenced by them and he echoed and imitated them quite consciously. In his young days he was almost a new Stuart Merrill, whom he greatly resembled in personality.

Matthew Josephson wrote a sort of Dadaist poetry, went back to America, became first a successful advertising man and then an even more successful biographer and forgot about poetry, Dadaist or otherwise.

Jolas spent several years trying to shift the basis of Surrealism from Freud and Marx to Jung and St. John of the Cross, publishing in *transition* Joyce's *Finnegans Wake* and imitating it in polylingual poems full of neologisms which nobody read. He and his friends launched "The Revolution of the Word," complete with manifesto (which he persuaded all sorts of French personages to sign), but nothing came of it and he went back to America. As an apologist for his own brand of Surrealism, he was, if anything, a more cogent and learned polemicist than Breton himself, and to his door can be laid the beginning of the present popularity of Jungianism, with its chaos of undigested symbology and its antinomian mysticism. Out of him come the pseudo mahatmas of *On the Road*—but, alas, all devoid of his curious and amusing learning.

Yvor Winters suffered from tuberculosis and was forced to go from Chicago, not to Paris with all his colleagues, but to the New Mexican mining town of Raton, high in the desert mountains. He actually knew more about French literature than any other practicing American poet of his generation and in his early work did a better job of intelligent assimilation of the whole tradition from Baudelaire to Aragon and Breton than anybody else. He cannot be said to have shown specific French influence. Like William Carlos Williams, his work was his own completely but it was part of the world of modern European literature. Only he of all poet-critics of the time in America had any comprehension of the profound spiritual crisis which this evolution embodied. Suddenly he identified himself with the antimodernism of Valéry or Maritain and became the strictest of contemporary Parnassiens. This is a phenomenon typically French again, so much so in fact that his poetic style and critical opinions are still very little understood in America. He once wrote a long attack on H.D. which was at the same time his own farewell to Imagism—hers and his own dissociative, Reverdy-like brand of it. Now this essay has an odd note about it of never quite comprehending H.D. and of somehow missing the whole point of her work. The reason is simple. In its original form it was not about H.D. It is very close to being a paraphrase of Charles Maurras' famous attack on Renée Vivien, "*Le Romantisme Féminin: Allégorie du Sentiment Désordonné.*"

In the meantime, there was growing up in Vanderbilt University, one of the few institutions of learning in the American South, a little coterie of political reactionaries, under the leadership of their English professor, John Crowe Ransom. Their roots were in Europe, too, though not in the antimodernism of Maritain and Valéry, but in the antimodernism of Léon Daudet, Maurras, and in the theories of Pareto, Houston Stewart Chamberlain and Major Douglas—the "social credit," "classless syndicalism" and "new agrarianism" which came to so disastrous an end in a gas station in Milan and a fiery hole in Berlin. Their idol was T. S. Eliot, "Classicist, Anglo-catholic, Royalist." They tolerated Fernandez, but thought he was too broad in his tastes. They approved of Ezra Pound but wished he paid more attention to the rules of verse. They believed Nigras should be kept in their place. Their real mentor, who imported these ideas for them—they lacked the languages—was a political professor named Donald Davidson, whose writings somewhat resemble those of a literate Senator Eastland and who is one of the leading think tanks of the modern South.

They numbered one genuine poet in their ranks, a then young girl named Laura Riding. The association was fortuitous. She did not share their ideology. Like Williams, Stein, Winters, she was a genuinely autochthonous American modernist. Her poetry bore a slight resemblance to Reverdy's but I am sure this resemblance too was accidental—convergence again. She left the Ransom group (who called themselves "The Fugitives"—fugitives from modernism, liberalism, humanitarianism, socialism, interracialism, and all the other cuss-words of the reactionaries), migrated first to London, where she was one of the early muses of W. H. Auden, and then to Paris and Majorca, where she ran a press and a magazine for several years with Robert Graves. She is without doubt America's most unappreciated good poet. Unfortunately her best poetry is small in bulk and came early. Later she broke down into a dull wordy chaos and then stopped writing altogether. She is one of the many casualties of the permanent crisis of the modern mind, like René Crevel, Rigaut, Artaud, Mayakofski, Hart Crane, Harry Crosby, Dylan Thomas, and the rest—but for a while she was one of the very finest poets of her day in any language.

Walter Lowenfels lived in Paris for many years and was one of the better American contributors to *transition.* He published a series of books—printed by Darantière, who printed so many of these people—called "Some Deaths," the deaths being those of D. H. Lawrence, Apollinaire, Hart Crane, Rimbaud and a couple of others whom I have forgotten. Structurally they bear considerable resemblance to Apollinaire. Lowenfels, a fairly wealthy man, returned to America after the Stavisky riots (he was one of the first signers of the famous manifesto), gave up poetry and became a correspondent for *The Daily Worker* and editor of its Pennsylvania edition. Only in recent years, arrested under the Smith Act outlawing the Communist Party, was he moved to return to poetry. In his young days he was certainly one of America's best poets, and one of those most in the current of contemporary French life. He is, incidentally, the hero of the very amusing episode "Jabberwhorl Cronstadt," in Henry Miller's *Black Spring*—which shows how much comprehension Henry has of the refinements of modernist verse. Miller, of course, is another writer so American he is completely assimilable to French culture and stands at ease in the small company of Restif, Céline, and Sar Péladan.

e. e. cummings lived in France after the First World War, but for him Paris seems to have been a place of beautiful streetwalkers and abundant liquor. He is a conventional and sentimental poet whose typographical and syntactic oddities are the pranks of an incurable Harvard Boy. They certainly have nothing to do with the sickness of the European heart which began in 1848 and became fatal in Père Lachaise in 1871. Everybody pretends not to notice that among his comical cut-ups are some of the most scurrilous bits of anti-Semitic doggerel in any language, including German. Anti-Semitism is unknown in America except among lunatics. So in the sense that he is a sane and educated man and an antidreyfusard, he may be said to show French influence. It is a little ominous that he is just beginning to be appreciated in France.

John Brooks Wheelwright was a different kind of Bostonian, a perfect descendant of the revolutionary humanists and eccentrics of the 1840's. Descended on both sides from ancient Mayflower families, and moderately wealthy, he lived for a while abroad and read a great deal of modern French poetry. But he had his own ideas about what kind of modernism he wanted, and he again was a true *indigène*, and so, a good European. Too hot for the orthodox, he became an impassioned Trotskyite, Anglocatholic and several other kinds of violent and peculiar exceptionalist. Walking home one night, he was killed by a drunken driver near the bridge across the Charles River in Boston which his father had built. Dead in his prime like so many American poets, he was not, like most of them, already burnt out. No one has ever taken the place of this dynamic, inexhaustible and lovable mind and completely original talent. Had he written in French, he would have died loaded with honors. As it is, few people have ever heard of him.

Already revolutionary politics has begun to intrude into this narrative. With the onset of the permanent world economic crisis, the rise of fascism and the development of war economies, the Americans went home from Paris, and other international movements than those founded by Picasso and Apollinaire captured the allegiance of American poets. Aragon's *Front Rouge* was recited to jazz trumpets and drums in John Reed clubs (the American Union of Revolutionary Writers) in San Francisco and Chicago—the "trip to Kharkov" caused all sorts of convulsions in advanced literary circles. Mimeographed magazines of Proletcult poetry flourished in provincial towns. The theses of Leopold Auerbach were passionately debated in unheated furnished rooms and rattling boxcars. This movement produced some excellent prose—the early work of Mike Gold, Dos Passos (Dos Passos was strongly influenced by the program, but not the practice, of Jules Romains' "Unanisme." In fact, "Unanisme," which had produced a poetry either monstrous or dull, or both, found in Dos Passos' *USA* its major realization), Farrell, Richard Wright and others, even Steinbeck in a sense—but the bitter fact is that it produced almost no poetry of any consequence whatsoever. The American Roman Catholic Church is the most ultramontane in the world. Similarly the American Communist Party has always been more Russian than the Russians, more Stalinist than Stalin. The witch-hunting—or "petty-bourgeois hunting"—of the bureaucracy, the tedious "let's play we all work at the Pulitov Iron Works" pseudo proletarianism of the Bohemians of Greenwich Village drove most bona fide writers away or out of proletarian literature and into actual trade-union work, and robbed those who stayed of the self-respect essential to poetry. With the exception of Mike Gold, who has not done any important writing in twenty-five years, all the novelists and short-story writers ended up bitter enemies of Bolshevism in all forms . . . many of them professional antibolsheviks, a very lucrative occupation in the States.

There was a moment when French influence was very important in American writing. From Kharkov to *Les Cloches de Basle,* all eyes were on Aragon. Would he be the leader of an assertion of the valid rights of literature against the anti-intellectualism of the bureaucracy? Nothing happened, and one by one the writers dropped away. The leading literary quarterly in America, bitterly reactionary, paranoid in its antibolshevism, was once an organ of the International Union of Revolutionary Writers and carried, along with myself, Louis Aragon on its masthead. No one of my generation is ever likely to forget Aragon's speech attacking Léger and praising as the pure representative of the working class—Gromaire!

When the split came, Breton did not carry any of the older American modernists with him. A whole new crop of American poets sprang up—specifically disciples of Breton's brand of Surrealism. The most important of these poets are Charles Henri Ford, Parker Tyler and Philip Lamantia, all still writing today. Together they edited one of the most dynamic magazines of "Surréalisme Outremer"—called *View*—which was livelier if less learned than *transition*. All three are certainly among the finest non-French Surrealists. Parker Tyler's *Granite Butterfly* is an excellent philosophic revery of the type written by Lowenfels, Zukofsky, myself, and others—a form which begins in France with *Un Coup de dés*. This poem of Mallarmé's, along with *Zone* and *Le Cimitière marin*, —even Carco's *L'Ombre*—have been of immense influence on American poets of my generation.

In the meantime, as a sort of effort to stave off disorganization, the poet Louis Zukofsky organized a "movement"—with manifesto—called Objectivism. It owed a good deal to Apollinaire and the Cubists and to the principles, but not the practice of the German *Neue Sachlichkeit*. Just at this moment people in France—notably Léger—were talking about "the return to the object." Zukofsky himself was deeply read in French poetry and had translated André Salmon, in fact, all of *Prikaz*. His own poetry somewhat resembled the Salmon of the days of *Prikaz* but owed even more to William Carlos Williams and Ezra Pound's *Cantos*. He has a peculiarly knotty, Kabbalistic sort of mind and his long philosophical-personal "epics," actually reveries, resemble nothing so much as the permanent crisis of the modern heart filtered through the baffling convolutions of the Zohar. Incidentally, he was a friend and translator of the great Yiddish modernist, Yehoash. Zukofsky included me, along with Williams, Pound, Horace Gregory, Lowenfels, Wheelwright, in fact, anybody who would say yes and didn't write sonnets, in his Objectivists—but after putting out a very stimulating anthology (printed by Darantière) the movement died for lack of interest on the part of its members. Zukofsky did discover the one American poet who is, without ever having heard of him, an almost exact replica of Reverdy—Carl Rakosi, who published one small book and then fell silent.

The Rakosi book was published by James Laughlin at New Directions. For over twenty years Laughlin alone imported French writers into America by the bucketful. He took up where Jolas stopped and has lasted four times as long. He has published everybody from Julien Gracq to Eluard, from Queneau back to Louise Labé. At one time he was very awake to what was going on in France. People were just beginning to talk about Michaux in St. Germain when Laughlin appeared with a bilingual *Selected Works of Michaux.* In 1940 the baby Surrealists in the American cornbelt cut their eye teeth on the *New Directions Annual* Surrealist number. In recent years he has been more interested in publishing the work of Asian writers in English and has turned away from the French writers of post-World War II. He is himself an excellent poet, a kind of *intimiste,* who owes much to the example of French poets as diverse as Toulet, Eluard, and Queneau.

The Second World War produced nothing in American poetry. Like most everybody else in the world, Americans seemed to be ashamed of themselves—fighting a war in the middle of the twentieth century; but unlike the more seasoned British, they were unable to write out this attitude in a mature way. Of course, there was nothing in America like the French press of the Resistance, which was by definition stimulating. However, anything that crossed the ocean by chance from North Africa was eagerly read and by the end of the war American poets who read French were well aware of the wartime work of poets like Char and Frénaud. *Les Editions de Minuit* and *Poésie* were easier to buy in America than in Paris.

Has the French poetry that has come after the Second World War had much influence? I think not. Modern American poetry now has a long tradition behind it and it is deeply involved in developments of its own. Poets like Allen Ginsberg, Robert Creeley, Denise Levertov, Lawrence Ferlinghetti, all of whom have lived for long periods in France, owe much to the classic period of French modernism, but they are now following roads which diverge widely from the poets represented in anthologies like Rousselot's and Bealu's. Ferlinghetti has translated Prévert and fancies that he himself writes like Prévert. Actually, if he resembles anybody, it is much more Queneau.

Kenneth Patchen is one of the Old Masters of the universe of discourse which is that of American poetry after the Second World War. Once again—see how often we come to these American writers, truly indigenous, who are so easily comprehensible to the French! The simplest definition of Patchen's style is that he writes as Aragon might have written if Lunacharski had been chairman of the Kharkov Conference. Aragon at the great turn said, "We do not need to concoct synthetic nightmares, the nightmares of the daily press can always surpass us in horror." Well, Patchen really captures that horror, in the way no social-realist ever could. He writes of a world in which every man has become Antonin Artaud, where René Crevel and Mayakofski shoot each other at every street corner, and where every body of water six feet deep contains its own corpse of Hart Crane and every barroom floor a bloated Dylan Thomas lost in a coma from which there can be no return.

Ever since the wave of world-wide reaction which is a reflection of the by now admittedly incurable economic crisis and the economy of permanent war, American poetry has been in the hands of a coalition of the pillowcase-headdress school which originated at Vanderbilt so long ago, and the ex-Stalinist paranoiacs of a small circle of cocktail drinkers in New York. These people control the scholarships and fellowships that bring American intellectuals to Europe and French intellectuals to teach in Iowa State University's School of Creative writing. They also publish lavish quarterlies subsidized by American millionaires. They also control that milk-soaked biscuit *Encounter*, which is not really what it seems—edited by John Foster Dulles—but is a publication of the international *beni oui-oui.* So they have given the impression abroad that this is what American poetry is today, a sort of hayseed imitation of Valéry at his most pompous, a bumpkin version of Patrice de la Tour du Pin at his most vapid. The truth is that, like the Proletcult Boys before them (many of them were Proletcult Boys!), they are not poets at all, but politicians, professors and manipulators of prizes, fellowships and scholarships. They are the present American Academy, even more ridiculous than the one which the Bull on the Roof recently entered as the last Dadaist joke of his extreme old age. No one of importance in American poetry takes them seriously, except their poor students, to whom, if they show any originality, they can always give a failing grade in "Creative Poetry 2679132 A."

The great trouble with transatlantic communication is that it is like short-wave radio—it gets distorted by the overpowering signals of the official stations. French people seldom really realize, having never seen the country, that America is a commercial civilization with a mass culture and an official literature which in no way reflects the actual life of the country. But its noncommercial culture is by no means underground; it is just not exported by the American State Department or Hollywood or the big slick magazines and the academic quarterlies. Except by accident, important American intellectuals never show up in Europe on Fulbright Fellowships. The entire official and academic, but not the privately sponsored, fellowship system is a kind of U.S. State Department Gold Curtain, through which only mice can pass.

Finally, although some of the people in the collection presented by *Europe* are important poets and good friends of mine, they show no perceptible French influence. Muriel Rukeyser, Langston Hughes, John Ciardi, Richard Eberhart, all speak French, are well-read in the language and have lived in France; perhaps for this very reason they have been little touched by French poetry. I myself have translated a great deal of French poetry and probably read more of it than I do American poetry, but since my early twenties I do not think I have been much influenced by it. French poetry influenced American in the days when it was changing rapidly, and when it, more than the poetry of any other language, was the first to catch the funeral music of the end of our civilization. Its influence was so powerful because it was so different from American.

Today America has not just been dragged into the orbit of Western Civilization. It, more than any other country except Japan, reflects the inner moral collapse of that civilization. Between Cartier and Champlain thousands of Indians in Northwestern Canada died from the diseases imported by a handful of men in a couple of small boats. The gulf that opened before Pascal, the black bile of Baudelaire, the *sacrificium intellectis* of Rimbaud, the cacodaemon in the bowels of Artaud, these are commonplaces in America today, as common as measles among the Iroquois. And just as common on both sides of the Atlantic are those highly exportable commodities, the castrated pimps of circumstance in the night of man. The world ill has long since smitten Bolivia and Afghanistan. French poetry and American poetry in the age of Strontium 90 are much alike.

Notes on Historians

FRANCIS PARKMAN

Only a few nineteenth-century American novelists outrank several historians of the same period as literary artists, as minds of power, depth and scope. Unfortunately, the nineteenth century was more leisurely than this one, and so their works are long, and length alone has made them inaccessible to many modern readers who, book by book, at odd intervals have managed to get through the complete works of Hawthorne, Mark Twain and Henry James. Parkman's great history fills fourteen volumes in the most common edition. I do not believe in pocket-book abridgments and selected passages, but nowadays only a limited number of adults are likely to take the time to read it all.

Samuel Eliot Morison, as one might guess from his name alone, is a product of the same milieu as Parkman. He shares many of his prejudices, and is as unaware of them. If there has to be a *Parkman Reader*, he is certainly as good a man as any to put it together. It is necessary, however, to take his preface with a grain of salt. He speaks of Parkman as a literary stylist worthy of respect. As a matter of fact, only when he was caught up in the circumstantial rush of his narrative did Parkman write well. His set pieces on the beauties of the forest primeval, the savagery of an Indian war dance or the vices of the little provincial court at Montreal are rather comic reading today. Although he set out to deflate the legend of the noble savage, whole pages might well have come from Chateaubriand's *Atala*—illustrated by Gustave Doré.

The Parkman Reader. Edited by Samuel Eliot Morison. Little Brown, Boston, 1955.

John Fiske, who introduced the last collected edition, speaks of Parkman's people as being far more real than Prescott's. Morison shares this view. Prescott's Mexico and Montezuma resemble *The Arabian Nights,* it is true. But this is realism. They really were like that. Parkman's heroes are moved by the highly stereotyped motives of a sort of Puritan Ivanhoe.

Again, Morison speaks of Parkman as a gentleman and an aristocrat. He may have been a gentleman, but he was certainly not an aristocrat. He was a bourgeois valetudinarian. Whether it be Procopius, H. G. Wells or Motley, the historian usually injects much of himself between the lines of his history. But Parkman comes close to having written a fourteen-volume invisible autobiography. He came from a rich, upper-middle-class family of Boston Brahmins. He seems to have been thoroughly indoctrinated in the liberal but nonetheless "puritan" Puritanism of Unitarianism and advanced Congregationalism. He was expected to make his way in the world, but early in youth he started going off to the woods. In college days he took several long trips in the New England and New York backwoods; then a walking trip across Sicily and much of Italy as the beginning of a year on the Grand Tour; then a trip far out on the Oregon Trail, where he traveled as a guest with the Sioux.

In later life Parkman was to attribute his variously described incapacitating illness to incidents on all three of these excursions. One way or another he always blamed his poor health on the strenuous life of his youth. What seems to have happened is that, first casually in Sicily and Naples, and then in all its glory at the headwaters of the Missouri, he met his Id, and it was too much for him. The memory of the abandoned, dark-eyed *signorine* by the Porta Capuana and the naked Sioux belles disporting themselves in the waters of the Missouri prostrated him for the rest of his life. For forty years he devoted himself to justifying the triumph of anal over oral sexuality—or, in the words of another great Puritan, the ways of God to man.

The thesis of *France and England in North America* is that drinking, running around with women, rising late and loafing in the woods must go down to disaster before the righteous onslaught of the forty-eight-hour day, the well-kept savings account, patriarchal domesticity, well-shined shoes and cold baths. During the nineteenth century this was probably true, but the nineteenth century is a very brief period in the long history of man. It is doubtful if this moral struggle had much to do with the defeat of France in the New World. French America was lost in Europe.

Parkman was not horrified and fascinated only by Frenchmen. He speaks of the quasi-aristocratic Dutch on the upper Hudson as boors (aristocrats, of course, are always pretty boorish in the eyes of merchants). That thoroughly feudal personality of his period, Sir William Johnson, the "Father of the Iroquois," he looks on as nothing but a rascal. He never mentions the Quakers without losing his temper over their obstinacy and pacifism. The type that wins is the go-getter. Now that New England is a dying land gradually filling up with Poles and French Canadians, we forget that once almost everyone who lived there was a go-getter.

Recently we have seen in American history "the rehabilitation of the Business Community." The Business Community is the avowed hero of Parkman's history. In his pages appear the archetypes of the nineteenth-century robber barons and the twentieth-century hypomanics who grace the covers of the newsweeklies and who, alas, to judge by the newsweeklies, rule America.

But Parkman didn't break down and become a lifelong neurotic because he was a good businessman. He was a man in profound conflict with himself. As with Milton, his heroes are unconvincing and his villains are heroic. Except at the top, where no sane men want to be, it is doubtful if the Puritan tradition has really been as determinative in American culture as the scholars of Yale and Harvard would like us to believe.

All Americans are not those monsters portrayed by Artzybasheff who rise at 4 A.M. and bring home a brief case full of homework at 3 A.M. the next morning. The systematic conquest of the old Northwest by red-coated soldiers and land speculators has moved few boyish hearts, even in New England. But the story of the boats of Champlain poking their way into the dark, leafy wilderness, the heroic death of Father Jorgues, the pathetic death of La Salle, the joyful portages of Marquette and Joliet—even the cognac, riot and abandoned women in besieged Montreal—are as moving as the tribulations and defiance of Milton's Satan. And these traditions are still powerful, however quiet, in the land.

It is the spiritual conflict in the author, as well as his reading of history as a war between two basic types of personality, which gives Parkman's work its power. The archetypal struggle gives it epic character. The personal conflict gives it the intricacy and ambiguity of a psychological novel. The real subject and background—redskins, redcoats and chevaliers—give it the fanfare of high romance.

Parkman is very far from being Homer or Proust or even Scott, but he does combine—perhaps in cheaper colors but on a canvas of tremendous scope—the virtues of all three. I first read Parkman with a chill along my scalp when I was but in skirts—or at least in short pants—and I've read him all several times since. Opening Morison's reader to the map of Quebec and seeing the words "The Plains of Abraham," and then rereading the words of Montcalm and Wolfe, the same old chill comes back.

Near the end of the last volume, *The Conspiracy of Pontiac,* in lines that echo Melville, Parkman sums up the real, not the putative, moral of his life work:

> . . . To him who has once tasted the reckless independence, the haughty self-reliance, the sense of irresponsible freedom, which the forest life engenders, civilization thenceforth seems flat and stale. Its pleasures are insipid, its pursuits wearisome, its conventionalities, duties, and mutual dependence alike tedious and disgusting. The entrapped

wanderer grows fierce and restless, and pants for breathing-room. His path, it is true, was choked with difficulties, but his body and soul were hardened to meet them; it was beset with dangers, but these were the very spice of his life, gladdening his heart with exulting self-confidence, and sending the blood through his veins with a livelier current. The wilderness, rough, harsh, and inexorable, has charms more potent in their seductive influence than all the lures of luxury and sloth. And often he on whom it has cast its magic finds no heart to dissolve the spell, and remains a wanderer and an Ishmaelite to the hour of his death.

Mr. Morison does not include this passage or anything like it in his selection.

EDWARD GIBBON

We have all heard the wisecrack about Gibbon's *Autobiography*, that he wrote of himself as though he were the Roman Empire. How true it is. Never, not even in Plutarchian Rome, did the public mask, the Social Lie, so completely obscure reality as in Gibbon's day and world. We expect our great politicians, some fraudulent old "tub of whiskey and stale nicotine," to be strutters on the stage, to be devoid of personal life; and who will ever number the heartaches of Arthur Godfrey? Again, we can enjoy in small doses the letters of that urtype of Fifty-seventh Street pansy Horace Walpole, whom many people consider the best letter writer in the English language. Certainly a little camp now and then is fun. But Gibbon is another matter. Somehow, somewhere, we get the conviction of a tragic, hidden self, nursed through life like an imbecile in a garret. I think the secret leaks through in the fact of the style. Here is one place we can say for sure, the style is the man. True, the *Decline and Fall* is pompous

The Letters of Edward Gibbon, Edited by J. E. Norton. Macmillan, New York, 1956.

at times, snickers at times, but by and large, it conveys, more than any other work in English, in sentence after noble sentence, the conviction of integrity and tragedy. The famous footnote on Theodora, "in the decent obscurity of a learned language," is not just a leer. The whole Theodora story is a muffled cry across time, sex, space and circumstance of one lost and frightened person to another. Reading it, you know Gibbon was haunted by those terrified Byzantine eyes in the Ravenna mosaic of the little circus girl growing old under her top-heavy crown. Gibbon was a strange lover—the man who proposed only once to a woman and then, too chubby to rise in his tight breeches, had to be helped from his knees by her. An apocryphal legend, but with its own truth.

It is of course to Gibbon's letters to Suzanne Churchod that you turn first, hoping for something new. Here they are again, just as they were before, set pieces of evasion. This Abelard, "a man naturally cold, or at best tepid," preferred to wait till old age and write the *History of His Calamities* in the guise of the terrible romance of the martyrdom of Boethius—the noblest pages of the *Decline and Fall*, and one of the greatest short narratives in any language. There are plenty of secrets in that big book; there are none at all in these twelve hundred pages of letters. Not a secret. Not a single leak. Not just Suzanne—it is romantic to think she was of crucial importance—there is nothing at all. All the right eighteenth-century opinions on all the right subjects at all the right times. Letters composed by a committee from the *Manchester Guardian*, or, if you prefer, the *Nation*. No wonder the college professors all love the eighteenth century, those untroubled days when nobody peeked, nobody spilled the beans. Nobody except Blake and Burns and ten thousand other witnesses from Cowper to Sade. Nobody ever let on. Nobody burned the Bastille.

So, to talk like a book reviewer, here at last is the personal Gibbon, as complete as he is ever likely to be—three volumes of consummate care and scholarship. Here is plenty of documentation for "Main Forces in Eighteenth-Century Thought and Life." Here is some charming, witty, often even wise observation, in a prose no less noble for being intimate. Here is all the editorial information and apparatus anybody could desire. As for Gibbon, he is somewhere else—on the throne, in the brothels of the Levant with Theodora, in the tower with Boethius. Miss Norton has worked to do what she could, but, as she says, speaking of certain letters to a fellow scholar, "Had Gibbon continued the pursuit of pure scholarship, he would no doubt have become more correct and more fastidious, and the present letters indicate that he might have become an accomplished Latinist with an individual style."

STEVEN RUNCIMAN

A couple of years back I had occasion to review Steven Runciman's *History of the Crusades,* and before that his *Medieval Manichee,* a study of the Christian Dualist heresy. From the very beginning of his career it has been apparent that Runciman is a historian of no mean order. He has done the thing all modern historians hope to do, and almost none manages: he has combined the writing of history as literature ("historiography" in academic argot) and the study of history as a scholarly discipline, if not an exact science.

Henry Adams, Francis Parkman, Prescott, Gibbon, Froissart, Tacitus, Thucydides, Ssŭ-ma Ch'ien—for many centuries the Muse of History was one of the chief of the minor goddesses and history was a major art. Alas for our day, she has fallen on evil times and become a maundering academic drudge. A writer like Arnold Toynbee owes his reputation as a stylist essentially to the outrageous barbarity of his style, its endless verbosity and eloquent muddle, like a country vicar on one of the duller Sundays after Trinity. His reputation as a philosopher of history is due to the procrustean rashness of his scantily

The Sicilian Vespers. By Steven Runciman. Cambridge University Press, New York, 1958.

substantiated hypotheses. In her old age the Muse has fallen into the hands of the Goths who know her not.

Steven Runciman is a horse of another color. He is an indisputably good writer, clear, perspicuous, able to marshall immense detail and vast casts of characters; able, again, to communicate that feeling of the very time and place which is perhaps the first virtue of good historical writing. His subject this time is the thirteenth-century struggle for supremacy among the states and cities of the Mediterranean; a struggle which centered in Sicily, but spread as far as Germany and the Holy Land, and which was watched with more than neutral interest by the powers of England and France. It may be an illusion, but we live again in the quarries of Sicily with the dying Athenians, and on the bloody causeway with Cortez and Malinche. So we are there, our iron shoes clanging on the arid stone floors of that immense architectural hallucination Krak of the Knights; in the desert of the Holy Land we watch the leper King of Jerusalem wither and die like the Fisher King of the Grail Romances—it is an infectious verisimilitude. You can see, smell and hear Manfred's and Conradin's armies, trapped in melees at narrow bridges, horses splashing through fords and swirling in high waters, the terrible sun on afternoon battlefields full of men in stinking armor, the Sicilian burghers running through the streets with torches and long knives.

This participation extends even to certain engaging prejudices. Runciman is now not quite as down on Frederick II as he was when he wrote the Crusade book, but he doesn't like him or his bastard, Manfred, either. You feel that this is for no bona fide historical, social or political reason, but the result of a residual British prudery. Both of them just might have made it at lurid Balliol, but never at Cambridge. They were frank atheists and practically wallowed in what Dr. Kinsey used to call extramarital sexual outlets. That Frederick II was the only civilized ruler in the West between classical and modern times is beside the point for Steven Runciman. He is awed by his magnificent appetites and the splendor of his mind, but he isn't going to be pleased if he can help it.

The Sicilian Vespers is much more than a study of that legendary revolt itself. It is the story of the final breakdown of the possibility of the Empire, as distinguished from the Imperial dream; of the moral compromise of the Papacy that was to lead eventually to Papal Courts worthy of Suetonius, and the disgust of the Reformation; of the beginning of the invidious and destructive role of France in the peninsula, that was to endure at least until Napoleon III; and, wistful enough in its special way, the last assertion of the spirit of the Greek polis, the last bright flicker of the precious city-state ethos in a Greek Italy then two thousand years old. Through it all glitter the brocades and marbles of the oriental, pagan, birth of the Renaissance, the songs of the troubadours and Arabic minstrels, the speculations of Hebrew Kabbalists and Greek-Italian Aristotelians, the mysteries of alchemists and magicians—the last two Hohenstauffen courts, where what the French call *l'esprit laique,* the character of Renaissance and modern man, was invented.

Plenty has been written about Frederick II and Manfred, some of it bombastically romantic, but this whole world—what was really the southeast borderland of Western civilization—has seldom been seen steadily and whole. It is the march, the pressure area, between Gothic, Byzantine and Arabic civilizations, all three in their decline or rather decadence. It is hard to think of a more splendidly caparisoned historical stage, or one more crowded with spectacular characters, or one more haunted by fascinating mysteries and immoralities. It provided Gibbon with some of his most encrusted and brilliant pages. It requires a tremendous amount of hard work to co-ordinate its documents and sources and to disentagle its dilemmas and disputes. It is certainly not overcrowded with historians. Steven Runciman seems to have staked a claim on it as very specially his own. Long may he flourish, for he certainly makes it fascinating reading.

The New Poetry

From fifty to forty years ago America went through a widely publicized Poetic Renaissance. The writing of Gertrude Stein, Ezra Pound, William Carlos Williams, made hilarious copy for the newspapers. Scandal sheets ran succulent exposés of the wicked doings of the avant-garde in sinful Greenwich Village. Even more lurid stories were retailed of those lost souls, the "expatriates"—actually young writers off on their traditional wander year abroad—in popular mythology combinations of Benedict Arnold and the Marquis de Sade. What was really happening was that American poetry was moving from an isolated provincial innocence into the mainstream of world literature.

The writers of those days have long since become our still living classics and are taught in all well-appointed schools. In fact, they are, in the eyes of the present younger generation, taught just a little too much. For one high-school English major who has read Longfellow, hundreds have parsed *The Waste Land.* The living utterance of the major American poets of the first quarter of this century has been buried under a polar ice cap of commentary and exegesis. Nothing like it has been seen since ancient Alexandria or the Chinese Empire in its decadence.

Once again today the doings of poets are hot copy. A popular myth has been built of bearded savages who shoot themselves full of dope in public places—preferably on television—and take off their clothes at fashionable soirees. Nothing could be further from the truth. Of course, once a vulgar stereotype has been manufactured, plenty of people will appear, anxious to conform to it. What has been happening in American poetry is another thing altogether.

The young poets who have come into notice since the Second World War have certain common characteristics, and they are certainly wholesome ones. Primary is an emphasis on direct, personal communication. All of them have something to say and are anxious to have other people pay attention. In some this has taken the form of a poetry of explicit social protest. Sensationalists have discovered something they have named the Beat Generation and have played it up as an outrageous novelty. The source of all this furor is a small group of poets, rather atypical of the present younger generation, who write much like the Proletarians of the Thirties—only considerably better.

Practically all revolutions in poetry since time began have been nothing but reassertions, after a period of academic sterility, of the abiding principles of all poetry everywhere. There is little difference between the *Preface to Lyrical Ballads* and the *Imagist Manifesto.* So today, the poetry of the latest renaissance seeks always to be "simple, sensuous and passionate." It is not the fault of the poets if scandalmongers have chosen to play up the nasty, brutish and turgid.

As always, those who strive to reassert simplicity and personal directness are accused of being difficult, obscure, "avant-garde." This is just the massive resistance of bad taste. The Jesuits call it "invincible ignorance." It is a widespread response to any and all new poetry. However, we live in a time of widespread literacy. The most astonishing thing about the contemporary poetry renaissance is its popularity. Once poets started saying things people wanted to hear, a vast, unsuspected audience appeared. In comparison with the writers of a generation ago, the academic, self-styled Reactionary Generation, whose leaders were lucky if their books sold in editions of three hundred, the postwar writers are genuinely popular poets, whose books sell like novels, and who could live off the lecture platform if they so chose.

Just as this poetry is at once popular and "avant-garde," so it is also intensely American, a powerful declaration of independence of the English tradition, recently so popular with the Reactionary Generation, and a return to the mainstream of modern verse as it has been practiced throughout the world—except in England—for the past half century. It is always that money which is most solidly based at home which functions as an international currency.

For most of the twentieth century there has existed a kind of pendulum swing, an alternation of style in American poetry. This might be called the periodic rise and fall of French and Populist and then English, Puritan and academic influences. The only trouble with such a simplification is that except for the brief period when W. H. Auden, Stephen Spender and Day Lewis were in their salad days, the Americans usually anticipated developments in Great Britain and sometimes in France. It has been forgotten that the first so-called abstract and cubist poetry was written by Gertrude Stein and Walter Conrad Arensburg. Gertrude Stein's *Tender Buttons,* poems which attempt to translate into poetry the vision of the analytical cubist still life, first apeared several years before the analogous poems of André Salmon and Pierre Reverdy. American Imagism was French in inspiration. The dissociative techniques of Ezra Pound's *Cantos* and T. S. Eliot's *Waste Land* were derived immediately from the work of a minor French (actually Belgian) poet, Jean de Bosschère, who was living in London and was part of their circle during the First World War.

Out of the work of Pound, Eliot and the French tradition from Guillaume Apollinaire to the Dadaists came a whole crop of American and British poets—Louis Zukofsky, Walter Lowenfels, Nancy Cunard, Samuel Beckett, J. G. Macleod, whose work appeared in *transition* and other avant-garde magazines of the Twenties. Contemporaneously with them Malcolm Cowley and Matthew Josephson and their friends on *Broom* had imported into America a rather collegiate version of Dadaism. At the same time Yvor Winters was writing a sparse, cubist, but intellectual rather than imagist, dissociated verse under the influence of, I suppose, Mallarmé, especially the metaphysical late poem *"Un Coup de dés."* A couple of years later, at first under the inspiration of *transition,* a wave of Surrealism swept over a section of verse in English. The best poets of this period were probably the American leaders of the movement, Eugene Jolas, Parker Tyler and Charles Henri Ford.

Throughout its entire history American avant-garde verse has compared very favorably with the work of its presumed masters across the Atlantic. As the years go by Philippe Soupault and Tristan Tzara seem pretty thin stuff. Unfortunately little of this work is available but samples can be found in anthologies in public libraries: *Others* edited by Alfred Kreymborg, Louis Zukofsky's *Objectivist Anthology,* Parker Tyler's *Modern Things,* William Carlos Williams' *Contact Collection,* the five numbers of the annual *American Caravan,* and a number of anthologies edited by Jolas. These by no manner of means cover the field. Certain poets like Walter Lowenfels do not appear at all. Yvor Winters forbids all publication of his early work. Hardly a man is left alive who remembers that Matthew Josephson started out as a poet. For almost twenty years it was as though these people had never been.

What obliterated them from memory was a world economic crisis. They were overwhelmed by the Proletarian Thirties. No sooner had the literary soviets collapsed in ignominy than, to mix a metaphor, another wave of the future swept over American verse. Revolution was followed by counterrevolution —both of them about equally real politically. Up until the end of the Second World War the dominant tendency in American poetry was politically reactionary and stylistically conservative. Its politics was derived from the novels of Walter Scott and those American imitations *Red Rock* and *The Clansman,* and the rasher political excursions of Mr. Eliot. Its literary models were the poets of the English Baroque and the Chaucerian Decadence. For a number of years the people in this group, rather like the man in Orwell's *1984,* rewrote the past on their own terms, and their immediate predecessors were forgotten.

Postwar years are characteristically periods of wholesale literary revaluation. Everybody knows that this is what happened after the First World War. It is only now becoming apparent that the same thing occurred after the Second World War. Looking back over fifteen years of fiction we can see now that we are in the midst of a period of impassioned social criticism in the novel, far more intense and far more mature than the stereotyped documents of the Thirties. No one has come up to the major writers of those days—John Dos Passos or James Farrell, for instance—but on the other hand we have been spared the badly written empty formulas of the old-time "strike novel."

The years immediately after the Second World War witnessed a sudden efflorescence of avant-garde "little magazines," a type of publication that it had been assumed had gone out of existence for good a literary generation before. In the course of time a whole school of poets was developed in these magazines. For several years they could publish nowhere else. The editors were young men of high principle and great devotion. One of them managed to pay his printers with his savings from the G.I. Bill. Another used most of a Guggenheim fellowship to print other writers. Another lived in poverty in Majorca and spent practically all of his income on a magazine and a series of handsomely produced books. Cid Corman, Robert Creeley, Jonathan Williams, Richard Emerson and their magazines *Origin, Black Mountain Review, Jargon, Golden Goose,* laid the foundations for a new minor renaissance in American verse.

One of the most interesting things about these young postwar poets is their decentralization (it has never been noticed that this is also true of the contemporary novelists). They grew up not only in independence of the capital—the literary market place—but far away from it and in deliberate antagonism to it. They couldn't very well do anything else. To this day few of them have been published in the respectable literary quarterlies. The only geographical focus was San Francisco, where a literary world with stronger connections with London or Paris had been maturing for many years. San Francisco had its own magazines, its own presses, its own literary reputation, but the rest of the country was unaware of this faraway ferment.

In San Francisco also began the now fabulously successful oral presentation of poetry. For years, in fact from long before the war, there have been more poetry readings every week in San Francisco than I for one have ever been able to keep track of. At the present time American poets run the danger of being assimilated to the condition of Les Brown's band, Mort Sahl or Singer's Midgets. I suppose this feverish activity—extremely well paid by the way—has its dangers, but as far as I can see it is all to the good. Poetry is an art of speech, and it can only be helped by its restoration to immediate contact with a living audience. The major factor in the building of a nationwide poetry circuit has been the onerous, self-sacrificing work of Elizabeth Kray at the New York YMHA Poetry Center, and on the West Coast of Ruth Witt-Diamant at the San Francisco Poetry Center, both of whom have received help from the Rockefeller Foundation. As the audience for poetry has grown smaller and smaller in England and France, it has become a genuinely popular art in America.

Now for the poets. Their books are still not any too easy to come by, most of them. Few have been published by the more conventional publishers. They have had to rely on their own presses or the limited opportunities offered by the two houses which specialize in the avant-garde, Grove Press and New Directions.

Unquestionably the best of the lot is Denise Levertov. She first appeared, a young Land Girl, working on a farm in Essex, who sent her poems to *Poetry London* and *Poetry Quarterly*. In no time at all Herbert Read, Tambimuttu, Charles Wrey Gardener, Alex Comfort, and incidentally myself, were in excited correspondence about her. In those days she was the baby of the New Romanticism. Her poetry had about it a wistful *Schwärmerei* unlike anything in English except perhaps Matthew Arnold's "Dover Beach." It could be compared to the earliest poetry of Rilke or some of the more melancholy songs of Brahms. At the end of the war she published a small book in England, lived in France for a while, married a literary G.I. and came to America. Almost immediately she changed her style completely. At first it looked as though she was going to be just another of the accomplished disciples of William Carlos Williams. But in a short time she had evolved a style of her own—clear, sparse, immediate and vibrant with a very special sensibility and completely feminine insight. She is not only the most subtly skillful poet of her generation, she is far and away the most profound, and what may be more important, the most modest and the most moving. She can communicate the same vertiginous rapture as the great imagist poet H.D. (Hilda Doolittle) but without the need of her rather theatrical stage settings.

Second only to Denise Levertov is Robert Creeley. Superficially his poems look like the cameos of Mallarmé—such still lifes as "*Autre Éventail*" or "*Petit Air*"—or the intense little epigrams of William Carlos Williams—the plums in the icebox, the wheelbarrow glazed by the rain or the cat stepping over the window sill. On close inspection Creeley's poems turn out to be anything but Imagism. They are erotic poems, but what gives them their terrific impact is neither love nor lust. Each is an excruciating spasm of guilt. It is obvious that so limited a subject matter hardly provides the scope for major poetry. But there is no question of Creeley's effectiveness within his self-imposed or perhaps inescapable limitations. In the last couple of years he seems to have become more at ease in the world and less haunted by his relations with others, and his poetry is, however slowly, gaining in humanity and breadth. What distinguishes it is the same thing that keeps Mallarmé important—remarkable skill and special sensitivity to the inflections of speech—however special a speech either Creeley's or Mallarmé's may be.

A slightly older man, one who has had great influence on the entire group as a teacher and theorist, is Charles Olson. Like Denise Levertov and Robert Creeley, in fact like all these people, he owes a great deal to William Carlos Williams. He owes even more to Ezra Pound's *Cantos*. For several years he has been writing a long spiritual epic, a tighter, drier, less gaudy descendant of the *Cantos*—the *Maximus Poems*. This work is in the same tradition as the "interior epics," actually philosophical reveries, of the Twenties—Zukofsky's *A* or Lowenfels' *Some Deaths*. Olson lacks the passion and trouble and concern of his predecessors and he lacks the intensity of Creeley and Levertov. No one could quarrel with his scope. His canvas is as broad as Pound's, but his material makes more sense in terms of actual life. I suppose the best comparison is William Carlos Williams' own "epic," *Paterson*. Olson's shorter poems have a ruminative complexity a little like the later long poems of Wallace Stevens.

Associated with Olson and Creeley are a number of poets, once students at the college or contributors to the magazine—the "Black Mountain group." The best of them are probably Paul Blackburn, author of some of the best translations ever made from the Provençal, and Jonathan Williams, the editor of the Jargon Press.

For many years poets in San Francisco had been satisfied with their own, very satisfying world. Local fame brought considerable general prestige and standing in the community. The rewards at home were so much greater than the results of a frantic pursuit of national reputation that nobody bothered. In the course of time at least three poets began to be heard of around the country—Philip Lamantia, once editor with Tyler and Ford of the Surrealist magazine *View*, Brother Antoninus (William Everson), a Dominican oblate, and Robert Duncan.

Brother Antoninus is a rough, urgent startlingly honest poet, with a passionate identification with the Californian landscape. His verse has the same kind of integrity as that of Whitman, D. H. Lawrence, the early Sandburg, or the best of Robinson Jeffers. In certain, what are called enduring moral qualities, he is one of the very best poets we have. In style he has achieved a sort of sublimation of the native Populist tradition.

Philip Lamantia has more of a reputation abroad than he has ever acquired in the States. He belongs to that small group of second-generation Surrealists who dedicated themselves to an actual quest for madness—Artaud, René Crèvel—the literature of Black Magic and destruction. Although Lamantia is little more than thirty, he already seems to belong to another age. By this I do not mean that his poetry is dated or unimpressive, quite the contrary.

One of the characteristics of the recently powerful Reactionary Generation was a willful provincialism, a deliberate cutting off of American verse from the main stream of world poetry of the twentieth century. Sidney Lanier was far more important to the Southern Agrarians than was Goethe . . . let alone Baudelaire or Apollinaire. Robert Duncan has that special quality of temper which he shares with Edmund Wilson or Pandit Nehru, he is a Good European. Although Duncan has been singularly open to all the influences of all times and places, and has learned from all the Old Masters of Modernism, from Reubén Darío to Yves Bonnefoy, his distinguishing characteristic is not the breadth of his influences, but the depth and humanness of his heart. Now that he is approaching early middle age he has begun to take on something of the forgotten grandeur of the great nineteenth-century "men of the world" of letters—Monckton Milnes or Walter Bagehot. I can think of no other poet of my time of which anything like this could be said—with most, the very idea is ridiculous. As mentor and example, Duncan's influence on the younger men of the new New Poetry has been incalculable.

The now widely publicized San Francisco Renaissance owes more to Duncan than to any other one person. Since writing poetry seems to have become one of the three favorite indoor sports of the city, it would take pages merely to list the teeming poets and poetasters. Among the better ones (and by no means a complete list) are: Helen Adam, Madeline Gleason, Michael McClure, James Broughton, Robin Blaser, Jack Spicer, Thomas Parkinson, Kirby Doyle, Ebbe Borregaard, William Margolis, Ron Loewinsohn, David Meltzer, Eve and Dan Langton—just a selection from the poets who have found some publication nationally. A large number of people perhaps as good have been content with local recognition and have never bothered to seek anything else.

This regional activity had been going full swing for many years when suddenly it received a number of spectacular recruits. First was Lawrence Ferlinghetti. He is a successful book dealer, secretly the possessor of three degrees, one from the Sorbonne, a most imaginative editor and publisher, whose "Pocket Poets" series has sold hundreds of thousands of copies, and a genuinely popular poet. His own *A Coney Island of the Mind* nudges *Howl* for first place as the most popular poetry book of the decade, and without the latter's somewhat dubious publicity. Resident for many years in France, he "thinks in French"; his verse bears strong resemblance to that of Raymond Queneau, Jacques Prévert and Paul Éluard. Its nearest American analogues are the work of e. e. cummings and James Laughlin.

In my opinion the most promising of the new additions to the San Francisco group are Gary Snyder and Philip Whalen, both from the Northwest. Both write poetry which has learned much from the Far East, and which is saturated with a feeling for the new, human significance of the landscape and the primitive peoples of the mountains and forests of the Pacific Coast.

About four years ago a young man in violent revolt against the polite literary world of Columbia University, where he had been the student "most likely to succeed" in literature, showed up in San Francisco and stayed for a brief visit. The permissive atmosphere seems to have exploded him. His name, of course, is Allen Ginsberg. I am not prepared to defend Ginsberg's fantastic public image, one of the most unfortunate *hallucinations publicitaires* of our time. Once he throws away the worn-out Davy Crockett cap of the Beat Generation, it will be apparent that he is a typical American popular poet, in the tradition of Vachel Lindsay and Carl Sandburg. Certainly the youth now gaining headlines in the journalistically fashionable "new revolt of Youth" accept him as a spokesman, and well they might. This does not mean that his poetry is not thoroughly traditional—in one of the oldest traditions, that of Hosea or the other, angry Minor Prophets of the Bible. The picture magazines to the contrary notwithstanding, his connection with San Francisco is of the most tenuous.

Ginsberg's associate, Gregory Corso, is a genuine *naïf*. A real wildman, with all the charm of a hoodlum Le Douanier Rousseau, a wholesome Antonin Artaud, or a "sincere" Tristan Tzara. At his worst he is an amusing literary curiosity; at his best, his poems are metaphysical hotfoots and poetic cannon crackers.

Recently there has grown up, in the very heart of the literary market place, a New York group of young poets, loosely identified with the people I have been discussing. They are more urbane, literally more citified, than the outlanders, and their poetry is pitched in a lower key, quieter, more modest, more sophisticated. (Of course, several of the people I have mentioned live in New York, but they are not part of this group.) The best, I think, is Barbara Guest (who now lives in Washington, D.C.), very like Denise Levertov, but less intense and skillful. Others are Kenneth Koch, Frank O'Hara (both associated with the Tenth Street Club of abstract painters), James Schuyler, Joel Oppenheimer, LeRoi Jones, Edward Field—again, the list could be prolonged indefinitely.

To sum up. If I were asked to characterize all these poets as succinctly as possible, and to distinguish them from the literary generation immediately before them, I would say that they are at once more European and more American, more modernist and more popular, more conscious of the social role of the poet and more ready to, as they say, sacrifice all for Art. Young as they are, they have been around more than their sheltered academic colleagues. They are all, in their way, men and women of the world. Most of them are familiar with the literature of at least one other language. Most of them make a living in ways as little connected with writing as is possible. One thing they are not. They are not compromised.

Critics, and some poets, especially in times when they feel like writing manifestoes, like to think of poetry as fulfilling some sort of program or other. Of course, poetry does nothing of the sort; the programs are all post-mortem. At last in fact there are just the poems, experiences that must compete with all the other poems ever written—Sappho or Horace or Dante or James Whitcomb Riley. I may have been able to deduce a sort of program from the poems written by the poets who have come to public notice since the war and so I suppose it could be said that their poems do exhibit a high degree of success in fulfilling the demands of such a program. What counts are the poems. By and large they are successful. They are fresh, direct, concerned and truly humane in a way in which the poetry of the preceding period was not. I am not at all sure that anyone has come up who is sheerly as good as the classic modernists of American verse—Eliot, Williams, Stevens, Moore and the rest—although Robert Duncan and Denise Levertov certainly approach their standards.

Someone once said of one of the older leaders of this new renaissance that he made poetry a social force in San Francisco. This is about as complimentary a remark as could be made about a poet. Whatever else they have done, our young poets have returned poetry to society. Today in America; more than anywhere else in the world, large numbers of people find poetry interesting. It says something to them, something meaningful in their dilemmas and exultations. This is no small accomplishment.

Simone Weil

Simone Weil was one of the most remarkable women of the twentieth, or indeed of any other century. I have great sympathy for her, but sympathy is not necessarily congeniality. It would be easier to write of her if I liked what she had to say, which I strongly do not.

For an alert non-Bolshevik radical of the years of the Second World War, the two most decisive insights, at least for those who read only English, were Paul Mattick's "The War Is Permanent," published in *Living Marxism* in 1939, and Simone Weil's "The Coming World War," published in the *International Review* in 1938, but written in 1934. Nobody who read them then is ever likely to forget them. Mattick's theme is obvious from the title and is a commonplace today. Simone Weil pointed out that modern technology had made social violence a supranational thing, so that, whoever "won," modern warfare resolved itself in actual practice into the lethal conflict of the man at the desk with the man at the bench. The workers get killed in shop or foxhole, the college graduates get commissions or join the OWI. Unhappily, she was herself to undergo a transvaluation of values and join the Gaullist OWI.

One of Simone Weil's books, *The Need for Roots,* was a collection of egregious nonsense surpassed only by the deranged fantasies of the chauvinist Péguy; it was written for De Gaulle —a program for the moral rehabilitation of France when our

The Notebooks of Simone Weil. Translated by Arthur Wills. Putnam, New York, 1956.

side had won. It attempted to enlist on our side the same dark irrational spirits who seemed then to be fighting so successfully for the other side. Today it is a weird, embarrassing relic of a too immediate past. Luckily, as it turned out, they lost and we won without much effective intervention from the spirits on either side. Realities of the kind called harsh rule France today rather than any vestige of Simone Weil's odd ideals.

Simone Weil was born in Paris in 1909 to well-to-do parents of Jewish ancestry but no religion. After a brilliant academic career in philosophy she became a secondary-school teacher. In 1934 she left teaching for a year to work in the Renault plant, "to experience the life of the workers." In 1936 she went to Spain, and fought, or rather did not fight, in the Republican Army. Between her return from Spain late in the same year and the outbreak of the Second World War she broke down in health, abandoned her revolutionary ideas—which were never Marxist in any orthodox sense, but rather Communist-Anarchist of the type we associate with Alexander Berkman and Emma Goldman—and began a sort of tortured prowling outside the doors of the Catholic Church—like a starving wild animal. In 1940 she settled in Marseilles with her family, who were arranging to escape to America. In 1941 she met Fr. Perrin, a Dominican, who introduced her to Gustave Thibon, a wealthy farmer and a leading Catholic intellectual. On his farm she tried, not very successfully, to work as a "land girl." In the summer of 1942 she came to New York, and left for England in the fall with a commission to serve in the Gaullist organization in England. In the spring of 1943 she entered a hospital, and in August she died in Ashford Sanatorium in Kent. Superficially this career sounds much like that of many idealistic and rather giddy upper-class college girls of those days. Probably many such girls who are successful lady executives today did live with the same burning intensity as Simone Weil; probably a good many others came to an equally sad end. But she, like Marie Bashkirtsev, who was her nineteenth-century double, and the perfect exemplar of the type in those days, left a record quite as classic and fully as poignant.

In recent years Putnam has published several collections of her journals and correspondence: *Waiting for God, Letter to a Priest, Gravity and Grace* and *The Need for Roots.* As they have come out I have read them all again, and with them her new, unabridged notebooks.

I have the greatest respect, indeed veneration, for any tortured soul seeking peace and illumination. But in 1934 she wrote this: "War in our day is distinguished by the subordination of the combatants to the instruments of combat, and the armaments, the true heroes of modern warfare, as well as the men dedicated to their service, are directed by those who do not fight. Since this directing apparatus has no other way of fighting than sending its own soldiers, under compulsion, to their deaths—the war of one State against another resolves itself into a war of the State and the military apparatus against its own army. War in the last analysis appears as a struggle led by all the State apparatuses and general staffs against all men old enough and able to bear arms." And later in the same article: "Revolutionary war is the grave of revolution."

When war actually came she was writing things like this: "In civil society, penal death, if death is used as a punishment, ought to be something beautiful. Religious ceremonies would be necessary for it to be made so. And there ought to be something to make it be felt that the man who is being punished, on receiving death, accomplishes something great; contributes, as far as he is able in the situation in which he has placed himself, to the orderly state of the community. Let him remain in his cell until such time as he himself accepts to die?"

What would Thomas Aquinas have made of this? Or any Sicilian peasant or Irish teamster? Very much, I fear, the same as you or I. This girl killed herself seeking salvation, a salvation she identified with Catholicism. The passage above, and there are hundreds of remarks like it in the notebooks, is far from Catholicism, in fact from any religion. It has a horrible similarity to one theory of the Moscow trials, but it is a sick kind of agonized frivolity. And there are other things: a captious, misinformed playing with Hinduism and comparative mythology, worse than the confabulations of Robert Graves; a toying with modern mathematics of infinitudes and incommensurabilities—a kind of post Cantor-Dedekind Neo-Pythagoreanism.

In her last years Simone Weil seems to have sought enlightenment by a systematic cultivation of maximum hypertension. Her thought proceeded by no other way than paradox. This is not new. There is a good deal of it in Pascal, that least Catholic of Catholic thinkers, and of course in Kierkegaard. In Chesterton it sinks to the level of a vulgar journalistic trick. Paul Tillich has created, beyond the "theology of crisis" of Barth, Niebuhr and the Neo-Lutherans, a "theology of tension"—perhaps the most viable expression of that ancient science for a modern man. But there is the tension of life and the tension of death. Simone Weil was a dying girl. Hers was a spastic, moribund, intellectual and spiritual agony. We can sympathize with it, be moved to tears by it, much as we are by the last awful lunacies of Antonin Artaud, but we imitate it, allow it to infect us, at our peril. This is a Kierkegaard who refuses to leap. *Angst* for *angst's* sake. Anguish is not enough. When it is made an end in itself it takes on a holy, or unholy, folly.

It is one thing, like John Woolman, to refuse sugar because it was made by slave labor; it is another thing to refuse to eat more than the starvation rations of occupied Paris when one is dying in an English sanatorium. (What sort of doctor permitted this?) It is touching, even tragic, but it is the farcical tragedy of Lear, equally distant from the tragedy of Prometheus on his rock or Christ on his cross.

What was wrong with Simone Weil? Our grandparents used to say of learned girls who broke down, "She studied too hard. She read too many books." And today we laugh at them. I think Simone Weil had both over- and under-equipped herself for the crisis which overwhelmed her—along, we forget, immersed in her tragedy, with all the rest of us. She was almost the perfectly typical passionate, revolutionary, intellectual woman—a frailer, even more highly strung Rosa Luxemburg.

Rosa was saved from personal, inner disaster during the great betrayals of the First World War by several, all rather tough-minded, characteristics. She had a tenacious orthodoxy: she was perfectly confident of the sufficiency of Marxism as an answer, though she was more humane about it than Lenin. She had a warm, purely human love of people—physically, their smell and touch and comradeship. And a kind of Jewish indomitable guts, that ultimate unkillability which comes only from grandparents in *yamulke* and horsehair wig. Simone Weil had none of this. She made up her own revolution out of her vitals, like a spider or silkworm. She could introject all the ill of the world into her own heart, but she could not project herself in sympathy to others. Her letters read like the more distraught signals of John of the Cross in the dark night. It is inconceivable that she could ever have written as Rosa Luxemburg did from prison to Sophia Kautsky. People to Simone Weil were mere actors in her own spiritual melodrama. I doubt if she was ever aware of the smell of her own armpits. She may have called her fantasy "the need for roots," but *yamulkes*, rosaries or plain chewing-tobacco atheism, none had ever existed in her past. She was born a *déracinée* and she insisted on remaining one. She was constitutionally disengaged—the Renault plant, the Spanish Republican and the Free French armies to the contrary notwithstanding. Faced with the ordinary but definite engagement of becoming a baptized Catholic, she panicked.

Religion has been called the gap between the technology and the environment. When her intellectual and psychological environment blew up in her face, Simone Weil discovered that she had no technology whatever, and the gap was absolute. She never permitted herself access to anyone who could help her. If I were planning to enter the Catholic

Church the last person I would ever approach would be the kind of priest who could make head or tail of her *Letter to a Priest*.

Fr. Perrin and M. Thibon may have been wise men in their generation, but they both fell into the trap of her dialectic of agony. They took her seriously—in the wrong way. They lacked the vulgar but holy frivolity of common sense of the unsophisticated parish priest who would have told her, "Come, come, my child, what you need is to get baptized, obey the Ten Commandments, go to Mass on Sundays, make your Easter duties, forget about religion, put some meat on your bones, and get a husband." Simone Weil knew the type, and she avoided them as a criminal avoids the police, and probably secretly disdained them as much.

Only such advice could have saved her. Only the realization of the truth—so hard to come by for the religious adventurer—that no one is "called" to be any holier than he absolutely has to be, could have given her real illumination. To anything like this she was defiantly impervious. She went to John of the Cross when she should have gone to plain Fr. Dupont, or Fr. Monahan, or Fr. Aliotto. Even Huysmans, with all his posturing, had sense enough to make St. Severin, that humble slum church, his home parish. Simone Weil assaulted the Garden of Gethsemane, and as is so often the case, was broken on the gate.

At least she speaks, again and again, of her absolutely sure sense of the suddenly descending, all-suffusing presence of God. So we know that somewhere, somehow, in all her agony, she did find some center of peace, a peace which, unless we happen to believe in God, we may find hard to explain.

A Public Letter for William Carlos Williams' Seventy-fifth Birthday

Dear Bill,

A letter comes to me here in Provence from Laughlin: "Went to Billyum's 75th birthday party, he very gay and bright and full of life and ideas." I suppose the first thing to say is, "How time passes! How the old days stay vivid." It seems so little a while ago that John Ferren and I, both then in our early twenties, hitchhiked across the country and came to dinner at your house in Rutherford. A whole movement was growing up around you. Louis Zukofsky was issuing his very subjective Objectivist manifestoes. Hilaire Hiler was painting Neo-Naturalist paintings. Robert MacAlmon was writing his sparse, poignant poems and stories—a sort of psychological distillation of the Midwestern Naturalism out of which he had come. Valéry Larbaud was publishing your poems in *Commerce*. Pierre Reverdy had recognized you as a colleague, seeking in American the same values he was introducing into French poetry. That was thirty years ago.

Now you are seventy-five and full of honors, and even the nonliterary world is discovering you. They say *Time* has had a cover story on you in the slot for several years now. You're successful. Even the medical profession is proud of you and all sorts of doctors who never read poetry know about you as the Doctor Poet. I can remember when even the doctors in Rutherford didn't know you wrote.

Successful—is it true that success always corrupts, and absolute success corrupts absolutely? I think not. Most people think of success in terms of power and there Lord Acton's epigram applies. It is the illusion of power that has made so many of your contemporaries soft and silly as they have grown older. They think they have power. Or one poor demented old man is crazy because he always wanted power and never got any. But you have never had any doubt about the nature of power—in life, in human affairs, in art. You have never even sought "influence."

I have read essays of yours that I thought were a little foolish with good feeling for some young writer. You can be pretty rash in your praise. Parker Tyler once told me, "You know, Bill Williams compares me to Dante." "Hell," I said, "that's nothing—he has compared me to Homer!" But you know, Bill, there was always one outstanding characteristic of those little essays and reviews of new writers. There was never the slightest hint of patronage, of being the "discoverer" of anybody. There are those who are inordinately proud of having discovered Basil Bunting or Ralph Cheever Dunning or Mary Butts. And believe me, those now neglected people were never allowed to forget they were being discoverd. Well, your introductions to first books, your essays about anybody from Jeanne D'Orge to Allen Ginsberg always sounded as if you were simply overwhelmed by the compliment of being asked to read the work of the new, young and struggling.

I have your first letters to me—you'd think I had done you the most tremendous favor in sending you a poem. And I've seen those poems, too, the kind an older writer gets—grubby, penciled, crazy doggerel on Big Five tablet paper, or immaculately typed vacuities in special bindings—all the heart-rending dim signals of the inarticulate. Where did you find the time to answer all those people, so considerately, so modestly?

A busy doctor, especially a baby doctor, has a life expectancy of about fifty-five years. He wears out and drops in his tracks. Most American poets in the twentieth century have died of drink, or by suicide, or gone crazy before they were forty. And here you are seventy-five and still going strong . . . and nobody lost in Waterloo, Iowa, or Ashtabula, Ohio, ever called on you for succor without getting it. Even the most awful amateurs could always get a couple of encouraging sentences out of you for a blurb on the cover of their little job-printed books. Now this hasn't been because you were softheaded. It is because you have never thought of literature as an instrumentality of worldly power. You have always looked on other writers, young and old, in exactly the same warm, loving, human way you have regarded the people in your novels and short stories—and all the innocent, the lost, the castoff, who come and go in your poems. You have always known where the only kind of human power that matters was to be found—in the creative act.

I am living here now in the most classical of all landscapes, Aix-en-Provence, where life has changed less its ancient Mediterranean way than anywhere else. Far more than Greece or Italy, here men live very much as they lived in the first centuries of the ages of cities and agriculture around this tepid, slopping sea. As Horace said, and Gautier after him, and even poor old Gogarty, and before them all, some unknown Egyptian—what survives? "Only the blithe hexameters . . . only a few broken columns." Vaison la Romaine, some fine chisel work and a theater looking out over the deep distant Rhone Valley—and even the nation of which it was the capital is utterly vanished away. Power lies in the work of art and there alone. Armies conquer the world and their names are forgotten. But how many educated soldiers, in every corner of the world, have thought of the grounded constellations of the watch fires before Troy as they stood by their own bivouacs, or have wept with Xenophon as they first came in sight of some outlandish sea?

You have always had the perfect security of that power. Reverdy long ago was right—you have always had the authentic marble-and-bronze durability of the poets who founded this Western Civilization all the rascals assure us they are defending. The rascals have always been defending civilization and they have had so little power and none to share, and so, in a little while, they have always eliminated each other. But the civilization has gone on regardless. It has a terrific power and an almost inextinguishable life, because it consists of things like your cats stepping over the window sill, or chickens by a red wheelbarrow, or a fire truck in gold and red, or plums in the icebox. And those things are like the soup pot in the fairy tale; there's strength in them to be ladled out inexhaustibly until the slow geological processes of the planet, or the follies of the powerful, at last extinguish them. That is why you've always had so much to give, because you've never wanted anything but what you knew you had already. And so, for this birthday, I remember that many a Pharaoh sat on his throne at seventy-five and everybody hollered, "Live forever, O King!" So—more power to you, dear Bill.

K. R.

Poets, Old and New

YUAN MEI

For forty years Arthur Waley has been the leading interpreter of the poetry of China, and much of its philosophy, to the English-speaking world. All his translations are valid poems in their own right. In fact, they are among the most beautiful English poems of the twentieth century. His influence has been tremendous, and unlike too many other very influential poets of our day, it has been all for the good. Following his lead, Ezra Pound, Witter Bynner and Amy Lowell have done what is, in each case, some of their finest work in the form of translations from the Chinese. Waley's books have been a powerful force for clarity, personal immediacy and purity of intention, in a poetic world where, all too often, those essential qualities have been at considerable discount. In Dante's phrase, he is "the better maker," the master of us all. His influence on my own work has been incalculable, and better still, he led me to the originals, both Chinese and Japanese, and opened up for me the whole wonderful world of Far Eastern poetry. This world possesses to the full precisely those qualities of which the literary sensibility of our demoralized Western culture stands in such obvious need.

Too often Westerners think of Chinese poetry exclusively in terms of its great periods, the Classical Era, the Han, T'ang

Yuan Mei: 18th Century Chinese Poet. By Arthur Waley. Macmillan, New York, 1957 (Evergreen paperback, 1958).

and Sung dynasties. Classical purists, much like our own Latin Ciceronians, tend to put down the literature of the modern dynasties as decadent and formularized. However, it was in the period after the Mongol conquest that those special characteristics we think of as "very Chinese" seem to have developed in the Chinese personality, or at least found literary expression. Lin Yutang has done much to popularize these aspects of, if I may be forgiven the use of a phrase in bad scientific repute, the "Chinese national character," and his wise, sensitive and pathetic "Six Chapters of a Floating Life" is a small, perfect exemplar of eighteenth-century Chinese sensibility.

Now we have, in Arthur Waley's life of Yuan Mei, interspersed with dozens of splendid translations, the presentation of the same sensibility on a considerably higher literary level. After all, literature is not just the Bible and Shakespeare, or the Book of Odes and Tu Fu. The art of, to quote Mr. Waley's preface, being convincingly "lovable, witty, generous, affectionate, hot-tempered, wildly prejudiced . . . a writer of poetry that even at its lightest always has an undertone of deep feeling and at its saddest may at any moment light a spark of fun," is a very considerable art indeed. And it is, for most of us, more useful as a model, whether as writers or human beings, than the lofty heights of the world's ten greatest books. Few of us are called to write such books, any more than we are called to be heroes or saints. But we are all called to be human. Yuan Mei was, and is, intensely human, and Arthur Waley's humane sympathy and literary skill make that humanity accessible to us. I wish every American poet would read this book and ponder it long. The poems are beautiful, the biography is absorbing—but most of all, the "lessons" it has to teach, both literary and moral, are precisely those which cost the most when purchased in the open market of hard knocks.

WILLIAM BLAKE

In the splendor of his innocence and irascibility, Blake sits naked under the arbor in his back yard, discoursing to his wife, Kate, of Powers and Emanations. Before him pass the ghosts of St. Just, Danton, Marat, Robespierre, Hébart, to be judged by his integrity. He was really all the French Revolution that England ever had. In fact, except for Shelley and a brief flurry in the adolescence of the country-house and UNESCO set, he is just about all the revolutionary poet England ever had, of any kind. It was John Wesley who gave symbolic form to middle-class revolt in England. Methodism was England's Jacobinism. Blake's revolution might be called the shadow side of the one across the Channel. The French enthroned the goddess Reason. Blake hypostatized the nonrational forces of the soul. They looked forward to a Utopia of contractual relations and delegated authority. He spoke for the integral person, the pure act, the vital relationship which Buber was to call "I and thou."

Following the ill-informed snobbery of T. S. Eliot a lot of nonsense has been written about Blake's lack of tradition, about how he made up his system as he went along. It has been dutifully repeated in most reviews of this book. Nothing could be less true. Mr. Eliot's tradition goes back to Aquinas as interpreted in the pages of *L'Action Française*. Blake's goes back to the Memphite Theology and the Pyramid Texts. It is the tradition of organized heterodoxy. It is all there, from the millennia-old Doctrine of Emanations to the current fantasies of the Neo-Druids. True, the heterodox have always thought of themselves as possessed of a kind of factual knowledge. They called themselves Gnostics. Actually, Blake or Hermes Trismegismus, this is the art of providing the heart with images of its alienation. If the individual or society can project the dilemmas which reason cannot cope with, they can be controlled if not mastered. This was Blake's function. He saw the oncoming Business Civilization and prepared

The Letters of William Blake. Edited by Geoffrey Keynes. Macmillan, New York, 1957.

a refuge, a symbolic fortress and haven. The dramatis personae of his *Prophetic Books* are of relatively little importance. Fundamentally he accomplished his mission by being a certain kind of person. And he did succeed. Shorn of its paraphernalia of myth, we call it Romanticism. Blake was really the first mythographer of Romanticism. It is no accident that the German philosophic fathers of the movement were to look back to the very similar Jakob Boehme. And Blake's judgment stands unaltered, whether in Baudelaire's wounded soldier unable to budge under the heap of the dead, or Dickens with his pure Blakean outraged innocence caught in the dark Satanic mills.

Because Blake was above all else the kind of person he was, his letters are of primary importance. Like most letters by most poets they are mostly taken up with efforts to get money. Exceptionally among British poets, Blake was genuinely poor—not very poor, but poor enough. The poverty of the British Romantic poets is seen from the point of view of the caste of literary gentlemen—the rectory, The Reform Club, the halls of Balliol. Keats was not really poor, but most unlearned people are under the impression that even Shelley was. Blake needed money all the time, just to live, and had to work to get it, at a trade. It was this independence from the caste patterns of his day that preserved his innocence and hence his rage and hence the validity of his judgment. What Blake's letters give you is the anatomy of uninvolvement. They should, and never will, be taught in schools, but they are pondered, I hope, in a school not built with human hands.

STEPHEN CRANE

In 1952 Columbia University Library acquired the immense mass of Stephen Crane papers which for fifty-two years had been in the hands of his wife, her heirs and other private persons, and were, until then, unknown to scholarship. All

The Poetry of Stephen Crane. By Daniel G. Hoffman. Columbia University Press, New York, 1957.

this material was at the disposal of Mr. Daniel G. Hoffman, and for this reason his *The Poetry of Stephen Crane* represents a very considerable advance over the earlier biographies of Thomas Beer and John Berryman. Beer infused his own intense and rather peculiar personality into everything he wrote, while Berryman has a number of psychological theories to demonstrate. Hoffman's book is considerably more judicious and evenly balanced.

Most of all, the perspectives opened up by the new papers, some of them of great intimacy, reveal whole new depths—and shallows—of Crane's personality, without the aid of any special psychologizing. Daniel Hoffman handles every aspect of Crane, as writer and man; his revolt from his family, his mastering of his craft, his philosophical beliefs (such as they were), his attitudes and responses to love and sex and marriage and the special and peculiar significance he gave to war. The book ends with three chapters of detailed literary analysis and evaluation, and finally, there is an appendix of the hitherto uncollected poems which are not given in the text. This, I should say, is about as full-dress a treatment as the somewhat slender shoulders of Stephen Crane can bear. He wasn't the world's greatest writer, and it is difficult to imagine much more in him than Hoffman has dug out. He weighs carefully all the possibilities of influence of decadentism, symbolism and realism stemming from France, or pervasively in the air at the end of the nineteenth century and, rightly I think, rejects them as not being important, let alone determinative. In Hoffman's opinion Crane was an essentially, characteristically American writer. This is certainly right. He was not just natively, but really self derived, and his problems, and their artistic resolution, were the problems so typical of the American writers of the end of the century—and of American philosophy, as exemplified in William James, for instance.

The central problem, from which all the others stem, is of course the problem of isolation—of the self as an entity, of the individual, first in the world, then in society, and finally even, in love, and in the great crucial rites of passage that give life its shape: birth, coming of age, love, vocation, death, events that all cohesive cultures, in darkest Africa as well as in the Catholic Church, mark with sacraments.

Daniel Hoffman is hard put to cope with the barbarism, the journalese of Crane's style. The inescapable fact is that he was a pretty vulgar writer. And he was vulgar because he wasn't cultured—not in the sense of being high-toned, or being able to tell Guardi from Canaletto—but in the way a Hopi Indian is cultured. Stephen Crane seemed to everyone who knew him to be marked for early death. It was not simply illness—he literally was not at home in the world. It was the terrible poignancy of his aloneness which made him a valuable writer, not any felicities of his style, for they did not exist. Behind irony and sympathy, the battlefields of Stendhal and Tolstoi, are theaters of wisdom, but there is no wisdom in *The Red Badge of Courage*, just lostness. The acute imagism of the poems is due to the hyperaesthesia of incurable isolation—each image appears as though it were a brightly lit hallucination shining in the darkness of a prison cell.

Even the adolescent "philosophy" is simply an attempt to organize the counsels of desperation. Poe, Whitman, Emily Dickinson, Hawthorne, Thoreau, Mark Twain, Ambrose Bierce —what a lot of lonely people! Always the question is the same: "Is anybody out there?" No one can understand William James or Peirce who thinks Pragmatism is an attempt to answer the epistemological dilemma. It was a personal mystery of the self and the other which beset those men. And this separation still haunts American literature, still produces, whether in B. Traven or Nelson Algren, Wallace Stevens or Allen Ginsberg, work of piercing significance. Amy Lowell looked to Crane's poetry for the sources of imagistic precision. She found a clumsy and slightly vulgar writer. But Crane, while it is true that he was not a great writer, was a good one, like F. Scott Fitzgerald, another lonely barbarian. He was a good writer almost because of his faults. It was not any fancied inheritance from Jules Laforgue, later to be passed on to T. S. Eliot; Daniel Hoffman shows that nothing like this existed. It was his own terribly moving folly and innocence and wrath which redeemed him.

VACHEL LINDSAY

This is a sad book. It is a life of Vachel Lindsay, and Vachel Lindsay had a very sad life. What makes it even sadder is the realization that all his heartbreaking expense of spirit was far too dear a price to pay for his poetry. His poetry was not very good. Approximately thirty poets of what might be called "anthology rank" have committed suicide in the United States since the beginning of this century. It is one of the commonest causes of death among poets. Most of these suicides have not been nonconformists, oddities, evil livers; most of them have been exactly the opposite—"dreamers of the American Dream," like Lindsay. Many have been quite conventional people, middle-class, socially acceptable and rather dull.

Lindsay was a sort of Whitman of the high-school assemblies. He took Whitman's dream of a utopian society, emerging from the enlightenment of the Founding Fathers, and the storm and stress of the radical eccentrics of the revolutionary Forties, and turned it into something folksy, a bigger and better and sweeter Hometown. He took Whitman's sonorous verse and turned it into tub-thumping circus music. High-school assemblies and women's clubs loved it. For a generation he was the favorite American poet of the *London Mercury*; he was exactly the loud barbarian whom John Squire wanted to exhibit to the world as the perfect poetic voice of America—he was made to order for Bloomsbury ethnocentrism.

Perhaps they were right. He was certainly typical of the hometown that produced him and that he always believed hated and feared and snubbed him. Today, I suppose, he

The West-going Heart. By Eleanor Ruggles. W. W. Norton, New York, 1959.

would be a mildly rightish liberal, a common-sense New Dealer. In his own time he was an accurate reflection of Midwest Populism. His best poem is written to Governor Altgeld: "Sleep softly, . . . eagle forgotten, . . . under the stone, . . ." As far as I know, he never wrote one to the Chicago anarchists whom Altgeld pardoned, nor even a little one to Gene Debs. He did write an innocent hero-worshiping dithyramb to William Jennings Bryan. It isn't much as a poem, but it is an accurate picture of the enraptured Middle West that thrilled to Bryan's cross-of-gold speech and his flamboyant and treacherous leadership. I suppose Lindsay looked on his "The Congo" as an epic of the Negro people. Today it seems ridden with chauvinism and it is a brave soul who would "put it on" in a high-school assembly in the civilized parts of the country.

That is it. Vachel Lindsay was hopelessly naïve, more naïve than Carol Kennicott in *Main Street*. It is true that the Founding Fathers and the enthusiasts and screwballs of the Forties had dreamed a great dream. It is even possible that that dream may some day in some measure come true. But in the first quarter of this century in the middle classes of Middle Western towns it had become pretty confused and sentimental.

Yet Lindsay knew better too, at least at times. One part of him was drawn off into what has since become Chamber of Commerce local patriotism and social service; but another smaller part of him knew better. I doubt that it was the conflicting pull of these two tendencies that broke him apart —I think he killed himself from personal troubles and illness (he was an epileptic who feared and even refused to admit his disease), augmented by the manifest evils of the lecture circuit that was almost his sole source of money. But the conflict was there and he knew it, and even if his was a vulgarized version of the vulgarly called "American Dream," it was infinitely less vulgar than the waking realization of that dream he saw always about him. Naïve, yes—who else would write a poem called "Why I Voted the Socialist

Ticket"? Naïve, but terribly sincere. By the time Lindsay swallowed Lysol it had begun to look as though there would never be any place in the world again for that naïveté and that sincerity, and that simple, even folksy, social vision.

Eleanor Ruggles has done what the reviewers call a thoroughly workmanlike job; the whole picture of Lindsay is here and he isn't too much inflated or sentimentalized. This was his life, and possibly its telling is another documented answer to the question, "Why have thirty poets of anthology rank committed suicide in the United States since 1900?"

ROBINSON JEFFERS

This book on Robinson Jeffers by Radcliffe Squires is what is known as a labor of love, as well as a tour de force. In recent years Jeffers' stock has fallen. For an entire literary generation it might be said to have plummeted and still be plummeting. He still has considerable popular following, but I believe that too is waning. Many years ago his only serious rival to the title of "California's leading poet" wrote an essay on him in the *Hound and Horn,* later substantially reprinted in the book *In Defense of Reason.* It was one of the most devastating attacks in modern criticism and Jeffers' reputation, then at its height, never recovered, but entered a slow decline. Today young people simply do not read him. Few young poets of my acquaintance have ever opened one of his books, and know only the anthology pieces which, I am afraid, they dislike. This is true even in San Francisco, where I live, and where Jeffers once had a large following. Now Mr. Winters' point of view was a sort of secular Thomism—at least it was rigorously classical—but these young people are not at all so motivated. They would be much more likely to prefer the Romanticism for which Jeffers is supposed to stand. But they do not.

The Loyalties of Robinson Jeffers. By Radcliffe Squires. University of Michigan Press, Ann Arbor, 1956.

Puzzling over how I could write this review and hurt a minimum of feelings, I have tried the verse novels and dramas on several literary friends of the present generation. All thought them ridiculous. I myself manfully have tried to return to them with an open mind, but I like them even less than when I first read them. I have read Mr. Squires with care and taken strict note of every item in his argument, his attempt to rehabilitate Jeffers as a poet and to present him as a serious thinker. I am totally unconvinced. In my opinion the verse is shoddy and pretentious and the philosophizing is nothing but posturing. I say this with distaste. I do not like to put down a colleague and a fellow Californian. Many friends of mine of my own or a slightly older generation, leading poets and critics of poetry, still like Jeffers. Some even think he is great. I simply cannot see it. His reworkings of the plots of Greek tragedy make me shudder at their vulgarity, the coarsening of sensibility, the cheapening of the language and the tawdriness of the paltry insight into the great ancient meanings. His lyrics and reveries of the California landscape seem to me to suffer in almost every line from the most childish laboring of the pathetic fallacy, elevated to a very system of response. This is the sort of sensibility which calls a sunset "a picture no artist could paint." His philosophy I find a mass of contradictions—high-flown statements indulged in for their melodrama alone, and often essentially meaningless. The constantly repeated gospel that it is better to be a rock than a man is simply an unscrupulous use of language. "Better," "is," "man," "rock," are used to promulgate an emotional falsehood, but they are also used with no regard whatever for their actual meanings. This is sentimentality in the sense defined in Malachi Mulligan's famous telegram, "The sentimentalist is he who would enjoy without incurring the immense debtorship for a thing done. Signed, Stephen."

I am afraid that Mr. Squires' case is not proved. He has labored long and hard to endow Robinson Jeffers with a coherent philosophy. He has searched the whose corpus of his work for lines that will pass muster as respectable verse. He fails. He does not seem to realize that poetic license does not mean the permission of intellectual dishonesty. In a typical passage he says, "It is easy to find fault with Spengler's history, to point to the dogmatism, the weakness of arguing from analogy, the oracular mysticism. These faults may in poetry be virtues." I think it would be hard to make many statements about poetry that would be less true. This question points up the basic flaw of the whole case. You can't make an intellectual silk purse out of fustian rodomontade. As for Mr. Squires' examples of Jeffers' poetic gems, the less said the better. To me they sound like the rhetoric of a Southern State Representative. I write this with acute awareness that people I respect will disagree and that, as the old woman said, there's no accounting for taste.

WALLACE STEVENS

Wallace Stevens was a great favorite with the wives of mediocre poets. "What do you mean," they'd say, "you can't stand it another year at Corncrake College? Next year you'll be an assistant professor, and besides, look at Wallace Stevens; he's head of a big insurance company and it don't interfere with *his* creativity. He's the American Laforgue and Valéry together. What more do you want?"

Now I don't much like either Laforgue or Valéry, but he wasn't. The terrible truth to tell, Stevens wrote precisely like an insurance executive. He is a philosophical poet, the Higher Critics notwithstanding—it is what he talks about that is important, not the way he says it. But it is hard to say whether it is better to call his philosophy Santayana civilized and interpreted by the Harvard Business School, or the metaphysical weighing of life's actuarial contingencies—"Animalism and Skeptic Faith," the philosophy of the securely arrived

Opus Posthumous. By Wallace Stevens. Alfred A. Knopf, New York, 1957.

businessman in one of the more dignified fields of money-making.

So many American businessmen are insecure that we forget that they aren't all Babbitts. After all, Henry Adams was a businessman of sorts; he certainly didn't live by the sale of his labor power. The pencil factory kept the wolf from Thoreau's door. Country bankers who can quote Leonidas or Toulet in the original tongue, insurance brokers who collect the minor Mannerists—there are plenty of them in New England to this day, even if there are few in Gopher Prairie. If Rimbaud was the poetic analogue of Walker the Filibuster or Cecil Rhodes, Stevens was the analogue of himself—vice-president of a safe and sane insurance company.

Don't misunderstand me; there is nothing wrong with being a business executive. In the heyday of Chinese civilization all sorts of bureaucrats, merchants and generals were very great poets, and in this demoralized time both Mao Tse-tung and Wang Ching-wei have been among the handful of excellent contemporary Chinese poets. America would be a far less naughty land if the custom would spread in the upper echelons of the Power Elite.

That is one of the points about Wallace Stevens. He wasn't in the Power Elite. His line was insurance. He stood quietly on the sidelines and took bets from the Power Elite on the chances of their meeting with disaster or the consequences of their folly. That is what his poetry says. Never believe for an instant that it has anything to do with the seven types of ambiguity and the pure, aesthetic, self-contained systems of his Higher Critic expositors. "Knowing and being are one," "reality is an activity of the most august imagination," "only in man's definitions of himself, only encompassed in humanity, is he himself." Always, in every poem, Wallace Stevens struggled to catch and hold and keep and be true to the simplest animal wisdom and hence the most human and humane—the profound skepticism of the organism that acts in perfect confidence.

He emphatically does not resemble Laforgue—an envious

carbuncular tutor in an ill-fitting collar—but he does curiously resemble the only actual American Symbolist, the best American poet of the twenty-five years before the First World War—Stuart Merrill, anarchist, good liver, skeptic and quiet dandy, who wrote only in French. However, if Stevens ever shared Merrill's desire to cut a swath (Merrill was a bit of a Stanford White), he disciplined it away. One thing he had above all else was good taste, the kind that is so good that nobody notices it. He too might have been happier, back in 1920 at least, writing in French. I am sure he never considered doing so, but if he had, I am certain he would have rejected the idea as too ostentatious, as bad form—all right for a Virginian like Merrill, but not done in Connecticut.

This collection contains some paraphrases of Léon Paul Fargue, another *bon vivant* with immense hidden reserves of power, and perhaps the only French poet since Jammes who was thoroughly likeable as a man. Had he not been a businessman, Stevens might well have been very exactly the American Léon Paul Fargue. To anyone who loves Fargue as I do the kinship is an obvious and happy one. I think Fargue is the better poet, perhaps ultimately because he was poor and spent most of his time in hotel rooms and on café terraces. Fargue was a fat man, he looked and acted a little like a French Ford Madox Ford, but he was a sly and wily poet. Stevens weighed less, but there was always a trace of fat about his heart, a debilitating security, and in his later years his agility and mischievousness seemed a shade forced.

I guess it is true that compromise tells, even for one whose very philosophy of life, whose very aesthetics of creation, is based on the axiom that life, action, thought, are themselves compromise. Certainly Stevens never, in a long and very distinguished career, came up to the high point from which he started in his first book, *Harmonium.* That little book sold only a few copies, but it hit my generation with an unforgettable impact. *The Waste Land* may have made more noise, but when it was over, it left only a pose. *Har-*

monium left wisdom—its own rather privileged kind of wisdom, but real nonetheless. I suppose the wisdom is riper in the late poems in this book; it is certainly very ripe, but the poetic excitement is a good deal less and sometimes is lacking altogether. Of course the mass of unpublished poems and prose of a lifetime is bound to include some things which were left unpublished for good reason. Considering this, the collection is less diffuse than might be expected. Many of the later poems are deeply moving, but they are, by and large, put together with what is called quiet mastery, one of art's less exciting characteristics. Once in a great while this quiet assurance envelops you in its own very special mystery, the mystery of animalism and skeptic faith:

A Child Asleep in Its Own Life

Among the old men that you know,
There is one, unnamed, that broods
On all the rest, in heavy thought.

They are nothing, except in the universe
Of that single mind. He regards them
Outwardly and knows them inwardly,

The sole emperor of what they are,
Distant, yet close enough to wake
The chords above your bed tonight.

This may not have the bravura and pomp of "The Only Emperor of Ice Cream" but it is no mean thing to have written, secure and successful and past seventy.

EDITH SITWELL

Edith Sitwell is the nearest thing to a major poet that the British Isles have produced since Hardy, Lawrence and

Collected Poems. By Edith Sitwell. Vanguard, New York, 1954.

Yeats. With the exception of Hugh McDiarmid she is now the only British poet who possesses that special accent of both individuality and scope which makes a writer a member of world literature. Possibly this is because, like the others, she is both intensely national, even local—in her case "county," if you will—and yet aware in a living way of the literature of the whole civilized community, its problems, its ambitions, its disasters.

It is all too common nowadays in the modern academy to talk of Edith Sitwell as though she didn't mean anything, as though her poetry was just art. Few poets have had more to say or said it more explicitly, even didactically.

She introduces her *Collected Poems* with a preface which doesn't help matters much. I have never known whether the prefaces poets write to their books are deliberately designed to mislead or are just written to give the professors something to talk about in Mod. Eng. Lit. 176493 B. She is very fascinated by, but hardly cognizant of, her own metrical practices. She describes herself in great detail as exactly what she is not—a mellifluous metrist. If she did the sort of thing she says she does, she would be about as good a poet as R. L. Stevenson, who wrote similar analyses of his own verses—rather better because his verses resembled his analyses.

What Edith Sitwell really wrote in the period when she made her reputation is a tense, inspired and highly sophisticated doggerel of the sort invented by Goethe and practiced so whimsically in our day by W. H. Auden. Most of all in her young days she was like Laforgue—the French poet no writer of verse in English seems to be able to outgrow—a curious problem in comparative literature with which some academician should concern himself.

In the poems of the first twenty years the people are made of chemicals, with bric-a-brac emotions, the vegetation is of glass, and everybody including the painted sun and the omnipresent ducks bleats and blats and quacks and rushes blindly about dressed in stereotyped costumes of the Italian comedy. Laforgue taught Pierrot to talk like a moony upstart—

Julien Sorel in his frayed cuffs. Edith Sitwell's Pierrots moan like donkeys, her Harlequins sob like bitterns, her Columbine giggles like a basket of breaking eggs. It all runs by clockwork.

French poetry before Apollinaire, and Edith Sitwell's with it, was a shocked cry of protest against the mechanization of life itself. Her early books may all be frightfully chic and so like glittering shop windows of tinsel and dummies and commodities. This wasn't what is called in American universities a value-neuter statement. Two generations of her fans who have been developed by the fashion magazines would be scandalized to know that what the poems say is that she doesn't like it that way at all.

The consumptive glitter and rattle may have been the latest thing from France, but the moral earnestness was British, "to the core," as they say—that earnest, moral, British core. Edith Sitwell may be a Dame and Osbert Sitwell may have been Reader to the late King. Still they saw the Thames-side garden parties, which they graced with their aristocratic eccentricities, and where the aging lions roared over the tea things, like nothing so much as the slaughter fests that ushered in and out the reigns of savage kings in Ashanti on the African Gold Coast. In fact, "Gold Coast Customs" is the best poem of social criticism written between Patrick MacGill and Joy Davidman. The only thing to compare with it is Hilaire Belloc's "The Rebel." As Aristotle said, you have to be an aristocrat or a reactionary to write a good proletarian poem.

There was a long period while the world drifted into political terrorism and war when Edith Sitwell wrote little verse. To judge from her prose works, she seems to have spent her time reorganizing her sensibility in terms of the deepest meanings of the English poetic tradition—far deeper meanings than the loose talk about the Mermaid Classics which passes for traditionalism in fashionable literary circles. War and the final catastrophe produced, to use Toynbee's term, the return from this withdrawal. So far Edith Sitwell had been little more than a feminine Laforgue from an old county family. Her later poems have absorbed the systematically deranged world of Rimbaud, the madness of Lautréamont, the ghoulish, rebus-picture fables of the Surrealists, all the insanity and agony of the modern world, the apocalypse of the morning paper.

In addition, they have an entirely different metric—a solemn music, lissome and weary, that owes much to her brother, Sacheverell Sitwell. Behind the vision, behind the new virtuosity, is something rare in modern verse, so artistic and so neutral: the moral earnestness that makes English poetry great and that made "*Hugo, hélas!*" Gide's "only major French poet."

Arnold is not to be despised as an ancestor, nor Sir Thomas Browne. A low sad music of mortality, a far less naïve "Dover Beach," is perhaps the most fitting idiom for what is no longer the human predicament, but something far worse. Back in the days of bombardment, when we read the terrifying line, "And then out danced the babioun," we may have thought she meant Hitler. She meant the human heart, frivolous, bestial and corrupt. Behind the still, sad music sounds the anguish of urgent responsibility and the cold dread of utter helplessness.

Always there were gardens in the early poems. The last in the book come back to gardens—no longer painted gardens peopled with polychrome chessmen and playing-card kings and queens, but gardens on Atlantis and the outer planets—unknown fluids for atmospheres, animals of light and death, foliage black as interstellar night. The burden: night has come to stay and we are failing; hope and faith are long gone; only love is left—love which is the daughter of compassion and magnanimity.

Seated here at Trimalchio's banquet in 1955, these are good words for the human race to hear. Life is incurably tragic, no more so, but certainly no less, now that we hold the end of the world and the failure of man in our most venal hands.

. . . that ghost of Abel whispers o'er the world,
"Brother, I come.
I have no eyes
But my all seeing wounds, and I am dumb,
But yet from all the open mouths of the world's wounds
  I rise,
I come to testify."

and in the last words in the book:

If every grain of my dust should be a Satan—
If every atom of my heart were a Lucifer—
If every drop of my blood were an Abaddon
—Yet should I love.

CARL SANDBURG

Everybody loved Carl Sandburg in our town. Nobody knows where he went. What ever happened to the author of the best poems in *Chicago Poems, Smoke and Steel, Cornhusker*? Whatever happened to the friend of dynamiters and grifters and whores, factory girls and icemen and broken-footed cops? The very indigene, the aboriginal of the prairie cornfields and the slums of Chicago, the one poet who started out absolutely right. The guy who came by the right answer naturally. What happened to him?

There has been a lot of speculation, but I think I know: the First World War; Chicago journalism. Sandburg was, it is startling to realize now, the youngest and last of the apostles of an utterly irreducible grass-roots libertarianism. Debs was the greatest, the most noble and tragic—but there were others of all degrees of intransigence and compromise: Clarence Darrow, Oscar Ameringer, Brann the Iconoclast, even William Jennings Bryan, that bag of spoiled grape juice.

The Sandburg Range. By Carl Sandburg. Harcourt Brace, New York, 1957.

Spontaneous agrarian socialism—the Greencorn Rebellion, straight out of Rosa Luxemburg. Josiah Warren, who preceded Prudhon, and who really made funny money work; Jim Buchanan, the last head of the First International, the Kansas railroad man who led the first great railroad strike; Bill Haywood; Parsons—they are the heroes of the years when it seemed, at least to a million or so people, that the fate of American society hung in the balance. They are all the heroes I ever had.

I can't make a hero of Sandburg. Programmatically, he is absolutely sound. His poetry was rooted in real speech, in folksongs and lore, in real people, with never the slip of literature showing, always tied to a concrete situation and event, distinguishing itself fundamentally and all along the line from the English tradition and diction, so foreign to the Middle West of Swedish harvest hands and French *voyageurs*. No one, not even Whitman, has ever embarked on an American literary career with sounder ideas and better intentions. What happened? The war; the Red Raids; Normalcy. The perfection of that monstrous hallucination piped into every head from Madison Avenue—The American Way of Life. Sandburg fell for it. When Debs went to prison, he lay doggo. I remember so clearly the Whitman Memorial dinner with Darrow in the chair, shortly after the war. Carl was to read a poem which "would make clear his position on the war." It was the poem to the Unknown Soldier which later appeared in *Slabs of the Sunburnt West*. After it was over, Darrow, slouchy and disheveled, growled to us youngsters, eager for the word: "It ain't enough." It wasn't. At that point Sandburg gave up all those clear bright people, Anna Imroth and Chick Lorimer and Inez Mullholland and J. B. McNamara and Billy Sunday, real sweatshop fires, real baseball games between the Chillicothe and Rock Island teams, for a sweet muddy abstraction, "The People." The sentimentality of the police-court reporter which had given his work the pathos of actuality overwhelmed him. He became the victim of his own formulas and evasions. Compare "I Am the People, The

Mob" with *The People, Yes.* It's enough to make you weep. In the early poem you see so clearly behind the abstraction the stark individuals of the other poems in *Chicago Poems.* Behind the second "*People*" is only mush, or at best the amorphous mass out beyond the lecture platform. It is a terrible pity, but after about 1925 there is nothing of value. Since most of the prose comes after that, Sandburg the historian, novelist, autobiographer, writer of children's stories simply does not exist for literature. I suppose the last thing was the *Songbag.* But the time would come when Sandburg would sing in the chorus of "Sam Hall," "Gol durn your eyes!" But as Spiridovna or somebody said of some lost Russian leader, "We had his youth."

ROY CAMPBELL

Roy Campbell was hardly a writer at all. He was a professional personality, a rowdy bully and creator of scenes. For many years he was a source of diminishing amusement and dismay around Bohemian London. We live in a society beset by many evils, some of them probably fatal. Our literature is ruled by cliques and swept by fashions, both equally silly and ephemeral. What passes for poetry in many circles of the literary bon ton is empty, pretentious, academic stuff indeed. What passes for criticism is often worse. We have lived for over a generation in a farce where poets are the dupes and puppets of politicians. All too true. I suppose it is salutory to have this all said, no matter who says it. Or is it? As Milosz has pointed out, negative criticism of Western society is shooting fish in a barrel—and more fun. Anybody can do it. Mr. Eliot and M. Valéry have been very critical of bourgeois values.

Roy Campbell belonged to that small school of swashbucklers who were very vociferously "on the other side." He fought in Spain—for Franco. He had nothing but praise

Collected Poems. By Roy Campbell. Henry Regnery, Chicago, 1957-60.

for totalitarianism until it became dangerous to praise it too loudly. He was all for plain verse that cats and dogs could understand and that scanned and rhymed. He was an obsessive anti-Semite. He liked to kill bulls. But most of all he liked to kick up a row. His ideas were all outrageous, and they did not have the excuse that they issued from a government hospital for the insane. But they were more than that—they were tawdry and cheaply antihumane. He didn't only despise Einstein, I am sure he despised Erasmus . . . or Florence Nightingale.

So too, his verse. I am all for simple, sensuous and passionate utterance. I am sure Racine had a good idea when he read his stuff to his cook and rejected what she couldn't understand. I think *The Bible in Basic* reads just fine, although I still prefer the King James. But this is not the verse of William Barnes, or Toulet, or Robert Frost, or whoever you like who writes simply. It is doggerel. It is not conscious doggerel, of the type Goethe or Heine once wrote, and Mr. Auden sometimes uses so skillfully today. It is just plain doggerel. Not even like Robert W. Service (a much better poet with somewhat similar tastes in life if not in politics). What distinguishes it is its persistent, insistent ill-temper. This has given Campbell a reputation as a satirist. To most vulgar people, Pope sounds like doggerel, and abuse sounds like satire. But this just means that there are a lot of people in the world like Roy Campbell—a lot of very coarse-grained people with tin ears. They just haven't worked it out in a political theory and they don't have a facility for rather clumsy rhyming, but there are lots and lots of people every bit as vulgar. Ill-temper is not satire. Ill-temper is not "savage indignation." As you can learn in any manual of the seven sins from a tract case, righteous wrath is not the sin of anger. Rocking-horse couplets that go bump at the end are not "skillful verse in the great traditions of English Poesy." You can't learn that in any manual. In the long run it requires sensibility to tell Campbell from Kipling.

That brings up a necessary comparison of Campbell and better poets with whom he might easily be confused. Hilaire

Belloc and Oliver St. John Gogarty were professional belligerents and by and large they were usually "on the other side." They wrote conventionally structured verse about all the old-time great themes. They wrote a great deal of satire and some very funny epigrams and limericks. Belloc was a very good poet indeed. His verse is actually extremely subtly put together; his ideas, in the days when he thought them up, were original, and underneath his bluster was a powerful, magnanimous mind. Gogarty was in every way a lesser man. He was corny and sentimental, like an Irish barfly, but like so many barflies, he was very winning sometimes, and he had a great way with the ladies. There is no magnanimity whatever in Campbell, and less charm. The first requisites for satire are greatness of soul, and a certain iron-fisted charm. Dryden is greater than Pope for this reason. Pope was neurasthenic and tinkles. Dryden saw life vastly and he resounds like an iron gong. Campbell sounds like somebody being thrown out of a pub or a Bolshevik meeting in Brooklyn in 1936. What moves us in Sam Johnson or Juvenal is their manifest nobility of soul and purpose. We feel they have the right to speak. They were both born with this right and earned it. Catullus and Martial may have been born with less, but we know they have earned more, and very painfully. And all these people wrote beautiful, beautiful verse.

There is no vestige of these in Roy Campbell. He early learned that the British—inveterate bird watchers and amateur entomologists—will buy anything odd. In a nation of polite snobs he made a career of being a rude boor. When the innocent intellectuals trooped out of Oxford and Cambridge and the London School of Economics after the brassy parade of one totalitarianism, he, not in innocence, but cynically, beat the drum for the other one. It's that simple. Had he been able to grow two heads, or at least four ears, he would have been even more successful. The islanders would have said, "What jolly fun!" and lined up for tickets, until they grew bored and newer oddities invaded Bartholomew Fair.

There is a great evil here. It wasn't Bartholomew Fair at

all. The Spanish War, the Moscow Trials, the extermination camps, Hiroshima—these are not side shows in Bloomsbury, literary freak fights staged in Russell Square. They are terrible tragedies in which the soul of man was wrung like a hangman's rope. I don't really care if Roy Campbell made Stephen Spender blush at a cocktail party. And I feel dirtied reading about it.

ANTONIO MACHADO

It is good that a representative collection of Antonio Machado's poems has appeared in English. The present generation, only moderately well informed at best, knows Spain and Spanish culture only as the field of terrible battles and devastating agonies and betrayals, of men in arms or of the forces within the human heart. In writing, even that is almost gone and the official literature consists mostly of the *grimoires* of bureaucratic piety, while the great exiles seldom rise above their heartbreaking homesickness. García Lorca is the perfect symbol of the decades of disaster, the hero of the Spanish *Nibelungenlied,* not just because he was martyred by a spasm of senseless and anonymous folly, but because he himself was in many ways the most perfect expression of the night side of Spanish culture. The baroque vertigo of Berneri's St. Theresa, the frightening confidences of St. John of the Cross, the careful analysis of the psychology of Spanish terror in the Netherlands of Bosch and Brueghel, all these are aspects of the traditional Spanish character which flow together in the *Angst* and *Gestalt* and *beget* of García Lorca and give his poetry its special relevance to the world after Hiroshima. Black Spain, it is usually called. I doubt if this is the right historical attribution. It was the Goths who produced the Nibelungen Spirit, not the Moors, who especially in Spain seem to have been eminently urbane. Anyway, this

Eighty Poems. By Antonio Machado. Translated by Willis Barnstone. Las Americas, New York, 1959.

dark world certainly exists, and certainly seems most appropriate and Spanish in our own still darker time.

But the silliness of the Hemingways notwithstanding, there is far more to Spanish culture than this. Sancho Panza, the humanist on a donkey, was only interested in avoiding death in the afternoon. No gold-braided, black-velvet britches could ever entice him into a bull ring. In no other country did the intellectuals so early diagnose the twentieth century's onrushing pandemic of dehumanization. In no other country have the solid, irrefrangible glories of sensually verifiable objectivity—and I use six redundancies advisably—been so central, so steadily held at the heart of life. Erasmus, Montaigne, Rabelais, Cervantes . . . who is the greater humanist? Although his life was disorderly, unsuccessful, even romantic, Cervantes wrote with the happy confidence of one who knew his side is bound to win. With the debacle of the end of the nineteenth century, the men of Machado's generation knew that the humanism for which they stood was very likely to lose forever. This constant awareness of doom gave them all a classic nobility, like the heroes of Plutarch. Machado never lost this grandeur. Dying in exile, everything that he valued in Spain reduced to slavery and ruins, his poetry retained its old calmness and order, the kind of formal magnanimity spread abroad by the shattered Parthenon.

More than any other poet of the Spanish resurgence after '98, Machado was part of world literature. This is obvious even in his most patent influences. What other Latin poet was influenced by Japanese poetry? Who else so well pared away the fancy core of symbolism to reveal the hard Imagistic core? Who else in Spain so completely freed himself from the cloying decadentism of Rubén Darío? Who else was so well able to return, unreservedly, to the pure bright irony of the folk *cancioneros*, the troubadour verse in Gallician and Catalan? Mistral is plain dull. Pound's Old Englyshe Tea Shoppe jargon is ridiculous, and his Pre-Raphaelite neurasthenia is at the opposite pole from the Provençal sensibility. For Machado, William of Aquitaine spoke with the wisdom of the heart—or, if you prefer, of the loins and belly. Clarity, objectivity, humanity—these were Machado's virtues to a most eminent degree, virtues he shared with the greatest poet of his period, Francis Jammes. Like Jammes, who was after all, in medieval terms a Navarrese, Machado is the poet of a way of life which has changed little and only grown each millennium more humane since the end of the Stone Age—the Mediterranean way of life which is all some people think our race of man has to show for six thousand years in Western Europe. The poetry of Machado always calls to mind for me a lunch which Marthe and I ate on our honeymoon, on the honey-colored floor of the big temple at Paestum—wine in a goatskin, bread like the Greek loaves in the casts at Pompeii, olive oil, olives, pickled squid, figs, honey—and the wine-dark sea, very bright and white that day, filling half the sky like a silver shield. Machado is dead, but that life goes on, as it went on in Iberian Spain, in the Phoenician and Greek settlements, in the Roman province, corrupting the Visigoths, flowering in the Caliphate of Cordova, and certainly still there, never to be obliterated by any poppinjay in a bemedaled uniform or any madman in a black robe.

BROTHER ANTONINUS

Here is a book of direct statements, overwhelming in their intensity. Most poetry of direct statement is Imagistic, "Objectivist," about things. These poems are simple statements about subjective experience. They are about the agonies and triumphs of a complete spiritual transformation. The easiest drama in the world to turn into melodrama is the drama that goes on inside yourself. It is terribly hard to be modest and honest about the most important inner experiences, especially if you sit down to write a book about them, most

The Crooked Lines of God, Poems 1949-54. By Brother Antoninus. University of Detroit Press, 1959.

especially if they have been difficult, even tortured experiences.

Brother Antoninus (William Everson "in the world") has had a hard life, interiorly speaking. He has come through a lot of agony to present peace. Honesty, simplicity, modesty, complete commitment to communication—these are the outstanding virtues of good poetry in any case. In the telling of a spiritual odyssey of the sort Brother Antoninus has traveled these ten years since his last book, *The Residual Years,* they make all the difference. They make, in fact, a collection of poems of stunning impact, utterly unlike anything else being written nowadays.

Brother Antoninus is a real monk, not a pseudo-Zen panhandler, but an oblate of the Order of Preachers. His poems are the record of grueling struggle to prepare himself for vision. Anybody can have an ecstasy, but the ecstasies which are crowned with vision are the fulfillment of the very ordinary process of being good. It is only too obvious why the Ancient and Inscrutable East with its drugs and gymnastics is so popular with our amateur visionaries—"Ship me somewheres East of Suez . . . where there are'nt no Ten Commandments," said Kipling.

As far as his verse is concerned, Brother Antoninus is more or less a disciple of Robinson Jeffers, but I think he has made a harder and more honest instrument of it than his master.

The book is published by the University of Detroit Press, but it was printed in superlative beauty by Brother Antoninus himself, on his own hand press.

DENISE LEVERTOV

In my opinion Denise Levertov is incomparably the best poet of what is getting to be known as the new avant-garde. This may sound to some, committed to the gospel of the professor poets—the first commandment of whose decalogue of reaction

Here and Now. By Denise Levertov. City Lights, San Francisco, 1957.

is: "The age of experiment is over"—like saying that she is very much better than her associates, Charles Olson, Robert Creeley, Allen Ginsberg, Cid Corman, Chris Berjknes, Gil Orlovitz and others who published in *Origin* and the *Black Mountain Review*. I don't believe these are bad poets—in fact, I think they are the best of their generation and the only hope for American poetry. It is just that Denise Levertov has several things they haven't got, at least yet.

In the first place, she is more civilized. One thing she has which they lack conspicuously is what Ezra Pound calls culture (which he himself is utterly without). She is securely humane in a way very few people are any more. This is not because she is English, of Welsh and Jewish parentage, although the fact that her father was a learned rabbi, a leading authority on the Kabbalah, who became an Anglo-Catholic priest, may have helped. She seems to have grown up in a household full of mildly Bohemian scholarship, freewheeling learning of the type Theodore Gaster made well known in his reminiscences of his own father (Rabbi Gaster and Paul Levertov were friends). Certainly this is a humanism older than the Renaissance, so well founded that it penetrates every bit of life. This is far from the humanism of Sigismondo Malatesta or even Henry Luce—it is more like Lao-tse. If it is really absorbed and manifest in an individual it becomes that rare thing, wisdom. I don't need to labor the point that there exist practically no wise poets nowadays and few for the last two hundred years.

This means that Denise Levertov knows more than her colleagues, far more than most; she is far sounder than Olson, whose learning suffers from the same sort of Frobenius-Lost Atlantis provincial oddity as Pound's. Many of them know practically nothing, not even French and algebra. Because it is humane, her knowledge is the result of doing what came naturally. She may have read Donne from her father's library at the age of ten—perhaps, like the Bible, for the dirty words. That is the way to read Donne. Cultured people do not discover him when they go to Harvard and use him to intimidate the yokels back home in St. Louis. This means too that she has an almost perfect ear. Reading her, especially hearing her read aloud, you feel she must have literally absorbed the rhythms of great poetry with her mother's milk. It is all so natural and so utterly removed from English 7649328 A—Forms and Techniques of English Verse (4 credits).

Nothing shows this better than the actual evolution of idiom and tone. During the years of the Second World War, Denise Levertov came up as one of the best and one of the most individual of the young English Neo-Romantics. Comfort, Woodcock, Gascoyne, Gardiner, Tambimuttu, Read, the whole "leadership" of the "movement" were quick to recognize her as something very special indeed. She was naturally "romantic." She didn't have to believe in it or belong to it as a movement. She was built that way. I said of her then that "in poets like Denise Levertov this tendency (a sort of autumnal-evening *Wienerwald* melancholy) reaches its height in slow, pulsating rhythms, romantic melancholy and indefinable nostalgia. Once these qualities would have been considered blemishes. Today they are outstanding virtues. For the first time, *Schwärmerei* enters English verse." The only thing wrong with this statement in those days was that there weren't any "poets like Denise Levertov." She was unique. None followed her. The next crop, represented, say, by Heath-Stubbs, seem like muggy little Böcklins cut out of cardboard in comparison. It was as though for a moment in the October moonlight a girl's voice sang faintly across the Danube, "Knowest thou a land where the pomegranate blooms. . . ." And then she gave it all up. "Hospital nurse, land girl, charwoman, children's nurse, companion to an alcoholic . . ." Hitchhiking over France the year after the Second World War ended, she married a GI and came to the States. "She'll probably end up a professor's wife," said a friend in London in 1949, "pushing a pram in a supermarket."

Denise turned out to be made of tougher stuff . . . and the GI, himself a writer, was on the side of the angels. At first she fell under the influence of the Southren Colonels and the Country Gentlemen. It didn't last long. We were all horrified. "So and so is a lot like our Empson," said she to me. Said I to her, " 'Ceptin' that he never seen a book until he went to school and his folks still got cotton seeds in they hair. And besides, you are a leader of the very generation of revolt against the impostures of Empson, Richards, Eliot and their sycophants." She allowed as how that was true. But nobody "influenced" her to turn away, pretty quick, from the smoking dogs and bicycling seals of the American academicians. It was her own good sense, the good sense of bona fide tradition and an infallible ear. W. H. Auden has spent years in America and never learned to use a single phrase of American slang without sounding like a British music-hall Yank comic and his verse has remained as British, as specifically "school," as Matthew Arnold. In no time at all Denise came to talk like a mildly internationalized young woman living in New York but alive to all the life of speech in the country. Her verse changed abruptly. It would be easy to say that it came under the influence of William Carlos Williams. It would be more true to say that it moved into the mainstream of twentieth-century poetry. She writes like Williams, a little, but she also writes "like" Salmon, or Reverdy, or Char—or Machado, or Louis Zukofsky, or Parker Tyler, or Patchen, or the early Lowenfels, or me. After all, as Shakespeare said, we are all civilized men. I think Miss Levertov is a better poet than Salmon, as Williams is a better poet than Reverdy. If all her work of the past ten years were collected, I suspect she would show as the equal of Char and as superior to all but a handful of American poets born in this century. Certainly she is better than any post-Second World War French poet—than Frenaud, or Cadou, or Becker, or Rousselot. Her only rival among the younger women in England is a poet once described by an older colleague as writing like an exquisitely well-bred lady's maid, and who hasn't been up to her early snuff in many years. The only trouble with *Here and Now* is that it is much too small a collection and it is a collection of her easiest verse.

The fact that Denise Levertov has had to wait so long for publication and now is able to publish so little* is a shame to American publishers, who year after year put out the most meretricious, pompous, academic nonsense, which gets meretricious, pompous, academic reviews in the literary quarterlies—and wins countless millions in Fellowships, Scholarships, Consultantships and Visiting Poetships. The official position is that people like Denise Levertov do not exist. Officialdom to the contrary, they very much do, and they will out-exist the jerry-built reputations of the *Vaticide Review* by many, many long years. Nothing could be harder, more irreducible, than these poems. Like the eggs and birds of Brancusi, they are bezoars shaped and polished in the vitals of a powerful creative sensibility. No seminar will break their creative wholeness, their presentational immediacy. No snobbery will dissolve their intense personal integrity. However irrefrangible as objects of art, it is *that*, their personalism, that makes them such perfect poetic utterances. Denise may never have pushed a pram in a Cambridge, Massachusetts, supermarket, but these are woman poems, wife poems, mother poems, differing only in quality of sensibility from thousands of other expressions of universal experience. Experience is not dodged, the sensibility is not defrauded—with any ambiguity, of seven types or seventy. One meets the other head on, without compromise. This, I was taught in school, many years ago in a better day, is what makes great poetry great. And the rhythms. The *Schwärmerei* and lassitude are gone. Their place has been taken by a kind of animal grace of the word, a pulse like the footfalls of a cat or the wingbeats of a gull. It is the intense aliveness of an alert domestic love—the wedding of form and content in poems which themselves celebrate a kind of perpetual wedding of two persons always realized as two responsible sensibilities. What more do you want of poetry? You can't ask much more. Certainly you seldom get a tenth as much.

*New Directions has since published Miss Levertov's *With Eyes at the Back of Our Heads* (1959) and *The Jacob's Ladder* (1961).

WELDON KEES

Weldon Kees was one of the more significant American poets of my generation, and although this book is a beautiful memorial and worth every penny of its high price, I hope that it will quickly be reproduced in a large cheap edition. This is not poetry for collectors of fine editions. Although Kees's poetry was only moderately popular when it first appeared, it is certainly the kind of poetry people today seem to want to read. It has many of the elements of the recently excessively popular poetry of social revolt—or rather rejection—and fewer conspicuous faults.

When Weldon Kees started to write, the alienated poetic hero was at the height of his fashion. Conrad Aiken and T. S. Eliot had launched him on his poetic career a generation before, and the young W. H. Auden had picked him up and put him on the science-fiction stage of a near future of universal disorder and decay. At first Weldon Kees's poems seemed to be unusually successful exercises in a very current idiom. Then, as they accumulated, it became apparent that they were something very different; in fact quite the opposite—this man really meant every word of it; he was not trying to frighten the denizens of a chic literary weekend in a Stately Home.

Where the narrator of Weldon Kees's poems is in the third person he is sometimes given a name: Robinson—modern man at the end of his rope. Kees is only distinguishable from his hero by his pity. However, he himself, as narrator-hero, is not lost beyond the end of night in a world of shoddy failures and low life. He is Robinson Crusoe, utterly alone on Madison Avenue, a stranger and afraid in the world of high-paying newsweeklies, fashionable galleries, jazz concerts, highbrow movies, sophisticated revues—the world in which Weldon Kees was eminently successful. When he said, in these gripping poems, that it filled him with absolute hor-

The Collected Poems of Weldon Kees. Edited by Donald Justice. The Stone Wall Press, Iowa City, 1960.

ror, he meant it. On July 18, 1955, his car was found abandoned on the approach to the Golden Gate Bridge. He has never been seen since.

Besides these moving poems Weldon Kees left behind an excellent play of the type now most successful off-Broadway, called *The Waiting Room.* I hope his heirs will make it available soon. Like his poems, it was just a few years too early.

ROBERT DUNCAN

Robert Duncan has published some ten or more books. This is the first to appear under the imprint of a national publisher, or at least a New York one. Since he was a boy, editing *Experimental Review* with Sanders Russell and *Phoenix* with James Cooney, he has enjoyed a considerable reputation among readers and writers of what is still unfortunately termed the avant-garde. From San Francisco and from Black Mountain College his personal influence on young writers has spread far and wide. Today he ranks with Denise Levertov, Robert Creeley, Charles Olson, Lawrence Ferlinghetti and Allen Ginsberg, as one of the leaders of the New Poetry —so recently discovered by the media. He has never received a major fellowship or prize, nobody has ever offered him a teaching job in a smart girls' school, and if he has ever been published in a quarterly, I missed it. In fact, until the last couple of years, the Literary Establishment in America pretended that he didn't exist. In further fact, whenever I used to mention him in an article, the name would always be corrected to some other Duncan, a minor member of the Establishment, of whom I had never heard. Since Duncan has been a mature writer with a fully developed style for a long time, this lonely grandeur is an odd state of affairs. To understand it requires a short lesson in literary history.

All during the twentieth century American poetry has alternately expressed two antagonistic tendencies. One has

The Opening of the Field. By Robert Duncan. Grove Press, New York, 1961.

been the *consensus orbis terrarum* of poetry in our time—a world idiom that the newspapers still call "modernist." Although this idiom was first worked out in France, in the decay of Symbolism and the reaction against it, the difference of time is slight. The development took place all over the world in the same years—from Blok to Mayakofski, from Rubén Darío to Neruda, it was in the final analysis the same process, a reorganization of the sensibility and accompanying it, a new syntax.

From 1912 to 1929 this was the dominant tendency in American poetry too. It was disrupted by the depression and the pseudo proletarianism of the Thirties and finally gave way to a counter tendency. At its best this latter was a return to the traditions of English verse, especially that of the Baroque period. By and large, however, it was simply a conservative reaction, a return to academic stereotypes that could be taught, "seven types of ambiguity" and the politics of the far Right—T. S. Eliot, Ezra Pound and the Southern Agrarians. Mostly it was just a teacher-placement bureau and a fellowship hunting club. Its prime article of faith was, "The age of experiment and revolt is over." Most of its members denied, quite sincerely, that poets like Duncan did or could exist. In fact, it was not until one of Lionel Trilling's students got in trouble for writing a dirty poem and made the picture weeklies, that any of them dreamed that anyone could be a writer any more who was not at least a teaching assistant.

In actual fact, the Reactionary Generation came totally bankrupt out of the Second World War, its power gone, despised by its students. Since its members held control of many channels of publication, fate took a little while to catch up with them. In the last couple of years, a movement that had come to fruition in the years immediately after the war is at last gaining public notice.

Of the postwar poets—this new generation of experiment and revolt—Robert Duncan is one of the most accomplished, one of the most influential and, it can be said of this and his last three books, *Caesar's Gate, Letter-Poems, Selected*

Poems, probably the most mature. Some of his colleagues are narrow, some are warped, some make a virtue of their immaturity, a couple are frivolous or desperately "immoral." There is nothing of this in Duncan. He is a grown man.

It's a little awesome, reading these poems. They have a noble gravity about them that we don't expect from our contemporaries; they have a deep sonority and a steady pace, like the plain-song processional, "*Media Vitae.*" It is not solemnity of subject, although many have that too, but a kind of inner life attitude of immense seriousness and devotion. At the same time the poems have a strangely uncontemporary worldliness, as though they had been written by one of those dignified and accomplished literary men-about-town of the Victorian era—Monckton Milnes or Walter Bagehot. It's not just dignity; perhaps it's wisdom. Wisdom is a virtue, like courage and magnanimity, that we have long since lost the habit of expecting from literary people, so it's hard to recognize it when it appears.

The previous generation of experiment and revolt had tended to treat the work of art as a construct rather than a communication. Duncan comes to poetry seeking the communication of an organic wisdom, as in the act of love. This is poetry which transcends the existentialist dilemma, a gift of the self to the other. Hence its religious, or specifically its reverent, tone, because it does, in poetic act, what the philosophers of personalism and communion discuss. It is responsible, as only the work of art can be and, alas, so seldom is.

INDEX

NEW DIRECTIONS PAPERBOOKS